THE WINGED WHEEL

THE WINGED WHEEL

A Half-Century of
the Detroit Red Wings
in Photographs

ROB SIMPSON

Forewords by Mike "Doc" Emrick and Mickey Redmond

John Wiley & Sons Canada, Ltd.

Library and Archives Canada Cataloguing in Publication Data

Simpson, Rob, 1964–
The winged wheel : a half-century of the Detroit Red Wings in photographs / Rob Simpson.

Includes index.
ISBN 978-1-11814-428-2

1. Detroit Red Wings (Hockey team)—History.
2. Detroit Red Wings (Hockey team)—History
  —Pictorial works.
I. Title.

GV848.D4W56 2012
796.96'2640977434
C2012-904133-5

Production Credits

INTERIOR DESIGN AND COMPOSITION:
  Costa Leclerc Design
MANAGING EDITOR: Alison Maclean
PRODUCTION EDITOR: Lindsay Humphreys
COVER DESIGN: Adrian So
COVER PHOTO: NHLI/Getty Images/Dave Reginek
PRINTER: Quad/Graphics

John Wiley & Sons Canada, Ltd.
6045 Freemont Blvd.
Mississauga, Ontario
L5R 4J3

Printed in the United States
1 2 3 4 5 QG 16 15 14 13 12

Photos

PAGE 2: *Nicklas Lidstrom* | PAGE 4: *Jim Rutherford* | PAGE 6: *Dan Cleary*
PAGE 7: *Niklas Kronwall, Brad Stuart* | PAGE 8: *Mickey Redmond*
PAGE 9: *Mike "Doc" Emrick* | PAGE 10: *Gordie Howe* | PAGE 11 (TOP): *Mike and Marian Ilitch*
PAGE 11 (BOTTOM): *Kris Draper, Chris Osgood* | PAGE 12: *Steve Yzerman, Sergei Fedorov*
PAGE 13: *Bill Gadsby*

To Nora, whom I first met in the Olympia Room at the Joe Louis Arena.

It was love at first sight.

Contents

Mickey Redmond, Red Wing sniper turned award-winning TV commentator.

Forewords

WHEN I WAS TRADED TO THE Detroit Red Wings in 1971, the once-storied franchise was in disarray, mainly due to absentee ownership that led to poor decision-making.

And despite the fact my career was shortened by injury, I had many highlights and pleasures, the simplest of which was playing with Gary Bergman, Alex Delvecchio, and Gordie Howe, and wearing the Original Six sweater of the Winged Wheel.

The franchise turnaround began when Mike and Marian Ilitch bought the team in 1982. They hired Jim Devellano as GM and he drafted Steve Yzerman in 1983 and Nick Lidstrom in 1989.

Jacques Demers, Bryan Murray, and Scotty Bowman were all a part of the turnaround as coaches, and Mike Babcock has continued that excellence since 2005. Ken Holland, first as a scout, then head of scouting, and now as GM since 1997, with help from Jim Nill and Hakan Andersson, has been a master at the draft table. Sergei Fedorov (picked 74th overall in 1989), Vladimir Konstantinov (221st in 1989), Tomas Holmstrom (257th in 1994), Pavel Datsyuk (171st in 1998), and Henrik Zetterberg (221st in 1999) are just a few of the examples.

I have been behind the microphone since 1979 for Wings games and some of the highlights include: the Bruise Brothers (Probert and Kocur in the late 1980s), the Yzerman era (more than 20 years), the magic of the Russian Five, the Grind Line (Draper, Maltby, and McCarty), and the seven Norris Trophies for Lidstrom.

The team results speak for themselves as of 2012: 21 consecutive years in the playoffs, 12 consecutive 100-point seasons, eight of the last 18 seasons in the final four, six of the last 18 years in the Stanley Cup final, and four Stanley Cups.

The history is here.

Little did I know that 41 years after arriving in Detroit, I would still be a part of this prestigious Red Wings organization with the best seat in the house behind the microphone. I also continue to wear the Winged Wheel while skating with the Detroit Red Wings alumni.

They don't call it "Hockeytown" for nothing, and I've been blessed to be a part of it. The ride continues.

See you at the rink.

— *Mickey Redmond*

WHAT YOU ARE HOLDING IS A half century of a storied franchise. What you are about to get are glorious photos and newly told stories!

In 1962, if you didn't plan in advance, you would go down Grand River on a busy weekend afternoon hoping for tickets for that night. If you did plan, you bought in advance, and they arrived at your house in a small white envelope with a return address in the upper left-hand corner and an actual stamp, 5 cents, in the upper right. Nowadays, if you don't go down Steve Yzerman Drive to the Joe Louis Arena box office, you may buy seats in a millisecond with one click on your keyboard.

Whether you arrive in a car with a license plate from Michigan or Ohio, or tunnel or bridge it from Ontario, you hold those tickets with anticipation.

Mike "Doc" Emrick, the voice of hockey on television in the United States.

Few fans wore jerseys to games at old Olympia Stadium in the '60s. In the upper tiers that were so steep they had to put railings in front of every row, you would see fathers who worked for the Big Three. Sometimes, they would be there with a hockey-playing son who wore his jacket from Ecorse Big-D, Westland, Fraser, or Little Caesar's. Sometimes, like Little Caesar's graduate and future NHL goalie John Vanbiesbrouck, they would take advantage of the NHL's biggest standing-room section, extending some 10 yards back from the last row of the lower bowl.

Eventual Hall of Fame goalie Terry Sawchuk had to battle for his job in the fall of 1962, trying to win it away from Hank Bassen. He did. Very much like Jimmy Howard had to win his way to the Red Wings crease half a century later.

And, when the Red Wings changed lodging to Joe Louis Arena in the 1979–80 season, all Vanbiesbrouck did was take up standing room at the top of the lower bowl there. And as a resourceful teenager, he would earn extra cash holding the places of adults who needed time to reload at the concession stand. Or whatever.

While fans in the '60s might stop in at Big Bill's sporting goods or Bob Perani's for hockey gear, fans of the modern time go to any one of the national franchises or Red Wings stores. And, unlike the '60s, most everyone comes dressed in red or white these days.

The common ground, as I mentioned above, was the anticipation. Would this be the night when Gordie or Alex or Mickey or Stevie or Nick would tear the net down with a shot?

Would it be a night when a late lead would be preserved by something magical in the goal crease guarded by Roger Crozier, Jimmy Rutherford, Mike Vernon, or Chris Osgood? Or, in an era when "the players policed the sport themselves," as Gordie's son Mark Howe so eloquently put it would this be a night when Howie Young, Bob Probert, Joe Kocur, or Stu Grimson had to take someone to task (and to the penalty box with them)?

It was anticipation that you had when you bought your ticket. And it's anticipation we all have as we go through the pages of pictures and stories that follow.

What we all get to enjoy is a team that moved from a perennial finalist … through darkness … to the light shed by new ownership that embraced history but wisely passed on its mistakes … to perennial Cup contender.

This will be fun.

— *Mike "Doc" Emrick*

Preface

COMPARING A HOCKEY CLUB AND its fan base to a family is cliché. There is no dinner with great-grandpa Gordie or skating lessons with uncle Stevie. But because of the unique northern geography, the generations of memories produced for Detroit area hockey families, and the uncommon interest, the Red Wings are as much a part of the region's existence and psyche as any sports team anywhere. Being a "Wings fan" is a comfortable and at times wonderful feeling. It's being a part of an extended red-and-white-blooded lineage. Whether you're an old-timer enthusiast or just cutting your teeth, it's undying faith that binds one and all.

For players, coaches, team personnel, and legions of fans, the Red Wings are indeed a second family.

The Winged Wheel is a half-century of this clan, at times dysfunctional, often times successful, made up of hockey people all attempting to pull in the same direction.

In 1982, Detroit's future hockey generations found themselves with a new patriarch and matriarch, Mike and Marian Ilitch. With great drive and determination, dutifully and diligently, the Ilitches built a business and brought new life to the clan. They took care of their blood relatives, their seven sons and daughters; they continue to take care of their home town with revitalization projects in downtown Detroit; and they've definitely taken care of their hockey brethren.

Hall of Fame defenseman Marcel Pronovost, who wore the crest with great success from 1949 to 1965, can attest to the Ilitches' unprecedented dedication.

"I got a real pleasant surprise back in 2008," recalls Marcel, "when Mike Ilitch had rings made for all the past guys that won the Stanley Cup with Detroit. All the guys that were still alive, that had anything to do with winning a Cup back prior to Mike buying the club. It wasn't a custom back then; it [the tradition of Stanley Cup rings] started with Toronto in the early 1960s. I was surprised as anything and I called Mike right away to thank him profusely. He's an awful good guy, and he did the same thing for baseball as he did for hockey."

Each keepsake was personalized, which meant Marcel had four Stanley Cups listed on his ring. What a way to tie your hockey family's history together, to bring all together as one.

In its own humble approach, that's the idea behind *The Winged Wheel*. It's a pictorial refresher for some, a primer for others, bridging 50 years.

Whether you're one of those kids from down river, as Doc Emrick recalls in his Foreword, who used to wear his hockey jacket to the games at the Olympia; a goalie who played three games for Detroit; or a Red Wings fan from Bloomfield Township who could never get enough, you've stopped in the right place.

This book is about family: an historical, photographic reflection of three or four generations of hockey; the brotherhood that has made up Red Wings society for the past half century.

— *Rob Simpson*

Acknowledgments

THANK YOU TO John Hahn and Todd Beam from the Red Wings media/communications department. To archivists Sharon Arend and Courtney McAlpine at Ilitch Holdings for their tremendous support and photographic contributions. Same to Craig Campbell at the Hockey Hall of Fame, more specifically, the D.K. "Doc" Seaman Hockey Resource Centre in Toronto. Thank you to the ultimate pro, the irreplaceable Paul Michinard at Getty.

Hockey people are the best in sports and there is no better example of hospitality and class than the Red Wings hockey department. Thank you to Jim Devellano for his assistance and Ken Holland and Jim Nill for their support. And of course to the 90 or so Red Wings alumni who patiently answered all of my questions on the phone or in person over the last 14 months. Thanks to George Bowman and the Red Wings Alumni Association. Indubitably, thank you Mr. and Mrs. Ilitch for buying the team and running it with such distinction.

Many thanks to the Wings broadcasters, team support staff, and folks at the Joe, many of whom appear throughout the book. Thank you to Red Wings photographers Bob "Red" Wimmer, Jim Mackey, John Hartman, Mark Hicks, and Dave Reginek. What a fun way to show your efforts and the efforts of others. To Greg Innis and Ayron Sequeira for pointing me in the right direction. To old friends Bill and Mary Valpey for the grand Traverse City hospitality and the McCanns for the digs in Motown.

Thank you very much to Doc and Mickey, two of the sport's all-time greats.

At Wiley, as usual, much appreciation and admiration to Karen Milner, to Lindsay Humphreys, Alison Maclean, Adrian So, Brian Will, and of course Meghan Brousseau and Erika Zupko in marketing. Thank you very much to Jacqueline Lee for turning Simpsonese into English and to Gorette Costa and Jeff Winocur at Costa Leclerc for the tremendous design and layout.

A long belated thank you to my older brothers Jim and Tom, Red Wings fans for life, for showing and teaching me the game. Again, to Nora for everything, which includes letting me be a little kid, and to Ian for being my favorite hockey pal and a fine stay-at-home defenseman.

— *Rob Simpson*

OPPOSITE: *Not a bad one-two punch at center: Steve Yzerman and Sergei Fedorov.*

ABOVE: *Hall of Fame defenseman Bill Gadsby scores on Gump Worsley in Montreal at 5:14 of the 2nd period of Game 1 of the 1966 Stanley Cup final.*

1 The Olympia and the Joe

"The Olympia was just beautiful; just the way a rink was supposed to be. I loved that building."

— Paul Woods, FORMER DETROIT FORWARD AND LONGTIME RADIO COMMENTATOR

ABOVE: *The Olympia, opened in 1927, sat 11,563 people until 1966 when seating was expanded to handle 13,375. With its legendary standing-room areas, actual capacity for hockey ballooned to 16,375. The Joe Louis Arena, opened in 1979, seats just over 20,000 hockey fans, but with standing room has been known to top 21,000.*

RED WINGS FANS HAVE BEEN BLESSED with great hockey buildings. Their "new" building is actually an old one, a well-weathered friend, while their former home is a distant memory, recollected only by those who have been around long enough and have been fortunate enough to have worked, played, or spectated there.

The Detroit Olympia, at Grand River Avenue and McGraw Street, was built in 1927, and although it welcomed a variety of events, in the winter it was reserved almost exclusively for puck pursuits.

"I loved the old Olympia," states former Red Wings scorer Danny Grant. "Like most of the older rinks, the crowd was right there. During the warm-ups you could stand by the boards or glass and you could talk to any of the fans who wanted to; it just seemed they were more involved. I think there were a lot more kids at the games back then and they were allowed to come down and ask for autographs and that type of thing. I loved the old Olympia. It was a wonderful place to play."

"When you play on ice like that all the time . . . oh there's no doubt, the ice was the best," says Wayne Connelly, former Detroit right-winger. "I think it's because they left it down, they didn't pull it up for events, or mess with it too much. You'd go to New York and there'd be a circus in the afternoon or something, and there'd be crap all over," he laughs. "It was mostly hockey at the Olympia, and it was a pleasure. Olympia ice stayed down and it was the best."

The "Old Red Barn," as it became known, was built in just seven months, and appropriate for its eventual moniker, its first event was a small rodeo. However, make no mistake: this was a hockey barn first and foremost.

After playing their first season, 1926–27, across the Detroit River in Windsor, Ontario, the NHL's Detroit Cougars, formerly of Victoria, British Columbia, opened their second campaign at the Olympia on November 22, 1927, losing 2–1 to the Ottawa Senators.

In 1930, the Cougars became the Falcons. They kept the name for two seasons, and then changed it to the Red Wings under their second owner, James Norris. The Wings won their first Stanley Cup in 1936 against Toronto, and clinched their first Cup on home ice the very next season against New York.

"There was so much history with the Olympia," reflects former Wings goalie and current Carolina Hurricanes general manager Jimmy

Rutherford. "They had won so many Stanley Cups, and so many great players played there, and it was so unique because of the ice surface. In all the modern buildings, all the ice surface is the same, so it's not even like playing a road game. In those days it was all different. The Olympia had the short corners and it was really to the home team's advantage once you knew how to play it."

"I was raised there, that's why I loved it," reflects Hall of Fame defenseman Marcel Pronovost. "It was the best ice in the circuit. The boards were perfect, you could bank everything, and we knew, being used to the boards there, we knew where to put it to come back to a player. You had to know the [Original] Six buildings. We studied them."

Players in the know took advantage of the Olympia's unique layout. For example, there was a place at the visitors' end of the rink that, if hit with the puck from center ice, would bounce the puck back to the face-off spot to the left of the goalie. According to former sniper Mickey Redmond, "Alex Delvecchio was a master at hitting that spot. I'd be streaking down the right side and just waling into it at the dot, with the goalie hopefully on his toes. I was looking to unleash a high, hard one," he laughs. "Once or twice a game we'd get to use that play."

Longtime Wing Nick Libett particularly liked the oval shape of the rink. "Plus," he says, "the fans were literally hanging over you. You didn't

ABOVE LEFT: *The Olympia marquee in 1963, featuring the Stanley Cup final between the Wings and Toronto, and an April wrestling match between Dick the Bruiser and popular Detroit Lion defensive lineman Alex Karras.*

ABOVE RIGHT: *The Olympia, at 5920 Grand River Avenue, sat on the corner of McGraw Street with Lawton Street running behind.*

realize it at the time, but when you started going into the newer buildings everyone was so far away."

"We practiced on that ice, so we had an advantage," states Rangers legend, Hall of Famer, and short-term Red Wing Andy Bathgate. "We had good crowds all the time, which made it fun and interesting. A lot of Canadian people would come over all the time."

Detroit opponents held a similar appreciation. ESPN analyst Barry Melrose fondly remembers the rink as egg-shaped, with a very small neutral zone.

"They had two defensemen when I played against Detroit, Willie Huber and Jimmie Korn," he recalls. "It seemed like the two of them could touch each wall, and reach across the ice while touching the other side. It was a great old building. You actually walked through the lobby, through the people, to get to the ice. All the things you couldn't do today you did at the Olympia. It was just a great old hockey barn."

"It was very exciting as a rookie having to face Gordie Howe, Ted Lindsay, and Alex Delvecchio," says Hockey Hall of Famer Rod Gilbert. "I enjoyed the ice in Detroit, plus there was lots of energy and the fans were very knowledgeable about the game."

"We played there a lot," states former Bruins captain Ed Sandford. "That was a tough rink. The other thing there was the really good ice,

probably the best ice on the circuit at that time. I don't know why, but it was."

Credit for the renowned ice surface should go to the original architect of the Olympia, Howard Crane. A legendary theater builder, Crane also constructed the Orchestra Hall and the Fox and State Theatres, both still in use in downtown Detroit. According to the Historic American Buildings Survey, Crane's engineering achievements were second to none. "Notably in the elaborate refrigeration system that made Olympia Arena the largest ice skating rink in the United States at the time it opened, with an ice surface measuring 110 feet in width and 242 feet in length." With almost the entire base of the building frozen, there was refrigeration to spare once the boards went up.

It was the best ice in the circuit. The boards were perfect, you could bank everything, and we knew, being used to the boards there, we knew where to put it to come back to a player. You had to know the [Original] Six buildings. We studied them.

"I was a skater and it was a great place if you could skate," reflects former Red Wing and longtime University of Michigan hockey coach Red Berenson. "We had the round corners and the smaller ice surface, and I always really liked playing in it. And the fans just hung right over you—that upper balcony, the sight lines were great. So it was a great venue to watch a game and it was a great venue to play. It was electric any time Montreal or Toronto came to town, in the Original Six."

"Between the balcony and the lower bowl they had a concourse there, and they had a concourse up on top of the balcony, so people could walk around between periods and chat with one another," reminisced

TOP LEFT: *"Hockey Sunday." Once inside, this crowd would experience a very steep escalator and very narrow concourses.*

TOP RIGHT: *The Olympia's refrigeration system created "the best ice on the circuit."*

BOTTOM: *Bill Gadsby on the left and Gordie Howe on the right flank Ross "Lefty" Wilson, the Red Wings trainer, equipment manager, emergency backup goalie, and jack-of-all-trades from 1950 to 1982.*

former Detroit player and coach, the late Johnny Wilson, during the summer of 2011. "When we first broke in, there was mesh from one side of the goal line around to the other end of the goal line, and on the side, there was no glass or mesh or screen. So if you were in the first row, you could put your arms on the boards. You could almost lean over and look down the boards as the play was going either way."

The small ice surface and the absence of glass around the boards in the early days, lent a sense of intimacy to the arena.

"The fans could hear the loud swearing on the ice at times, and they could yell at the officials too," remembers Wings announcing legend Budd Lynch. "The intimacy of the fans. And they always had to walk by the visiting dressing room on their way out, whether it was Montreal, or Toronto, or Chicago, to get to their cars. They'd see [the players], shake hands with them, win or lose."

"In Montreal, before the game, the only people allowed in the dressing room were the coach and great former hockey players who might stop by very quietly, nobody else," states Bryan "Bugsy" Watson, who went from the Canadiens organization to the Red Wings in 1965. "When I went to Detroit, in the first game, there was a damn band out in the hall, a Dixieland band; Sonny Eliot, the weatherman from TV, comes into the room with his buddy, and Bruce Norris comes in with all his friends. It was like a parade. The country-club aspect was there to start off, but the first time you got knocked on your butt on the ice, you forgot about the band and everything else."

Sitting in the aisle, or standing in it, became fashionable at the Olympia.

Greg Innis, longtime "Minister of Statistics" for the Red Wings, also appreciated the feeling of involvement one had as a spectator at the Olympia. "I had season tickets, and I was in the first row of the balcony, out by center ice, the first two seats in the row, and you could actually hear the players talking to each other, that's how close you were. It was just amazing how close the action was."

"It was like a small Chicago Stadium, where the seats went up, as opposed to back like in the new buildings," adds Redmond. "Sixteen thousand sounded like 21,000 today. I could go on about the Boston Garden, and the Forum, and the old Madison Square Garden; they were all the best to me in every way for sure."

And like all of those other Original Six buildings, the Old Red Barn had peculiarities and sight-line issues because of its "old-world" construction.

"The only NHL game I ever went to before college, I sold the most raffle tickets in peewee and I got to go to Detroit and sit behind a big girder," explains former Red Wings forward Paul Ysebaert. "They played Buffalo that night and I remember Gilbert Perreault had a hat trick.

"I just remember a lot of smoke," he continues. "I think you were allowed to smoke, even cigars and pipes, and I just remember our seats

behind a big girder. Other than the smoke and sitting behind the girder I don't remember much. I wish I had kept the program."

Livonia, Michigan, native and eventual Hall of Famer Mike Modano, who ended his on-ice career in Detroit, also has some childhood memories of the Olympia.

"The only thing I really remember there is running between the chairs and knocking some teeth out," he says. "I remember Nick Libett, I remember that name, and I remember Reed Larson. Knocking my teeth out was my memory of the Olympia." Modano, the all-time leading scorer among American-born NHLers, was 9 years old when the building closed.

"It was a great building," says Walt McKechnie, a former Red Wing from London, Ontario. "I remember when Baun scored on his broken leg [in overtime of Game 6 of the 1964 final], we were there. My mom and I came down from London for the game, it was packed; we were sitting up in the balcony. The usher let me sit in the aisle. I still remember that vividly, Baun scoring that goal." McKechnie was a 16-year-old Maple Leafs fan.

Sitting in the aisle, or standing in it, became fashionable at the Olympia. Standing-room-only was a popular, discount alternative to having seats at the rink, and a phenomenon that could balloon attendance by two or three thousand people a night.

"The building was actually condemned at one time, for a couple reasons," points out Lynch. "When you went up to the first level to go to the concessions, if two people were in line, the fans couldn't get to their seats. It was just one of those strange things, but the firemen overlooked it, and they would sit in the aisle and watch the game."

It was neither the building itself nor the ice surface (obviously) that led to the closing of the hockey venue. The surrounding neighborhood had become a little too rough in those days—at least one man was stabbed in the parking lot at nearby Northwestern High School—and

TOP LEFT: *The Olympia ice and interior.*

TOP RIGHT: *Public address announcer Bob Liggitt, who worked in the rink for most of 1964 to 1971, went on to own several radio stations, a newspaper, and the Big Boy restaurant chain.*

BOTTOM: *Concessions man Pete Sentelia in 1965.*

for the comfort and security of visiting suburbanites, the Wings were forced to find a new home.

"It was pretty rough in our playing days," says McKechnie. "I remember there being shots fired outside of the building one day, after we had parked inside. It wasn't the safest neighborhood at the time."

Former Red Wing Dan Maloney compares the Olympia's surroundings to those of similar arenas of the time, including Chicago Stadium and Boston Garden: "They were all pretty rough areas, but we all had to go to work, we did so, and everything worked out pretty well."

"I was very lucky, I had some friends that worked at the Olympia. And the police," reassures Grant, "when the girls came down to go to the game, the Detroit police were there, guys that worked at the Olympia for years, they made sure everything was all right. I never had a problem the four years I was there, and neither did our family. We were well taken care of; there was no problem that way."

Over 50-plus years, the Olympia saw presidential speeches (Herbert Hoover), numerous championship boxing matches, including two between Jake "The Raging Bull" LaMotta and Sugar Ray Robinson, and many rock concerts, including two appearances by The Beatles. Its last NHL game culminated in a 4–4 tie between the Red Wings and the Quebec Nordiques on December 15, 1979. An Oldtimers' game two months later, on February 22, 1980, was the last event ever held at the sold-out rink.

"They had a little game between the regular team and the alumni there," remembers former Detroit left-winger Errol Thompson. "Red Kelly, Ted Lindsay, and I think Alex Delvecchio was there as well. Some of the older Red Wings were playing against, at that time, the present team. It was a night on its own. Kelly, Lindsay, and Marcel Pronovost had all coached me, and to have a chance to play against them, that was kind of neat.

"I was very lucky, one of the last guys to play the last game at the Olympia and one of the guys to play the first game at Joe Louis," continues Thompson. "There would only be a team worth of guys, 20 guys, or 22 guys that had that opportunity. Probably one of the highlights of my career."

The Red Wings lost their first game at their new home, the Joe Louis Arena, or "the Joe," 3–2 to St. Louis on December 27, 1979. On February 5, Detroit hosted the NHL All-Star Game, which included the memorable return of legend Gordie Howe, who received an elongated, tear-jerking standing ovation. As a toast to Howe's greatness and popularity, and in the spirit of "no real introduction necessary," public address announcer John Bell intentionally left off Howe's name at the end of the player introductions. Instead, he said, "And from the Hartford Whalers, representing all of hockey with great distinction for five decades . . . number 9 . . ." and the building went ballistic.

Months prior to this revelry, there was a completely different kind of drama. It came near the end of the new arena's $57 million, 31-month construction process.

"They forgot the press box," smiles TV play-by-play man Ken Daniels.

"The press box was built as an afterthought," points out Innis. "They finished the arena, and then all of a sudden somebody said, 'Well, everything looks good,' and the other guy said, 'Wait a minute, we forgot to build a press box, what do we do?' So they tore out two or three rows of seats, made one long row, and it's been this way since 1979."

At the Joe, members of the press have to coexist in fairly close quarters.

"There's only one single-person bathroom, so it's a long line at intermissions," Daniels adds. "It's a small area; guys have fought for their broadcast booth. We never lost our booth, number 208, to the network guys. That was thanks to Mickey [Redmond] before I got here, and I'm grateful for that. You get used to one spot, and we've had it."

Lynch, the team's public relations director at the time of the move, describes a couple of silver linings. "In the press box, you've got eight pillars to navigate, and hardly room to walk, but you've got a good view from every spot up here," Lynch says. "The other payoff was, we had the Republican National Convention here in 1980, and they put TV and audio cable in, one end of the press box to the other. I told them when

TOP: *The Red Wings hockey brain trust: assistant GM Jim Nill, senior executive and advisor Jim Devellano, and General Manager Ken Holland.*

BOTTOM: *Ken Daniels, Red Wings TV play-by-play man since 1997.*

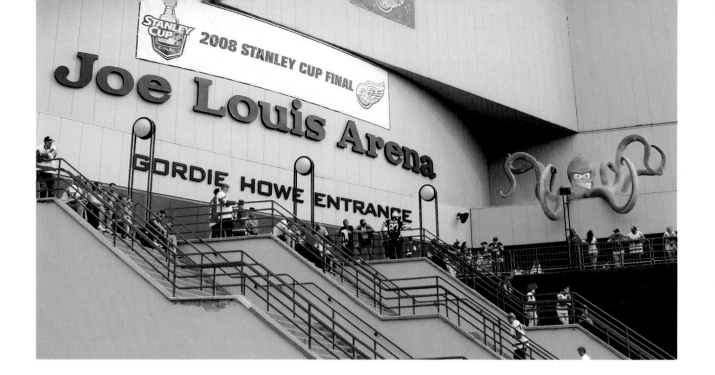

they were leaving, 'Leave that there, you don't need it.' And they did. They left it."

Another problem when the Joe Louis Arena first opened: the team stunk. Two years later, in 1982, the Norris family sold the franchise to Mike and Marian Ilitch. The turnaround was on.

"At all 40 home games, we gave away a car every game," says former team PR man Bill Jamieson. "Anything to get butts in the seats. The season-ticket base was less than 2,000. Mrs. Ilitch herself was working the phones in the box office trying to drum up publicity and business, trying to sell season tickets."

Also off the ice, the hockey department was changing, led by a new general manager and eventual senior vice-president and owner's adviser Jimmy Devellano. His first draft choice: Steve Yzerman.

> *Obviously it doesn't have the amenities of all the new arenas, but just taking a look up in the rafters, you get a sense of history, and it still gets very loud in the playoffs.*

Gradually, not enough fannies became not enough seats, and the standing-room-only tradition began anew.

The support of the fans is what former head coach and general manager Bryan Murray remembers most: "It was full, it was an older building but it was full all the time. An interesting and a fun place to play. My last year there they were adding seats to the aisles to accommodate all of the people attending games. People in Detroit were fabulous in terms of supporters."

"I remember the old Olympia and I used to go there during high school and nothing could beat that old building," says Ken Kal, radio

voice of the Red Wings since 1995. "It took me a little while to really take in Joe Louis Arena, but in the '90s until now, with the Red Wings being so successful, when the crowd's in here cheering, it's noisy, it's loud, it's a great building and atmosphere."

"We did a survey of local arenas and this was the favorite," points out the club's senior director of communications, John Hahn. "We have Comerica, Ford Field, and the Palace, but the fans like Joe Louis Arena the best. It's not because of the lack of modern amenities that make them say that, it's because of the atmosphere and the tradition."

"Still a great place to come and watch a game," confirms Wings media relations manager, Todd Beam. "Obviously it doesn't have the amenities of all the new arenas, but just taking a look up in the rafters, you get a sense of history, and it still gets very loud in the playoffs. All the seats are pushed down toward ice level, which is unique compared to the newer buildings."

Fans and players alike enjoy the idiosyncrasies of the Joe. "When you go to all the cookie-cutter buildings and compare, this is nice," says Daniels. "It's not the same. A lot of places you can stand at center ice and have to guess where they're playing."

"I think any building that has been around for 30 years is part of the team, part of the tradition," Hahn adds. "It has that atmosphere. You talk to the other teams, the players, the media that come in here, they love the new buildings and the spacious press boxes to work in, but they love being in here because of the great atmosphere."

The Olympia and the Joe Louis Arena: two distinct buildings joined by tradition and a love of the game.

"We played junior hockey there with the junior Red Wings, so we had a couple years in the Olympia; it was a great place," remembers Hall of Famer Mark Howe, referring to himself and older brother Marty. "I spent a lot of time there on my own. I used to get rides down there to the rink, when the Wings were on the road and no one was at the building.

TOP: *Building operations manager Al Sobotka made twirling octopi famous, so much so the team named its huge synthetic mascot "Al the Octopus." The tradition of fans throwing cephalopods onto the ice started at the Olympia in the postseason in 1952. Eight legs represented the eight playoff victories it took at that time to win the Stanley Cup.*

BOTTOM: *Nashville at Detroit, March 2010, at the Joe.*

ABOVE: *NHL referee Dan Marouelli greets legendary broadcaster Budd Lynch on November 5, 2009. The date marked the 60th anniversary of Lynch's first Red Wings broadcast. Players (from left) Kris Draper, Kirk Maltby, Justin Abdelkader, and Tomas Holmstrom look on. Lynch was still handling public address announcing duties in 2012 at the age of 94.*

The guy that used to run the concessions there, Jessie, he used to open the door for me. A lot of days, I'd be there six, eight, ten hours, skating all by myself, so I spent a lot of time at the Olympia."

"Being with Little Caesars [elite youth hockey program], we came down to the Joe every weekend and had practices," remembers future Hall of Famer Modano. "We rummaged through all the extra sticks the guys [Red Wings] didn't want, we thought we'd just died, we had all the tape, all the sticks. Going to represent the Wings in the Pee-Wee Tournament in Quebec, being with Little Caesars all those years, those were some great times, we loved coming down here practicing."

Regardless of an arena's longevity, or the depth of memories associated with it, no single building, or two, (just like no single player) is bigger than the organization itself. The buildings are just one part of what makes up the team.

"Being involved in an Original Six franchise is really special," reflects Paul Woods. "And those that haven't, they don't realize the history that has gone on in the franchise. It's beautiful just to be a part of it and just to learn about that history and to understand it a little bit."

2 Mr. Hockey

"Gordie was God to us."

— HALL OF FAMER, FLYER GREAT **Bobby Clarke**

THIS IS A TESTIMONIAL: To the greatest hockey player who ever lived.

During Gordie Howe's 25 seasons in Detroit he won four Stanley Cups, five goal-scoring titles, six overall scoring titles (Art Ross Trophy), and six Hart Trophies as National Hockey League MVP. He also earned First Team postseason All-Star honors 12 times, and Second Team All-Star honors nine times.

Two other NHLers would go on to surpass his career scoring statistics, but Howe's greatness transcends these numbers. Yes, Gordie was the leading scorer of his time, but he was also the toughest and most feared player on the ice in an era when toughness mattered most. The word "unique" falls well short of depicting the significance of this combination.

For many kids in the 1950s and '60s, and adults for that matter, from peewee players and road hockey enthusiasts to future NHL All-Stars, Howe was the embodiment of pure hockey hero.

"Gordie Howe was a household name with our family," remembers Hall of Famer and six-time Stanley Cup champion Mark Messier. "My dad [Doug] actually attended a couple of the Red Wings training camps so he had a lot of respect for Gordie Howe. Dad talked about him often. He was part of the folklore, how tough he was as a player and how good he was, and my dad had a lot of respect for Gordie."

Gordie really set the benchmark for every hockey player for what he was able to accomplish, not only in longevity, but his numbers were pretty staggering as well.

Messier passed Howe in Cups, in total career NHL points, and in penalty minutes. Mainly because of their combination of toughness and talent, the two are sometimes compared.

"I always have a tough time with comparisons, even at the best of times," Messier states. "Gordie really set the benchmark for every hockey player for what he was able to accomplish, not only in longevity, but his numbers were pretty staggering as well. It's always a compliment [to be compared], but I think it's tough to compare players because

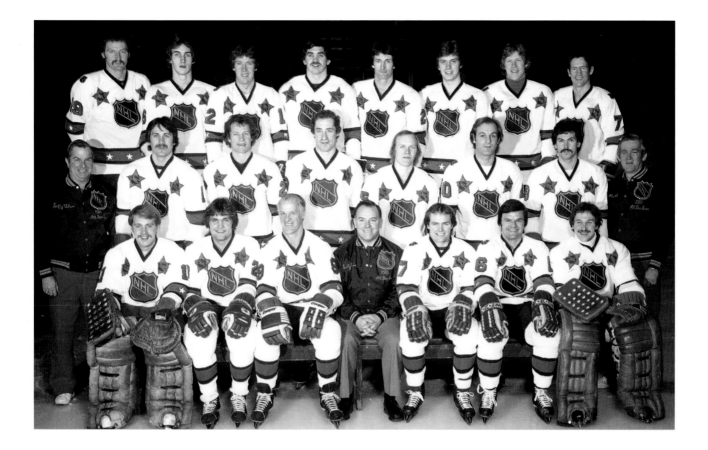

everyone in their own right brings something, a quality, when they come to the rink."

It's often said that it's tough to compare players from different eras. However, the players that were active during the Original Six era should be the standard by which all other players are judged. It's a frequently overlooked argument: before the league was watered down by the addition of new teams, Gordie Howe put up his numbers, and his elbows, and dominated during a period when the NHL was limited to the absolute best 120 players in the world. This was long before the time when a quarter of the players in the league would have been a better fit for the AHL.

"He was such a great player, and so charismatic," reflects Ontario-born Hall of Famer Bill Barber. According to Barber, who watched *Hockey Night in Canada* as a young boy, Howe was "easy to follow as a star player. I admired him so much that I ended up going to his hockey school for two years, and when I turned pro I ended up playing against him. That was a great thrill. I know him now and he's a great man, Mr. Hockey, simple as that."

"We didn't have television, we listened to the games on the radio," remembers Bobby Clarke, a Flin Flon, Manitoba, native, Barber's teammate in Philadelphia, and fellow Hall of Famer. "Of course Gordie, from Western Canada, was as big as you could possibly get for us kids. I don't think anyone then ever evaluated skill or toughness, it was just Gordie. He was just Gordie."

ABOVE: *NHL All-Star Game Prince of Wales Conference team photo, 1980. Front row, from left: Don Edwards, Red Wing Reed Larson, Gordie Howe, future Red Wings coach Scotty Bowman, future Red Wings captain Danny Gare, former Red Wing Marcel Dionne, Gilles Meloche. Middle row, from left: Detroit trainer Lefty Wilson, Gilbert Perreault, Darryl Sittler, Bob Gainey, Butch Goring, Guy Lafleur, Real Cloutier, Detroit assistant trainer Dan Olesevich. Top row, from left: Larry Robinson, Dave Burrows, Mike Murphy, former Red Wing Ron Stackhouse, Steve Payne, Craig Hartsburg, future Red Wing Jim Schoenfeld, Jean Ratelle.*

ABOVE: *Ambidextrous Howe stick handling through Black Hawks Chico Maki, left, and rookie defenseman Keith Magnuson in 1970.*

OPPOSITE TOP LEFT: *There's a goalie stick, but no goalie, leaving Chicago defenseman Gilles Marotte to fend for himself against Howe. Red Wing Alex Delvecchio looks back.*

"He was hard to play against because he was so well positioned," adds Barber. "And the respect factor. That's the biggest thing. You're playing against Mr. Hockey and you followed him since you were 5 years old—it was hard to play against a great player like that, but I'm glad I had the opportunity."

Centerman Garry Unger was 19 years old when he joined the Red Wings in March of 1968. "So about three years prior to that, Gordie was signing autographs for Eaton's in Canada, in Calgary," recalls Unger. "He was in the basement of an Eaton's store, I stood over and watched him for a while and then stood in line for about two hours, kids all over. When I finally got up to the front of the line I was afraid to ask him for his autograph, so I left. Gordie was always my favorite player growing up, probably like thousands of other kids."

"The biggest thrill was coming in and getting to play with Gordie Howe," says former winger Wayne Connelly. "That was a big thing, going in that dressing room and seeing Gordie Howe and Alex Delvecchio and Frank Mahovlich. That was my biggest thrill up to that point in the NHL, getting to play with Gordie and sitting in the room with those guys."

Hall of Fame left-winger Johnny Bucyk, who has spent 50-plus years with the Bruins organization, says of Gordie Howe, "He was my idol and still is. Detroit was the team I came up with, and for a couple years I had a great time there. When I walked in I was in awe. I listened to him

play on the radio and I was in the Detroit system for many years, and to sit behind Gordie and Teddy and get on the ice at the same time as them—that was something special."

Bucyk, also known as "Chief," has been the man in charge of everything in Boston for decades. Need a new car? Need an apartment? Need a deal on a suit? "Need an elephant"(as some have joked)? Chief is the man to get it done. It's a quality he learned in Motown.

"Gordie Howe and Teddy Lindsay took me under their wings and taught me an awful lot," Bucyk explains. "It's what you do for the team. Teddy and Gordie always used to look after the kids, and that just reflected on me. I went to the Bruins and I've done what I can for the players."

When you can be the toughest guy in the National Hockey League and the best player at the same time, it's a combination that never ever happens at that level.

Meanwhile, as kind and considerate as Howe was off the ice, his demeanor on the ice was often exactly the opposite. His elbows were legendarily dangerous, and he was tough as nails. Although Howe only completed the triad a couple of times in his career, to this day a player who accomplishes an assist, a goal, and a fight in a single NHL game is said to have performed a "Gordie Howe hat trick."

Howe didn't win all of his early fights, but after 1959 he was rarely challenged. In February of that year he destroyed New York Rangers tough guy Lou Fontinato so thoroughly with fisticuffs that his reputation for being one of the most, if not the most, intimidating and toughest players in the league became cemented. Howe's combination of abilities was beyond compare.

TOP RIGHT: *Howe scored his 500th career goal shorthanded in New York against goalie Gump Worsley of the Rangers on March 14, 1962.*

BOTTOM: *Howe, with coach Sid Abel, also scored his 600th goal against Worsley, on November 27, 1965. It came in Montreal against the Canadiens, who won the game 3–2.*

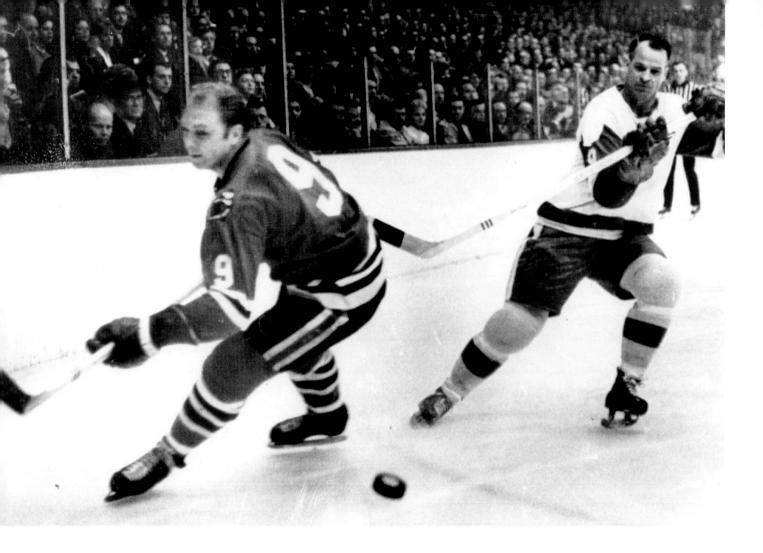

"When you can be the toughest guy in the National Hockey League and the best player at the same time," points out Wings broadcaster and former player Paul Woods, "it's a combination that never ever happens at that level."

Wayne Gretzky had Dave Semenko and Marty McSorley for protection. Steve Yzerman had Bob Probert and Joey Kocur. Gordie Howe had Gordie Howe.

[Howe] was tough, he could hit, he could do anything.

"There's a lot of great players, the Gretzkys, the Lemieuxs, you can name them," stated the late, great Original Sixer Johnny Wilson during the summer of 2011. "None of them could go out there like Gordie, and if they harassed him or a teammate, he'd go over and fight the guy and beat the hell out of him. Not too many hockey players could do that and be the leading scorer. He's what I call the complete hockey player because he was tough, he could hit, he could do anything."

Howe lived by two personal on-ice standards: get them before they get you, and if they happen to get you first, never forget.

Teammates and opponents alike have stories of Howe's penchant for rough play. Harry Neale, longtime NHL coach and commentator, remembers a story that Bobby Baun once told him about playing against Detroit at the Olympia when he was a rookie for the Leafs. Baun was something of a tough player himself, and at one point in the game, when Howe was in the middle of a slap shot, Baun knocked him down.

"He wasn't unconscious, but he was down for a while, which was uncommon," relays Neale. "But he finally got up and went to the bench. That was 1957 or '8."

Ten years later, Howe finally got even. Baun was playing for Oakland, explains Neale, "and Gordie was still with Detroit. Almost the same thing happened, only this time Gordie saw him at the last second and put his stick out, and Baun ran right into it with his neck. He said, 'I'm laying there on the ice thinking I'd never breathe again, I couldn't breathe, and I'm trying to catch my breath.' Howe skated over and kind of half straddled him and said, 'Now we're even, you son of a bitch.'"

Hall of Famer Dave Keon was one of many players who found themselves on the wrong side of Gordie Howe's vicious elbow.

"[Keon] had this patented hook check where he'd come up and sweep the puck away from you," explains Gordie's son Mark Howe. "Keon said in

LEFT: *Howe swoops in and scores five-hole (between the legs) on Los Angeles Kings goalie Wayne Rutledge after evading Bryan Campbell in 1968. Howe finished top-five in NHL scoring for an unparalleled 20 consecutive seasons ending in 1968–69. That season, he finished third, with 103 points, at age 40.*

TOP RIGHT: *Howe with Los Angeles Kings captain Wayne Gretzky, after the latter broke Howe's career NHL scoring mark of 1,850 points, on October 15, 1989.*

BOTTOM RIGHT: *Howe with Penguins legend "Super" Mario Lemieux at an awards ceremony in 2000. Howe is third on the all-time NHL scoring list, Lemieux seventh.*

ABOVE: *Howe first had his number 9 retired by the Wings on March 12, 1972. Here, his banner is hoisted at the Joe Louis Arena. From left, Wings owner Mike Ilitch, NHL president John Ziegler, Howe, and former teammate Johnny Wilson.*

OPPOSITE LEFT: *Howe faced-off against the Red Wings on January 12, 1980, as a member of the Hartford Whalers, nine years after he retired from Detroit. The NHL absorbed four teams from the WHA for 1979–80; the Whalers, Quebec Nordiques, Winnipeg Jets, and Edmonton Oilers. On his left wing, his son Marty, on his right wing, his son Mark. The Red Wings from left to right on the draw, Jean Hamel, Dennis Polonich, and Bill Hogaboam.*

one game, Dad was skating with the puck and Davey came up and hooked the puck from behind and took it away. He went and sat on the bench and all the players looked at Davey and said, 'Nah, you can't do that.' Davey said, 'Look, I've seen Gordie Howe on *Hockey Night in Canada* on Saturday nights and I'm not going anywhere near him, just playing the puck.' And they said, 'We're telling you, just be careful.'"

But Keon ignored his teammates and repeated the manoeuvre. Again, his teammates warned him. "'He's going to get you, we don't know when or how, but you are going to pay for what you're doing.' So Davey said he went to try it again later in the game, and the next thing he remembers is waking up in the hospital in Toronto. I guess he reached a little too far, Gordie knew, caught him with an elbow and knocked him cold."

Howe retired from the Red Wings and the NHL in 1971, complaining of a bad wrist, when, in reality, his departure had as much to do with his relationship and frustration with Red Wings coach turned general manager Ned Harkness.

"I was in my early 20s," remembers Nick Libett. "Gordie was near his mid-40s and everyone thought he might be close to retiring, but then he was kind of forced to retire . . . Ned came in and that was another issue, not sure exactly what it was between Ned and Gordie, but Gordie basically got shuffled into a little back office with no responsibility and that just finished him in Detroit."

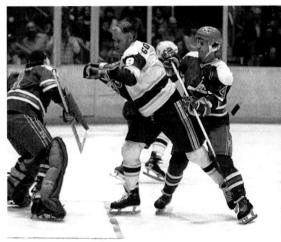

Three seasons later, Howe came out of retirement to join his sons Mark and Marty with the Houston Aeros in the upstart World Hockey Association (WHA). Despite the league featuring a number of superstar NHL expatriates, the WHA's statistics have never been recognized by the NHL. During six seasons playing for Houston and then New England, starting his "second career" as a 45-year-old, Howe won the league MVP award in 1974 and helped Houston win two championships. He tallied 508 points, 174 goals, in 419 WHA games.

Even more remarkable than his production, was the unprecedented fact that Howe wasn't only looking out for himself, he was looking out for his offspring.

"When we were playing together, Marty, Dad, and I, the first year down in Houston, that's when there used to be a lot of brawls," says Mark.

He recalls one game in particular, when an Edmonton player pinned Marty to the ice and knelt on his arms. "Dad and I were trying to get over, finally got over there, and Dad looked at the guy and said, 'It's time to get up. It's all over and done with, get up.' The guy kind of gave Dad that mind-your-own-business look, go do your own thing, I'm in control here. So the next thing Dad does, it surprised the heck out of me, he took his hand, he has massive hands, he ran two fingers up the guy's nostrils and threw the guy backwards, ripped his nose half off his face. This guy went flying, Marty got up, and I'm looking, thinking,

TOP RIGHT: *The three Howes's (left to right, Gordie, Marty, Mark) first WHA team was the Houston Aeros, where they played from 1973 to 1977. Gordie, at age 46, was the league MVP after their first season and the Aeros won back-to-back Avco World Trophy championships.*

BOTTOM RIGHT: *Howe as a New England Whaler in the WHA in 1978, taking a bump from Winnipeg Jets captain Lars-Erik Sjoberg, in front of Jets goalie Joe Daley.*

'Oh my God, who would even think to do that, to pick a guy up by the nose!'"

When four teams from the folding WHA, including the Howes' Hartford Whalers, were absorbed into the NHL in 1979, 51-year-old Gordie Howe was back in the National Hockey League. He was one of just four players on the team that season to play in all 80 games, tallying 15 goals and 26 assists.

"He was still good," states former WHA and NHL defenseman Barry Melrose, "and his two sons were on the team, and if you ever did anything to Mark or Marty, Gordie made you pay a price. Gordie was tough, was a great player. He actually did the thing [shot effectively left- and right-handed] with both hands, saw him do that many times. I saw him at 50, so the guy must have been unbelievable at 25."

On February 5, 1980, Howe played in his record 23rd NHL All-Star Game, 33 years after playing in his first one. The game was played in Detroit at the new Joe Louis Arena. Howe was introduced last, and

ABOVE: *Bruins defenseman Leo Boivin tries to elude Howe behind the Boston net.*

the ensuing standing ovation lasted almost three minutes before being interrupted.

According to Sabres All-Star Danny Gare, "It was awesome. I sat next to Gordie in the dressing room. I remember Reed Larson was the one Red Wing in the game and he was introduced and then Gordie, Mr. Hockey. What an honor. The crowd went nuts, and went on and on, for all the things he had done, and he was still playing well and not missing any shifts. A great player and a great person, and he deserved it. We all had chills. It was unbelievable standing there on the blue line."

Two months later, on April 11, 1980, at age 52, Howe played his final NHL game.

"Greatest hockey player that's ever played," says Hall of Famer Ted Lindsay. "I will say that until the day I die. Bar none."

From that point forward, Gordie naturally became hockey's all-time greatest ambassador. He's probably signed more autographs than any human being in history. He and his wife, Colleen (who passed away in

2009 after 55 years of marriage), the true businessperson and "boss" in the family, went about being Mr. and Mrs. Hockey.

"I'm just in awe every time I'm in his presence," states network broadcaster and former Wings play-by-play man Dave Strader. "The most recent time that I was working and was around Gordie was the 2009 All-Star Game in Montreal, and I was on the bench doing some interviews for NHL Network. I think he had just turned 80, and he was the same as he was 30 years ago. It's incredible how he is. He had never changed one bit as a human being, and is as great an ambassador as there has ever been. It always feels good, when you're a hockey person or someone that's been around the game, and you go to an event and Gordie is there. You can't wait to go up and shake his hand, and he tells you a little story. He makes you feel great."

Greatest hockey player that's ever played. I will say that until the day I die. Bar none.

Legendary head coach Scotty Bowman remembers how Gordie would visit the Red Wings during playoffs to encourage the players: "I do remember one playoff series. It was 1997, the year we won. Fedorov got a shoulder injury in one of the early rounds. It wasn't a serious injury, but it was painful and he wasn't sure of himself. I'm thinking, 'We've gotta get this guy going.' So Sergei came down one afternoon to skate on his own and Gordie came by and talked to him and boosted him up and said, 'You know, this doesn't happen all the time. You're going to be in the playoffs, and you're very valuable.'"

Fedorov finished with 20 points in 20 games to help the Wings end a 42-year Cup drought.

"I got to meet Gordie a lot of times in Detroit and he's just a great person," affirms Gerard Gallant. "And everything you hear about him, it's definitely true. He's just a great ambassador to the game and just a great man."

Budd Lynch agrees. "Amazing individual, outstanding player, team player, respected by everyone around the league."

"It's hard to find a finer gentleman than Gordie Howe, the ultimate ambassador for hockey for all those years," states Mickey Redmond. "We'd always see a lot of him in the press box and he'd always have a smile and a quick remark and a high elbow to say hello to you."

For Paul Woods, Gordie Howe sets the bar for all other players in terms of public image and overall behavior. "It's incredible how he treats people and how he handles the public," he says. "And again, it goes back to the history of your organization, and what a great lesson for the young players to see a guy like that handle himself that way throughout his life. Especially after all of his accomplishments, it's truly something."

Gordie's son Mark agrees that his father has set a high standard. Yet there's something about Gordie Howe that is nearly impossible to emulate. Mark reflects that it has "nothing to do with anything on the ice, everything to do with off the ice. He does have a certain thing—I've

only met three or four people in my life, they just have a certain way with people, and Dad is one of them. He makes people feel special, and to me it's an unseen, unknown thing. I was reading a letter he got a month ago, a guy waited in line for an hour to get his autograph. It was something like the 15th autograph he had from my dad, but he said he just wanted to get five minutes to visit with him again.

"People who know my dad never ever talk about him as a hockey player, they talk about him as a person," Mark concludes. "That, and a tremendous husband and father that he was, that's what I appreciate most about him."

Gordie Howe: simply the greatest ever.

ABOVE: *Howe wore number 17 as a rookie with the Red Wings. He wore number 9 for his following 31 professional seasons.*

Terrible Teddie

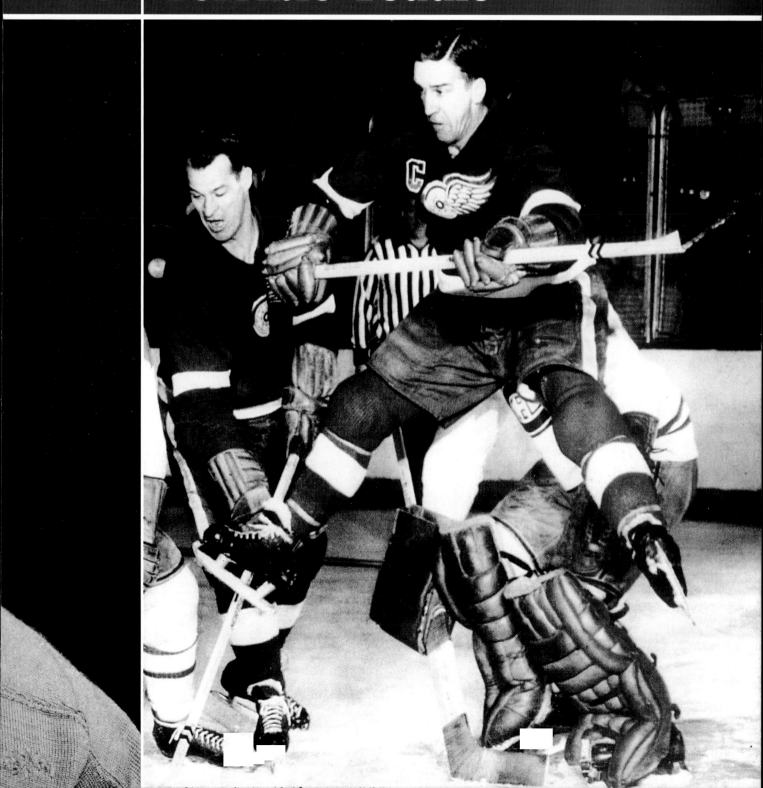

"They say I had 600-plus stitches put in my face. Not too interested in knowing the exact number." — Ted Lindsay

ABOVE: *Ted Lindsay was the Red Wings captain for four seasons and two Stanley Cups in the 1950s.*

NOT THE LARGEST PLAYER BY ANY MEANS, at 5' 8" and 160 pounds, Ted Lindsay survived and flourished in the National Hockey League due to his zealous, competitive nature. Ted became "Terrible" for persistent disruptions and eruptions; for the punishment he doled out over the course of 17 seasons with his stick, his elbows, his forearms and, when necessary, his fists.

Yet Teddie wasn't so terrible after all. In the spirit of "love thine enemy," Lindsay actually had in mind the best interests of his on-ice adversaries all along.

The latter stages of Lindsay's Hall of Fame playing career, which ended for the first time in 1960, were defined by his efforts to start a players' association beginning in 1957.

Unhappy with the way the players of the NHL and farm teams were being treated by the six-team league, Lindsay and Montreal's Doug Harvey attempted to make a change. Unfortunately, their efforts were met with contempt and outrage by league ownership.

I went to Chicago, but I was a Red Wing. I had it tattooed on my forehead, over my heart, and on my backside.

"I was traded to Chicago, as punishment," Lindsay explains. "We players never really spoke to each other with the different teams, but Doug and I were on the pension board, and I saw some of the things that were happening to the kids in Detroit. Our farm teams back then were Edmonton in the Western league and Indianapolis in the American league. These kids were making probably $2,700 or $3,000 [a season], and management could send you down anywhere they wanted, and they didn't owe you anything, and if they didn't want to pay you, they didn't pay you."

Decades before free agency, long-term, multimillion-dollar contracts, and no-trade clauses, there was Ted Lindsay attempting to gain some simple rights for the NHL players.

"That's the way it was," Lindsay continues. "It was a dictatorship in the six-team league. We wanted a say in pension. We weren't interested

in running their league, we just wanted a voice. We were no better off in the long run than a guy standing on the street corner selling pencils."

Essentially through threats and intimidation, especially aimed at the younger team members, the owners squashed the players' first attempt to organize themselves, and Lindsay was cast aside for his leadership role. The short-term end result for his involvement was on-ice misery. Along with his ally, young goaltender Glenn Hall, Lindsay was traded to Chicago. After 13 years, an Art Ross Trophy, 11 All-Star Games, and four Stanley Cups with his beloved Detroit club, Lindsay was shuffled off to the lowly Black Hawks.

"I was a Red Wing. I played hockey, not because of [Detroit GM and coach] Jack Adams, I played because I loved hockey," Lindsay urges. "I went to Chicago, but I was a Red Wing. I had it tattooed on my forehead, over my heart, and on my backside."

Prior to the Black Hawks deal, Lindsay and fellow Detroit left-winger Marty Pavelich had started a business in the Motor City as manufacturers' representatives in the automotive industry.

"So when I got traded, Adams told Marty he had gotten too slow—Marty could have played another four years for four other teams in the league—and we had our business just starting and Marty retired and he went to run our business," Lindsay explains. "The business would support him at the time, but we weren't in it long enough for it to support both of us, so I went ahead to Chicago.

"The third year I was in Chicago, I was existing," he concludes. "I wasn't through playing, as far as my body, legs, or brain, or whatever, but I decided to retire and come back home and go to work. So that's what I did."

The players' pension concerns resulted in a lawsuit against the league and a settlement in 1958, but a permanent players' association wouldn't come into being until a decade later. Lindsay had laid the groundwork using much of the same determination and spirit he used throughout his years on the ice.

When Nick Polano, a Red Wings head coach in the early '80s, was a kid, his favorite player was Ted Lindsay.

"I liked Ted Lindsay because of his drive and his determination to win," says Polano. "He wasn't a big man but he had a big heart and he combined that with a lot of skill. I liked Ted so much that when I got the head coaching job I asked him to come on some road trips with us. He'd come on the road once in a while with the team and I told him, 'Any time you want to talk to any of the players, just chat with them; I want them to play like you.' He was really great about that. A great man."

In 1958, Lindsay's former linemate Sid Abel became head coach of the Red Wings, and in 1963 he also became general manager. This was a stroke of luck for Lindsay, who, because of his impeccable conditioning and some good timing, found himself in a Red Wings jersey once again in 1964.

"Four years after I retired and moved back [to Detroit] I went in to see Sid," Lindsay explains. "They had just started doing television then, little six-inch screens, black and white, snow all over it. And I said, 'Sid, I want to be remembered as a Red Wing, but I don't want to do radio and travel all over because Marty and I have our business.' They were only doing about seven or ten games on television a year and I said I'd like to do color commentary on the television between periods. Sid answered with, 'Why don't you come back and play?'"

Despite skating on a regular basis and playing in an industrial league since his return to Detroit, Lindsay wasn't convinced.

"I laughed at Sid, but he said, 'No, I'm serious, I really think you can help us.'

"The day before the season opened we were at the press club, and Sid said, 'We've got a young rookie that we're going to sign to a contract

OPPOSITE: *Lindsay wore number 15 when he came out of retirement to play for the Red Wings in 1964–65, because teammate Norm Ullman had assumed number 7 back in 1958. A total of 20 other Detroit players wore number 7 after Lindsay, but it became his forever when the team retired it in his honor on November 10, 1991.*

ABOVE *(left to right):* Right-wing Gordie Howe, center Sid Abel, and left-wing Ted Lindsay; the famous Production Line from the late 1940s having a chat. At this point, in 1964, Abel was long retired from playing and had taken over as Detroit's general manager and coach.

ABOVE: *For his role in trying to start a players' union, Lindsay was traded, or in his mind banished, from Detroit to Chicago in 1957. Here, as a Black Hawk, he attempts to elude New York Ranger Bill Gadsby, a Hall-of-Famer and future teammate for one season in Detroit.*

tomorrow, and his name is Ted Lindsay.' And that was the first time anybody really knew about it."

Terrible Teddie was obviously still feisty nearing age 40. In 69 games, he scored 14 goals and 14 assists and piled up 173 penalty minutes—the second-highest single-season total of his career.

Lindsay remembers the newspaper headlines that came out at the start of the season. NHL president Clarence Campbell called Lindsay's return "a black day for hockey," because a 39-year-old man would be playing alongside teammates half his age.

Terrible Teddie was obviously still feisty nearing age 40. In 69 games, he scored 14 goals and 14 assists and piled up 173 penalty minutes—the second-highest single-season total of his career.

"He's entitled to his opinion," Lindsay says now. Also, he gives Campbell credit for coming out with a public apology after seeing the team play. Clarence was quoted as saying, "Lindsay has done what I thought to be next to impossible. His comeback is one of the most amazing feats in professional sport."

Campbell wasn't the only one who doubted the wisdom of Terrible Ted's return.

ABOVE: *Teddie waiting to get his publicity photo taken.*

"Everybody in the six-team league picked us for fifth or sixth spot, nobody thought we were too good," Lindsay says with a laugh. "We played each other 12 times a year, and after we went around the league circuit once, I'm thinking to myself, 'Who's any better than we are?' After we went around twice, I got the guys thinking that we could win this whole thing if we put our mind to it. So, we went on to win the league [regular-season] championship. We beat Montreal, home-and-home, the last two games of the regular season to win the championship."

The Red Wings hadn't finished first in the league since Lindsay was dealt away.

"We should have won the Stanley Cup," Lindsay continues. "If it wasn't for that jackass referee Art Skov. I'm serious, I'm serious. Seventh game of the series in Detroit against Chicago [Cup semifinal], we're ahead two–nothing, the game is half over, and Chicago never got it over center ice up until that time."

And then, as Lindsay recalls it, Skov gave Chicago two power plays in a row.

"They had Hull and Mikita," Lindsay explains. "They got one goal and that picked them up, and then they went from there, and they beat us. Montreal then beat them for the Stanley Cup. We would have won the Stanley Cup, if he hadn't called those two penalties. Everybody thinks I'm pipe-dreaming, but that's a fact of life. We dominated Montreal that year."

Despite winning Cups in 1950, '52, '54, and '55, Lindsay, as it is with many players, remembers the losses more than the wins. Falling short, for whatever reason, sticks in the craw.

ABOVE LEFT: *A friend to generations of hockey players, Lindsay shakes hands with Guy Lafleur at the 1977 NHL postseason awards ceremony. Montreal great Jean Beliveau sits between them.*

ABOVE RIGHT: *On Ted Lindsay Night at Joe Louis Arena, on October 18, 2008, Ted greeted the Red Wings on the bench, (right to left: Darren Helm, Tomas Holmstrom, Tomas Kopecky, and Kirk Maltby.*

"When we won the championship in 1955 against Montreal in seven games, the 'experts' all said we were lucky," Lindsay recalls. "I don't care whether we were lucky or not, we were the Stanley Cup champions. So, Adams traded nine players away from that Cup team—half of it. Three or four to Boston, three or four to New York, and a few guys to Chicago."

The Montreal Canadiens would win the next five Stanley Cups.

"Every time I see Henri Richard, and he's got 11 Stanley Cups, I've got four, I say 'Henriiiii . . . you're luck-eeee,' and he says, 'Ted-deeee, I know, I've got the rings.' We would have won those five, or we would have won four of them. It bugs me to this day."

Lindsay's comeback lasted just the one season. Twelve years after his second retirement from playing, and after a stint commentating in New York for the Rangers and on network telecasts for NBC, Lindsay jumped back into the real hockey fray in 1977. He was hired as the general manager of the Red Wings in an effort to rejuvenate a moribund franchise.

When he returned to run the club, his efforts were accompanied by a popular public relations campaign: "Aggressive Hockey Is Back in Town." In Lindsay's first year as GM, the Red Wings made the playoffs for the first time since 1970, and only the second time since 1966.

"Ted was a very straightforward and hard-nosed and tough guy," states Paul Woods, the longtime Wings radio broadcaster and a rookie on the 1977–78 team. "But he was an honest guy too. I look back at life and the situation when I played, and I really understand now, he was just a good man."

Woods remembers Lindsay's honesty during his contract negotiation. "I had come from Montreal [the Canadiens' farm team] and my deal was running out, and I didn't have an agent, and did [the negotiations] myself. Ted said, 'Here's what we're gonna do: you just write down on a piece of paper what you want, and I'll write down on a piece of paper what I want to give you, and we'll just trade pieces of paper and we'll go from there. That'll get it started.' It's funny, his paper was better than mine, so we went with his."

In 1980, Lindsay stepped down as general manager and became head coach, an experiment that lasted just 20 games. With only three victories, Ted became part of a revolving door of coaches in the early '80s.

From that point forward, Lindsay continued to grow a successful automotive business, he became an honored hockey ambassador, and, as always, he remained a Red Wing through and through. All the while, he never stopped working out at the rink.

"He would stay out of our way," remembers former Red Wings coach Scotty Bowman. "He would figure out when we were practicing and get in there [the weight room] before us. Ted was probably in his early 70s then, he used to come in and work out all the time, and that's why he looked so fit."

There's a long list of former and current Red Wings who ran into the elder statesman in the workout room. Kris King, a longtime NHL hockey operations executive and a Red Wing in the late '80s, remembers seeing Lindsay while the team prepared for games. He reflects that, "Every time we were there early, Ted Lindsay was there working out, and he could lift more than most of us. He was like a machine. I forget how old he was at that time, but he was in there almost every day from three thirty to five before the team showed up, working out in the changing room. Wonderful guy, real nice man, and it was kind of neat just being around him."

There's a long list of former and current Red Wings who ran into the elder statesman in the workout room.

"That's where I met Sergei Fedorov," recalls Lindsay. "I'm in the room in the summertime, and who comes walking into the room, but Sergei. He couldn't speak English; it was Sergei and his interpreter. Good guy, really a good guy.

"And then I was working out there another time and Tomas Holmstrom came in," he adds. "It was summer, and those Swedes are very, very intelligent people. They speak better English than I do. I'm in the room working out and Tomas comes in and asks the equipment guy, 'Who's the old guy by the name of Ted Lindsay?' That's where I met Tomas the first time. He really is a great guy and a good friend."

Tomas Holmstrom remembers meeting Ted also. "He comes down to the rink it seems like every second or third day," Holmstrom points out. "He's fun to talk to; he always has some good stories. I've learned a bit about him for sure, a little guy like that, he was feisty, a really good hockey player when he played."

Being a good friend and advocate to generations of hockey players is inherent in Ted Lindsay's character. In his playing days, when the NHL season was over, Lindsay would visit his sisters in Kirkland Lake, Ontario. During one visit, he asked one of his sisters, a teacher, about some of the local youth players.

"So she gave me the names of Dick Duff, Ralph Backstrom, Larry Hillman, and a kid by the name of Jack Whittle," Lindsay explains. "Jack Whittle never became a hockey player, but now he lives out in Seattle, Washington. He's a writer."

Leave it to Ted to keep track.

Being a good friend and advocate to generations of hockey players is inherent in Ted Lindsay's character.

About 90 miles from Kirkland Lake was Schumacher, Ontario (Frank Mahovlich's hometown). Lindsay recalls that at the end of June each summer, the best figure skating teachers in the world would descend on the northeastern Ontario town, and on Friday nights they would provide skating and training to the public. Lindsay used this as an opportunity to mentor the students recommended to him by his sister.

"I talked to the parents of these guys and I said, 'We'll skate, and after we're through skating, we'll stop and have a hot dog or hamburger and a pop, and I'll get them home by one thirty, two o'clock Saturday morning.' So we did that for a couple years, never dreaming that these three guys would end up in the National Hockey League, and Dickie would end up in the Hall of Fame."

Ted Lindsay's accomplishments and honors are diverse. He won a Memorial Cup as a junior player with the Oshawa Generals in 1944. He scored a Stanley Cup final record four goals in Game 2 in 1955 against Montreal. He was the first captain to hoist the Cup and take it for a skate following a championship. He was inducted into the Hockey Hall of Fame in 1966. In 1978 *The Hockey News* named him NHL Executive of the Year, and in 1998 named him the 21st greatest player of all time. The Red Wings retired his number 7 in 1991, and in 2008 his statue was unveiled inside the Joe Louis Arena.

But the honor that epitomizes Lindsay, the one that takes him full circle, from those training road trips in Northern Ontario, to the clandestine association meetings, to getting to know generations of new players and making new friends: the 2010 renaming of the Lester B. Pearson Award to the Ted Lindsay Award—a prize given annually by the National Hockey League Players' Association to the league's "most outstanding player."

He was the first captain to hoist the Cup and take it for a skate following a championship.

Ted Lindsay has earned the respect of countless hockey players and fans over the years. Future Hall of Famer Chris Chelios says he would be proud to be compared to a player like Lindsay. "Seeing what he went through with the players' association and knowing how he was on the ice, a great team guy, what he represents, I like being compared to him. I always thought I was like Stan Mikita, because he was kind of the same way when he first started, but they finally toned him down on the ice as a dirty player, as they say. I wouldn't compare myself to him [Ted], but if I were to be compared, that would be one of the guys that I'd really be proud to be associated with."

"He's just such a nice gentleman," states former Wings grinder Kirk Maltby. "'Terrible Ted' just doesn't seem right, you know?" he laughs. "As players, we've always tried to golf in his golf outing that he has [the Ted Lindsay Foundation has raised more than $2 million for autism research]. Ted is really just a great person who is a big part of this organization."

For a man who has given so much time, energy, and charity to the game, Lindsay never fails to appreciate, with some astonishment, just how much the game has given back.

"I was born in Renfrew and grew up in Kirkland Lake," Ted states. "I never dreamed of playing in the National Hockey League. I grew up playing every day in the school yard, we had two rinks in every school yard. Our normal temperature would be 15 below. You skated, then we had warming huts at center, between rinks, and you'd go in there to warm up. I wasn't playing for the league, or to get to the Stanley Cup. It was the little black puck, and with a stick you'd chase it."

4 Sawchuk

> *"An unfortunate accident, but he certainly was a top, top, top goaltender."* — HALL OF FAME RED WINGS EXECUTIVE Jim Devellano

ABOVE: *Sawchuk, from Winnipeg, Manitoba, took up goaltending because his older brother, Mike, who died at age 17 of a heart ailment, was a goaltender. Sawchuk was scouted by Detroit at age 14 and signed four years later.*

OPPOSITE TOP: *Sawchuk began wearing a goalie mask full time during the 1962–63 season, his 13th in the NHL. Here, he slides across to confront two rushing New York Rangers, Andy Hebenton (12) and likely Earl Ingarfield. Red Wing Howie Young is in the background.*

OPPOSITE BOTTOM: *Sawchuk sans-mask and deep in his crease against the Maple Leafs in Toronto, with some help from defenseman Marcel Pronovost (number 3) and wing Vic Stasiuk.*

TERRY SAWCHUK OPERATED LONG BEFORE the days of overbearing celebri-tologists and instant social media, in a time and place when rumors and gossip took a while to track. Who knows—had the greatest and most acrobatic goalie in the world been unwillingly monitored day and night, and scrutinized every moment, maybe he would have survived his reckless lifestyle. Instead, he was a tragic character, a fallen hero who died at the age of 40.

"Sawchuk I watched as a kid, one of my favorite goalies," remembers Jimmy Rutherford, who played 314 games as a netminder for Detroit. "They play the position different now, quite a bit different, but the great goalies of their era could still play in this era, especially with the big equipment. Conditioning and all those things are so much different than when we played, but clearly a guy like Sawchuk could have played at any time."

When Harry Neale was growing up, he loved to watch Sawchuk play. "I always thought he was the most stylish goalie of all the ones playing in those days," says Neale. "And goalies had to move a lot more then to stop the puck than they do now. I've heard from some players who know a lot more about hockey than me, that they thought he was the best at the time and maybe the best ever."

> *I always thought he was the most stylish goalie of all the ones playing in those days.*

Over a career that spanned 21 seasons, Sawchuk piled up 446 wins (now fifth all-time) and an astounding 103 shutouts (now second), both NHL records entering this millennium. Martin Brodeur of New Jersey, who broke the shutout record in 2009, has 119, sixteen more than Sawchuk, but as of the spring of 2012, Brodeur had played in 219 more games. Meanwhile, Sawchuk played at a time when tie games ended in ties, and shoot-outs and overtime didn't determine victories.

"I go back to 1956 in my memories and knowledge of the NHL," reflects Wings executive Jim Devellano, "and I think if you're going to talk about the game, and you're going to talk about the best goaltenders to ever

play the game, Terry Sawchuk might be at the top, and if he's not at the top he's very close to it."

After a seven-game rookie stint with the Detroit Red Wings in 1950, Sawchuk took over full-time the next fall, and over his first five seasons won three Stanley Cups in 1952, 1954, and 1955.

"I think most people remember the 1952 team—they won the Cup in eight straight games," continues Devellano. "It was two best-of-seven series to win the Cup. Detroit won eight straight, but what was remarkable is that in the four games at the Olympia in Detroit, Sawchuk never allowed a goal. You can look that up."

It's true. The Wings swept the Habs in the final, 3–1, 2–1, 3–0, and 3–0, with the latter two games occurring at the Olympia. In the semifinal, Detroit had swept Toronto as well, winning at home 3–0 and 1–0, followed by wins on the road, 6–2 and 3–1.

Hockey writer Stan "The Maven" Fischler remembers Game 3 of the 1952 semifinal in Toronto. "We heard Sawchuk's one weakness was shots over his shoulder. So Detroit is up one–zero in the game and Joe Klukay, 'The Duke of Paducah,' ties it up for the Leafs one–one with a shot over Sawchuk's shoulder. We were thinking, 'Okay, here we go, we found his weakness.' Fat chance. The Wings go on to win the game six–two and the Cup in a double sweep.

"He was innovative," Fischler adds. "Screen shots became more prevalent in those days, and instead of standing up tall or leaning and looking over players' shoulders, Sawchuk would get down in this deep crouch, and look through legs and around bodies."

Sawchuk's teammate and Hall of Fame defenseman Marcel Pronovost believes that the goaltender's older brother, a minor-hockey goalie who died in his late teens, had a lot to do with the quality of Sawchuk's game.

"He wanted to exemplify his brother," says Pronovost. "He was acrobatic and fearless. He was very, very competitive. You wouldn't believe the saves that he made. Boy, he would bail you out—I know because I played D in front of him."

As part of general manager Jack Adams's post-Stanley Cup purge in 1955 (described earlier by Ted Lindsay), Sawchuk was shipped to the lowly Boston Bruins in a nine-player deal. The new conditions were tough, to say the least, and Sawchuk missed part of the 1956–57 season due to what was termed "nervous exhaustion." Then, in a trade that sent eventual Bruins Hall of Famer Johnny Bucyk to Boston in 1957, the Red Wings brought their goalie back.

> *He was acrobatic and fearless. He was very, very competitive. You wouldn't believe the saves that he made. Boy, he would bail you out—I know because I played D in front of him.*

"He had some problems in his private life," explains Pronovost. "It's too bad. I was very good friends with him, I tried to straighten him out, but I wasn't able to . . . He had a beer when it was time to have a beer, he was out and about, and he loved the girls. I kind of curbed him—he was an important part of our club—and I said, 'Terry, take it easy,' and he did for a while."

"His biggest problem was actually his head. And he had some bad luck," reflects Fischler. "When he was traded to Boston he got mono

ABOVE: *Sawchuk with a glove save as Rangers center Camille Henry looks for a rebound in 1961. Many a hockey "old-timer" swears Terry Sawchuk was the greatest goaltender of all time. Comparisons are difficult, as equipment, styles, player size, training, and the game itself have all changed dramatically over the years. But one thing is for sure, as it relates directly to the act of "doing whatever necessary to stop the puck": very few netminders have mustered up the guts, flexibility, and athleticism that Terry Sawchuk exhibited during most of his 21 NHL seasons.*

[mononucleosis]. He was a pretty big goalie for his time, about five eleven, almost 200 pounds, but when he got sick he lost weight down to about 170 and never gained it back."

Players and reporters alike remember Sawchuck as moody and at times unfriendly. Apparent heavy drinking and the depression that ensued played a large role.

"He was squirrelly," explains Lindsay. His behavior was a marked contrast to teammate Marty Pavelich, "who would be smiling 365 days out of the year. And Terry would come in and Marty would say, 'Howdy Uke,' [*Uke* or *Ukey* were common nicknames for Western Canadians of Ukrainian descent] and Terry would say, 'Hi Marty.' He might do that for two weeks, but then for two months he'd say, 'Go to hell, kiss my ass,' you know? So then Marty would wait until Terry said hello first. He was a bit miserable at times."

"Gordie Howe told me this one," says Neale. "The one thing we learned quickly in the warm-ups is never hit him with the puck. If you did, and you skated by, you might get the goal stick . . . If you used to shoot in close, he went wild. Our team must have looked like the greatest scoring team in hockey—in warm-up we always missed Sawchuk and scored, and he used to just stand there."

Sawchuk's second run in Detroit went through the 1963–64 season. To that point, he had won the Calder Memorial Trophy as NHL Rookie of the Year, had won three Vezina Trophies as best goalkeeper, had been

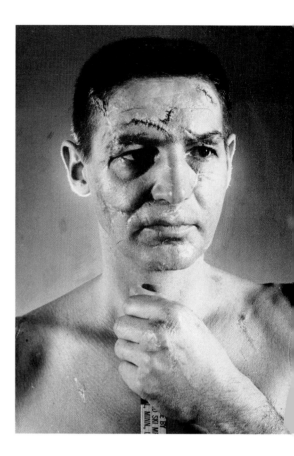

a First Team All-Star three times, a Second Team All-Star four times, and had played in 10 NHL All-Star Games.

At the age of 34 he was claimed off waivers by Toronto. He'd win another Vezina, this time with Johnny Bower in 1965, and another Stanley Cup with the Leafs in 1967. He won six of his 10 playoff starts that spring and had a goals against average of 2.65.

Following his brief resurgence, Sawchuk would continue to bounce from team to team. After three seasons in Toronto he was left unprotected and was claimed by Los Angeles in the original expansion draft, where he'd go 11–14–6 with the first-year Kings franchise. Then, just before the season in 1968, he was traded back to Detroit where he played 13 games, only to be traded again the next summer to the New York Rangers. That is where his career, and his life, would ultimately end.

Off the ice his existence had gradually become more difficult. His 16-year marriage, which bore numerous children, ended in 1969. Drinking was his demise. In the infamous incident that led to his death, he was intoxicated when he got into a fistfight with Rangers teammate and housemate Ron Stewart. Sawchuk fell onto some barbecue equipment and was seriously injured and taken to hospital.

Shirley Fischler, Stan's wife, then a writer in New York for the *Toronto Star* and *Hockey Illustrated*, was the last journalist to see him alive. She arrived at his hospital room unannounced, flowers in hand, and remembers thinking that he was looking better.

ABOVE LEFT: *Sawchuk in his third and final hurrah with Detroit, a one-season stint in 1968–69. He was the first Red Wing ever to wear number 29.*

ABOVE RIGHT: *These marks and scars aren't real. In 1966, a makeup artist simulated what Sawchuk's face and body would look like with the cumulative injuries from 16 years of professional hockey.*

ABOVE: *Sawchuk was waived by Detroit in 1964 and snatched up by Toronto. Here he battles to follow the puck while playing against his former team. That's former Red Wing Marcel Pronovost (number 3) on defense, along with Tim Horton (number 7) for the Leafs. Alex Delvecchio (left) and Paul Henderson crash the net for Detroit.*

"He had two women at his bedside," Fischler recounts, "neither of whom, in any way, shape, or form, related to him. But he also had a bottle on his bed stand. I gather it was literally the night after I saw him that he probably consumed that bottle. He had cirrhosis of the liver, had been a hard drinker much of his life, and when he and Ron had their tussle, and he fell over the barbecue, he injured his liver. So he was in very dicey shape and apparently he consumed that bottle of whiskey that I saw on his nightstand and totally went into some kind of terminal situation. That's when they moved him to another hospital and he died a day or two later. When I saw him he was officially in recovery."

In Fischler's opinion, Sawchuk's move to New York was a disaster. Ted Lindsay agrees. "Should have been home with his family," he says.

Sawchuk's life ended just as his career was coming to an end. Given the physical breaks and bruises, and the tumultuous road emotionally, the timing of his demise, though tragic, seemed appropriate. He was alive as long as he was goaltending.

In his last season in New York, he appeared in eight games, won three of them, lost one, tied two, and recorded a shutout.

"You could see remnants of how brilliant he must have been," Shirley Fischler points out. "He had good nights still, but as an interview or as a human being, he was kind of mean and surly most of the time."

It hadn't always been that way. Marcel Pronovost remembers a teammate who had another side: "One night . . . I was playing with Toronto and so was he, and we ended up losing two to one," Pronovost recalls. "I was on the ice for the two goals they scored, and boy I felt bad—it was a year we really weren't supposed to lose. I come into the room and I said, 'Jeepers, Terry, I'm sorry. I let this guy go and I should have had him.' 'Don't worry about it,' he said. That was Sawchuk: never placed the blame on anyone else.

In 1971 he was inducted into the Hockey Hall of Fame. Three decades later The Hockey News *placed him ninth on the list of the 100 greatest hockey players of all time. Sawchuk was the highest-rated netminder.*

"There's another instance that stays in my mind," Pronovost continues. "There was a kid that stood on the far side of the boards at the Olympia, and he got hit right between the eyes by the puck. They brought him into the dressing room and Terry came in and gave him a puck and his stick and everything. Terry had a family of his own, so he could relate. The kid got hit right between the eyes."

Sawchuk's empathy also stemmed from his personal experience. As a child, he had suffered a broken arm that required multiple surgeries and that never healed correctly. As an adult, he had taken more than his fair share right between the eyes—and everywhere else in the face, and head, and shoulders, and arms, and legs. Photographs and documentary testimonials tell of his cuts, scars, and bruises—multicolored bruises that ran the length of his body. It's no wonder this fearless man was a little bit, or a whole lot, ornery.

In 1970 his pain ended when he passed away. In 1971 he was inducted into the Hockey Hall of Fame. Three decades later *The Hockey News* placed him ninth on the list of the 100 greatest hockey players of all time. Sawchuk was the highest-rated netminder. And on March 6, 1994, the Red Wings retired his sweater, number 1.

For Ted Lindsay, Terry Sawchuk was the "greatest goaltender that's ever lived. I know a lot of people want to talk about goaltenders. There's a lot of great ones, believe me, but for the first five years he was in the league, there'll never be anyone equal to him."

"Some say the greatest ever, but it was different hockey then," says Stan Fischler. "But he's among the top five all time, and if someone were to insist the greatest ever, I wouldn't argue with them."

ABOVE: *Sawchuk's last publicity headshot came with the New York Rangers, for whom he played eight games in 1969–70 after being traded from Detroit. He died on May 31, 1970.*

5 | "Fats"

"Alex was quiet and to himself, a good teammate and just a real good guy." — Peter Mahovlich

OPENING SPREAD LEFT: *Delvecchio and Howe attacking against Montreal goaltender Phil Myre.*

OPENING SPREAD RIGHT: *Known for his good sportsmanship, Delvecchio was the Red Wings captain for 12 seasons starting in 1962–63.*

CONSISTENCY SHOULD BE Alex Delvecchio's middle name. He was a constant for fans at the Olympia for a quarter century. From his single-game debut during the 1950–51 season, through to his retirement as a player in November 1973, "Fats" averaged 58 points a season and missed only 43 Red Wings games due to injury.

"Alex was the most methodical player you'd ever want to watch, one of the greatest centermen to have ever played," states Hall of Famer and Delvecchio's former linemate Ted Lindsay. "When he laid passes, he laid them on your stick. You'd have to be a moron not to corral that puck and get a good chance. He was tremendous. Never got involved, not a physical guy in any way, shape, or form . . . that's why he played 24 years, and he was a great, great hockey player."

Of his 1,549 games played, all with Detroit, 548 of them came consecutively; a team record.

After another Hall of Fame center, the late Sid Abel, who had his number 12 retired by the club in 1995, was sold to Chicago to join the Black Hawks as player-coach in 1952, Delvecchio took his spot on a line between Gordie Howe and Ted Lindsay for most of the next five seasons. Filling the pivot on what had been the famous "Production Line" was heady stuff, but Delvecchio answered with seasons of 59, 29, 48, 51, and 41 points. The 29-point season, just his third in the league, was his career low, and after 1956–57, he never finished with less than 53 points for a season during the next two decades.

According to Garry Unger, his teammate from late in his career, Delvecchio made it look easy: "He looked like he played effortless. It never looked like he was sweating."

During Unger's rookie year with Detroit, 1968–69, Delvecchio, as a 37-year-old, finished with a career high 83 points. Four years later, at 41 years old and in his last full season in the league, he finished with his second-highest point total, 71.

Delvecchio was Red Wings captain for 12 years. During the 1973–74 campaign he gradually went from player, to practice player-coach, to coach. He played in 11 games that season and was head coach for 67. His demeanor didn't change much.

"You had [Toronto coach] Punch Imlach, who was a dictator," states Unger, who first came up with the Leafs. "He walked in and nobody

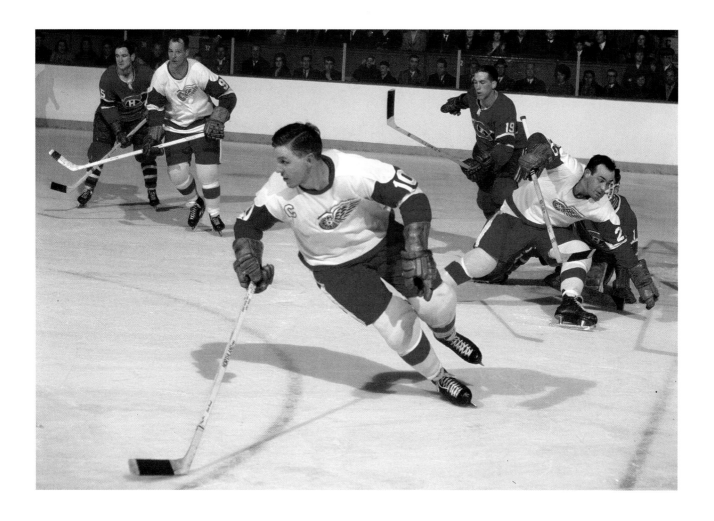

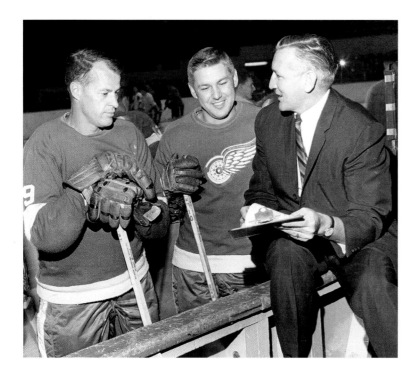

ABOVE: *Delvecchio pursues the puck in the Canadiens zone at the Montreal Forum with linemates Gordie Howe (left) and Parker MacDonald. The Habs goalie is Charlie Hodge with Bobby Rousseau (number 15) in front and Claude Larose.*

LEFT: *Gordie Howe, Delvecchio, and coach Sid Abel. In 1952, Delvecchio replaced Abel centering Howe and Ted Lindsay on what quickly became known as the "Production Line 2," a line that led the Wings to two Stanley Cup championships.*

ABOVE: *Delvecchio and D-man Matt Ravlich of the Black Hawks.*

talked. And then you go to Detroit, and you've got Sid Abel coaching, and Doug Barkley, and Bill Gadsby coaching a bit, all really laid back, good guys and good coaches. A whole different mentality, the dressing room, it wasn't run by this one guy who came in yelling and screaming in between periods. Gordie would have something to say, Alex would have something to say, Gary Bergman would have something to say, it was always calm. It was an atmosphere I loved. Alex and Gordie, mainly those two guys, set the precedent for the dressing room."

Of his 24 years playing in Detroit, 20 of them were spent with Howe, 19 of them on the same line for the most part. Playing next to the greatest player in the game at the time—and some would argue the greatest ever—might bother a skater looking for the limelight. However, Delvecchio remained the consummate team player.

"Alex had great hands, just a terrific playmaker and a smart player," says Pete Mahovlich, who broke in with Detroit in 1966. "He had great vision. Like many say, when you're playing with Gordie, who at the time was dominating the sport . . . you can be in the shadow. But Alex was just a tremendous teammate, a great captain, and great leader."

He didn't search out notoriety. He'd always go about his business very quietly, as best as a guy can, being a Hall of Fame player.

Current Red Wings general manager Ken Holland agrees: "He's just a quiet guy; he just went out and played. He was overshadowed a little bit, but he was a special, special player. Anyone that has their jersey at the top of the rafters . . . first class, unbelievable person and an incredible career."

"I think Alex was happy in that [secondary] role," points out teammate Bryan "Bugsy" Watson. "Gordie was always gonna get all the attention. But Normie [Ullman] and Alex were fantastic centermen. I think it might have helped them. He played with the greatest player in the world, and that's just the way it was."

Delvecchio's personality had a lot to do with how well he handled sharing the ice with Howe. His former linemate Mickey Redmond says,

ABOVE: *Delvecchio, with the early '70s hair and 'stache, heads up ice against Garry Monahan of the Leafs.*

OPPOSITE TOP: *In 1966, Delvecchio has pinned a Leafs defenseman as Doug Roberts attacks. Goalie Bruce Gamble struggles over as Frank Mahovlich looks on.*

OPPOSITE BOTTOM: *Delvecchio may have won three Lady Byng Trophies for "gentlemanly conduct," but he wasn't averse to creating havoc around the net, taking on (left photo) Kings defenseman Gilles Marotte and (right photo) North Stars goalie Cesare Maniago.*

"That was Alex . . . He didn't search out notoriety. He'd always go about his business very quietly, as best as a guy can, being a Hall of Fame player."

When Redmond became the first Red Wing to score 50 goals in a season, Delvecchio, in his final full season, was Redmond's center.

"Alex just did his job for 20-plus seasons," adds Redmond. "And did it much better than most, that's for sure."

Watson remembers talking with his Montreal teammates about other teams and players. At one point he mentioned Gordie Howe, and Jean Beliveau said to him, "Hey, watch Delvecchio, okay? Don't have it in your head that it's all Gordie. Believe me, it's not." Of Alex Delvecchio, Watson says, "I have great respect for him—Alex was a hell of a hockey player."

"I loved Alex, Alex was a great guy," adds Unger. "[The lack of attention] didn't seem to bother him one bit. He went about his business and was great. He and Gary Bergman . . . they were the type of guys who could have a couple beers . . . and you'd never notice anything different—he didn't change. He'd get up in the morning, go to practice, and never notice the difference. He was a special guy, had an incredible metabolism. He was always positive and upbeat in the dressing room."

Ullman adds, "He wasn't that quiet around the guys. Maybe in public, he may have been a little reserved in public. He had a long, long career.

ABOVE: *Dave Keon of Toronto won his two Lady Byngs back-to-back. Here, he accepts congratulations from previous winner Delvecchio at a brief ceremony at Maple Leaf Gardens.*

RIGHT: *From 1966, Delvecchio and Leafs defenseman Red Kelly tie up behind the net of Toronto goalie Terry Sawchuk. Detroit winger Dean Prentice looks on.*

There were a lot of different years where they were talking about trading him, but he survived."

"He was very sound and he had a hell of a line with Gordie," states Hall of Fame defenseman Bill Gadsby. "I enjoyed playing with him. He always got in good position coming out of your own end, things like that. He had a lot of moxie."

Delvecchio channeled his "moxie" into scoring and helping out on the backcheck. As Lindsay pointed out, physical play wasn't his forte. But Delvecchio combined skill with fair play to win the Lady Byng Trophy "for the best type of sportsmanship and gentlemanly conduct combined with a high standard of playing ability" in 1959, 1966, and again in 1969.

In 1955, had there been a Conn Smythe Trophy for playoff MVP, he likely would have won it, with 15 points in 12 games.

Among a younger generation of Detroit fans, many might be surprised to see the name "Delvecchio" near the top of most of the hockey organization's record lists. Besides Yzerman, he's the longest-serving captain in team history. Old Number 10 is also second in games played for the Red Wings, and still has the third-most goals, assists, and points. As for league numbers, as of 2012 Delvecchio was top 10 in games played and top 30 in points (1,281).

Delvecchio won Stanley Cups in three of his first four full seasons in the league. In 1955, had there been a Conn Smythe Trophy for playoff MVP, he likely would have won it, with 15 points in 12 games. Not bad for a guy who didn't learn to skate until he was almost a teenager.

"I broke in with him, so when we'd play with the alumni, he and I would play together because I knew where he was going to be all the time and he knew where I was," said Johnny Wilson during the summer of 2011. "One time we're coming off the ice and he said to me, 'Johnny, you see those guys out there we're playing against?' And I said, 'Yeah, what's wrong with them?' He said, 'They're 45, 50 years old. We're 70! What the hell are we doing here?'"

Wilson passed away at the age of 82 in December of 2011, just about the time his good friend turned 80. Alex still helps run his own business, Alex Delvecchio Enterprises, with his son Alex Jr. in Troy, Michigan. Friends and cohorts will find him in his office most every morning.

Also, as he is accustomed, Delvecchio still makes appearances as an ambassador for the hockey club at events all over the Detroit area. In turn, public accolades for this Red Wing "lifer's" career have continued over time as well. The team retired Delvecchio's sweater in 1991 and dedicated a statue of him in the concourse of the Joe Louis Arena in 2008. The artwork stands as a steadfast reminder of Delvecchio's life as a Red Wing; a model of consistency.

TOP: *The grey-haired captain toward the end of his 24-season Red Wings career.*

BOTTOM: *This statue honoring Delvecchio was unveiled at the Joe Louis Arena on October 17, 2008. His number had been retired on November 10, 1991.*

6 Stevie Wonder

"Although my stats declined, my confidence grew incredibly."

— Steve Yzerman, WITH A SMILE, ON BECOMING A STRONGER
TWO-WAY PLAYER UNDER HEAD COACH SCOTTY BOWMAN

ABOVE: *Steve Yzerman wins a draw against Adam Graves of the New York Rangers.*

OPPOSITE: *Yzerman was named captain of the Red Wings in 1986 (at age 21), a responsibility he held for the next 19 seasons, an NHL record.*

STEVE YZERMAN PLAYED 22 SEASONS in Detroit, captained the Red Wings to three Stanley Cups, and finished his career in 2006 as the sixth leading point getter (1,755) and the eighth most prolific goal scorer (692) in NHL history.

These achievements are beyond impressive, but it's not the on-ice accomplishments alone that make Yzerman a hero to men, women, and children who follow the Winged Wheel; it's the way he went about his business. Yzerman's demeanor and approach, heavy on courtesy and humility, is what truly attracts the adoration and respect.

In a world of whiners, Yzerman played on one leg. In a world of "bling," Yzerman was an understatement. In a world of "look at me," Yzerman always put team first.

When asked at the 1997 All-Star Game about emerging as the new face of the Red Wings, moving to the forefront, replacing Gordie Howe as the franchise's icon, Yzerman looked pained.

"I don't . . . I can't think about that. That's impossible," he said.

However, to that next generation of Wing Nuts, he was the franchise, the star, the leader, the captain.

And to think he may have been traded . . . twice.

"There were two times that there were fairly heavy discussions in moving Steve Yzerman," states longtime Red Wings hockey executive Jimmy Devellano. "The first time would have been in the early '90s, Bryan Murray was the general manager of the franchise, and I know there were talks of moving him to Buffalo for Pat LaFontaine."

LaFontaine had been drafted third overall, just ahead of Yzerman, in the 1983 draft, and would have been the Red Wings' choice had he not been selected by the Islanders. The graduate of Waterford Kettering High School in Michigan had been monitored by the Wings for years.

"The second time would have been 1994," Devellano continues. "We got upset in the first round by San Jose, a series that we were favored to win by quite a bit, and there were extensive conversations between Detroit and Ottawa. I would say the conversations went on a long time, a lot of names bashed back and forth, but it didn't happen. It didn't happen mainly because Ottawa couldn't take on Steve's contract and they didn't have anything to give up. They thought we were gonna make a deal and pick up part of his contract . . . we weren't trying to get rid of him *that* bad."

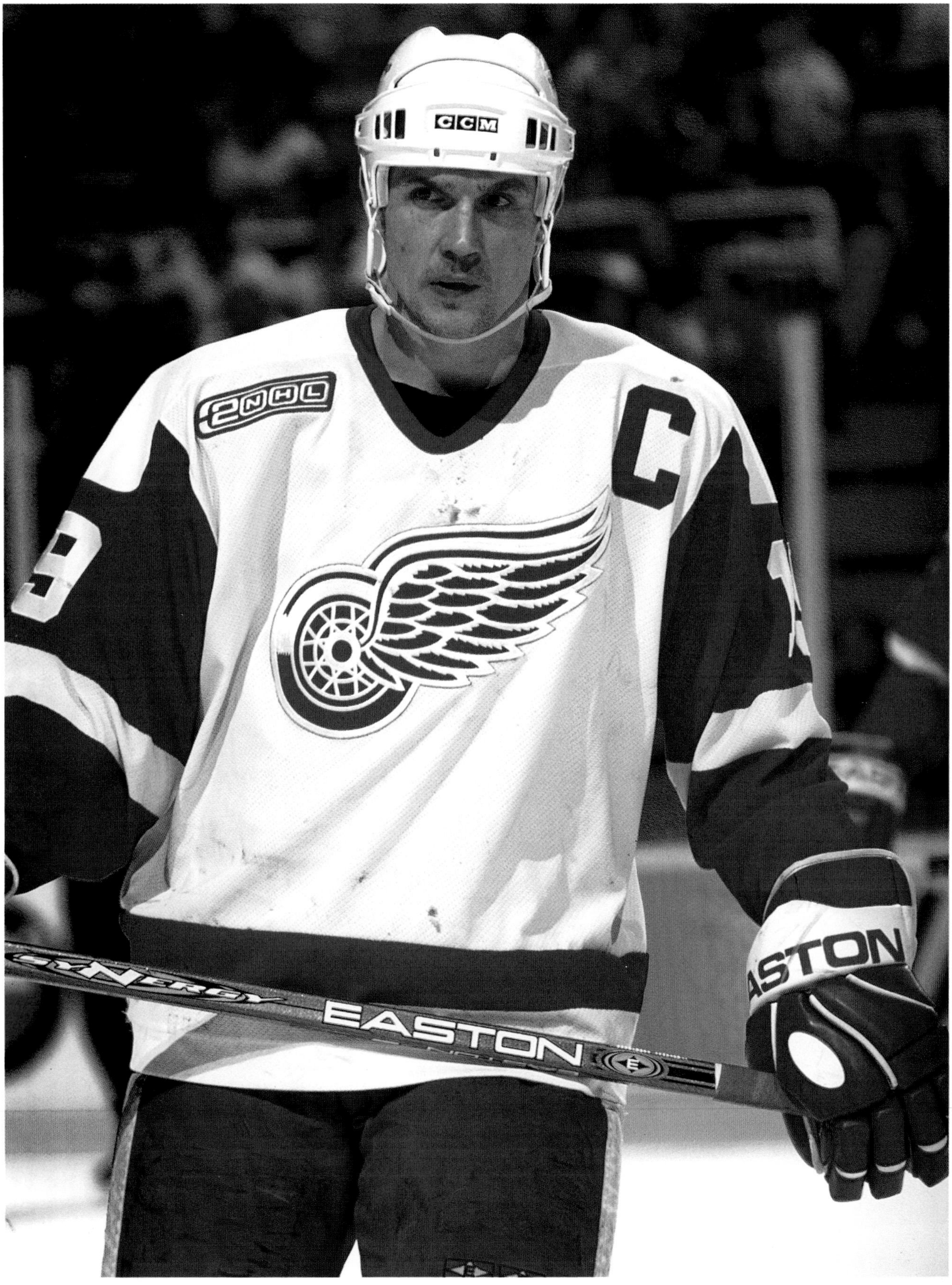
CCM
EASTON

The trade discussions in '94 came as the Red Wings front office was in flux. Bowman had finished his first year as Red Wings coach under general manager Bryan Murray, who, along with assistant GM Doug McLean, was fired after the playoff loss to the Sharks. Bowman added director of player personnel to his responsibilities, Devellano was named director of hockey operations, but neither man had full control of the hockey team.

"The Wings put in a new president, a guy by the name of Bill Evo," remembers Bowman. "All of a sudden he became the president of the team. He had a pretty strong voice, he was a league governor, and he went to those meetings. He was a fine guy, but he wasn't really a complete hockey guy.

"I'm pretty sure the guy they [Ottawa] were offering was [Alexei] Yashin, center for center," Bowman recalls. "It got talking, but then Jimmy said, 'This isn't gonna fly because Ilitch is not trading Steve Yzerman, you know, he's like his own son, he's like another son to him.'"

Instead the Wings improved their goaltending, a sticking point for Bowman, by adding Mike Vernon in a trade with Calgary. Over the next three calendar years they'd also add Slava Fetisov, Igor Larionov, Kirk Maltby, Brendan Shanahan, and Larry Murphy.

While management was busy reorganizing itself and the team, Steve Yzerman was undergoing an important transformation of his own: he was reinventing his style of play.

Former Red Wings forward Bob Errey remembers when he arrived in Detroit in 1995: "The Red Wings were still trying to find themselves, as was Stevie," he says. "But as a leader he was always great because he always asked questions, he relied on people around him, and he really led by example."

Yzerman collaborated with coach Scotty Bowman to make the Detroit Red Wings a more well-rounded team. During his jersey-retirement ceremony at the Joe Louis Arena in 2007, Yzerman spent a full three minutes of his speech singing the praises of Bowman.

ABOVE: *(Left to right) Kirk Maltby, "the Wizard" Ray Whitney, and Yzerman.*

"As I handed him the Stanley Cup," Yzerman recalled, "he just whispered in my ear, 'Steve, that's it, I'm retiring. I'm done, I've coached my last game.' And in all the hysteria of that evening, and the celebration of winning the Stanley Cup, I feel we never rightly got the opportunity to express our gratitude and our thanks for him leading us to three Stanley Cup championships."

That coaching leadership had meant convincing Yzerman, his star player, to alter his game.

Steve bought into the program, and became a terrific two-way player.

"After my first year [in Detroit]," Bowman states, "I said 'Steve, the team is playing incorrectly to make a real charge. It's not the first time a player has made a big change, but this is going to affect your individual game.' He had 65 goals and 160-plus points that one year."

Bowman recalls giving Yzerman a history lesson.

"When I was coaching junior, Jacques Lemaire came up as a 16-year-old player," Bowman starts. "I was coaching the Junior Canadiens in Montreal and I had him for at least three years junior. He was a terrific junior player, but I couldn't play him against other top centers in the league because he didn't check. So I got upset with Lemaire and I told him one day, 'You're not going to make the Canadiens if you keep playing like this.'"

Playing for the Canadiens was Lemaire's ultimate dream.

"So over time," Bowman continues, "he started to pick up on it and by the time he finished junior he was beginning to really get anxious to play defensively as well. The reason I think the team did so well later in the '70s, is we had [Guy] Lafleur, we had [Steve] Shutt, but we never really had a centerman who could play with those guys. Once we put Lemaire at center with Lafleur and Shutt, that line was one of the best lines."

Bowman explained to Yzerman that "Lemaire had done a transformation and became a terrific two-way player, and that was a reason—not the only reason, but a big reason—why the Canadiens won so many Cups."

If Yzerman wanted his team to win the Stanley Cup, he would have to change his focus. "So he did the big change and players kind of got in line with him," Bowman concludes. "We were very fortunate because Sergei Fedorov was already very good defensively . . . So we had two guys, Yzerman and Fedorov, both of them. And Colorado had [Joe] Sakic and [Peter] Forsberg. So you can see the big rivalry. There's four of the best centermen that may have played in that era on two different teams."

Along with goaltending, this strength up the middle is an essential team attribute general managers seek and covet. It's no surprise that with the aforementioned talent, Colorado won the Cup in 1996 and the Red Wings won the next two that followed.

"Steve bought into the program, and became a terrific two-way player," declares Devellano. "He wasn't always that kind of player. That wasn't his fault, either. Part of that was my fault because when I drafted

ABOVE: *Yzerman puts on the brakes in the offensive zone at Chicago Stadium on March 3, 1990, against Blackhawks defensemen Dave Manson and Doug Wilson.*

him in '83, this team wasn't a Stanley Cup contender. I needed to sell tickets, okay, the building was half empty, couldn't make the playoffs, so I needed him to get 150 points. There were no complementary players so I was part of the problem. I wanted offense, and it was good for Steve Yzerman because he would get good contracts—you get paid for goals and points."

You talk about a combination of skating, and puck skills, and hockey sense all in one package and he had it.

Yzerman piled up the points at a rate never before seen in Motown. For starters, he set the team records for most goals (39) and most points (87) by a rookie.

Nick Polano, Yzerman's first head coach in Detroit, remembers how well the player lived up to expectations early in his career: "What he could do with the puck and his hockey sense was so much better than anyone else on the ice. You talk about a combination of skating, and

puck skills, and hockey sense all in one package and he had it. We started the season up in Winnipeg. He was on the fourth line starting the game. By the end of the game he had scored the tying goal—he went through the whole team to score, and he never got off the first line again."

Five years later, in 1989, he shattered established team season records with 65 goals, 90 assists, and 155 points. Yzerman credited his teammates.

"Any personal success I had was because of the wonderful players that I played with," stated Yzerman at his jersey-retirement ceremony. His humility may be the only quality that surpasses his competitiveness.

But his teammates know that Yzerman deserves every honor that he received. "On the ice he was a tremendous player, an individual player, he had all the skills, the work ethic," says future Hall of Fame defenseman Nick Lidstrom. "But I think what sticks out most with Stevie is his determination on the ice. If he . . . felt he could go to the net, whether it was against [Derian] Hatcher or [Mark] Tinordi or one of those big guys, he could do that. Just his determination is something that really sticks out."

When you put team first, a lot of good things happen to you, and I think Steve had that from day one.

Henrik Zetterberg sat next to Yzerman in the locker room toward the end of Yzerman's career. "It was pretty neat just to see him every day, just to see how he prepares and how focused he was every time," says Zetterberg. "His last year [2006] the battles he had with his body, but he was always going 100 percent out there and he never gave up."

An earlier example of Yzerman's body battles and determination came in 2002, the year Zetterberg won the Conn Smythe Trophy as playoff MVP. Many observers believed Yzerman deserved the award, as he led the Wings to the Cup while essentially skating on one leg. Knee surgery followed that summer.

"What I saw him go through when he came back off those injuries in his last couple of seasons, and saw how hard he worked and what he did to try to come back to play was incredible," marvels Wings commentator Paul Woods.

He remembers how Detroit lost to the Edmonton Oilers in six games in the opening round in 2006. Yzerman was injured and had trouble taking face-offs. "But he played anyway. It's funny with these great guys, something just seems to happen and they take it to another level. He was limited, but Edmonton got the lead on us, so the next thing you know Steve starts playing better, and he became our best player inside that game. The team responded and started coming back. He was doing everything, taking face-offs, and it was magical. And it's hard to say it's a great moment when you lose, but it was something."

Yzerman exhibited this type of leadership from day one.

"The first time I met Steve I was thinking, 'This kid is 18 going on 30,'" states Bill Jamieson, the Wings' PR man when Yzerman was drafted. "So mature."

It's why he became the league's youngest captain in 1986 at age 21, replacing veteran Danny Gare.

"I didn't mind," declares Gare. "It was an honor to be a captain for an Original Six club and what a great kid Steve was, and what a success story he's gone on to be. You could sense it then, and he was obviously the big reason the franchise started to turn around. It was fun. I sat with those kids in the room for a while, 17, 18, 19, right in a row, me, [Gerard] Gallant, and Yzerman in the dressing room."

Steve Yzerman's former teammate turned assistant coach Colin Campbell enjoyed skating with both the young players.

"I liked Steve. He was a well-based, great family foundation, good work ethics guy," he says. "Gerry Gallant the same way, great kid, hard worker. They were looking for some direction and they just watched us, veterans left and right, coming and going. You're always worried about the young players when there are a lot of veterans: What are they going to learn? What habits are they gonna take? But both Gerry and Steve had real good upbringings and they weren't going to be swayed the wrong way. They knew what was right."

"It wasn't about him getting 60 or 70 goals, it wasn't about the 150 points or whatever it was," says longtime teammate and friend Gallant.

ABOVE: *The Captain, proving he wasn't immune to the mullet.*

OPPOSITE *(counter-clockwise from top):* *Presenting President Clinton a Red Wings jersey at the White House, January 28, 1999, while the team was being honored for the 1998 Stanley Cup championship.*

Yzerman carrying the Stanley Cup while rolling past hundreds of thousands of fans in downtown Detroit on June 10, 1997. The four-game sweep of the Philadelphia Flyers in the final ended a 42-year Cup drought for the Red Wings.

The next year Detroit swept Washington in the final, this time hoisting the Stanley Cup on the road, June 16, 1998. As of the start of the 2013 playoffs, the Wings are the last NHL team to win back-to-back Cups.

"That obviously made our team better and gave us a chance to win, but it was always about team with Stevie, and I think all the guys knew that. We respected him, and he carried it on his whole career. He was well liked. When you put team first, a lot of good things happen to you, and I think Steve had that from day one."

"Stevie and Gerry know those qualities well," adds Campbell, "and that's why they're having success now in management and coaching. Their ethics are good, their intentions were always right, and their gut feelings were always right about hockey. You have to have those basic foundations and qualities, and those guys did."

Yzerman, however, downplays his leadership.

"I feel my image as a great leader was greatly overblown," he stated during his retirement speech over loud groans of disagreement from the crowd. "And I realized that because I played with some of the best hockey players that will ever play in the league."

Lidstrom is one of those players who disagree with Yzerman's humble claims: "Off the ice he was one of the best leaders I've been around," he says. "First leading by example, doing the right things on the ice, but he said the right things too, in the locker room. He wasn't an overly vocal

guy in the room, but he said the right things at the right time and he went out on the ice and did them."

"Steve was no myth," adds former teammate and current NHL executive Brendan Shanahan. "He kept it simple and basically led by example. He just played and never complained, and he made the rest of us better leaders."

Wings play-by-play man Ken Daniels is impressed that in his 14 years in Detroit, he never heard gossip about Steve Yzerman—not from teammates, and not from reporters.

"Guys just respected him enough, or were scared of him a bit in their own little way, not to say anything," he explains. "Injuries . . . backstabbing, none of that out of the Red Wings, and I think that went a long way to the current group and other players wanting to be here."

From teammates to media, and even to opposing fans, Yzerman seemed to garner a unique form of respect.

Red Wings forward Kris Draper remembers getting off the bus in Vancouver for the playoffs in 2002, a couple months after the Canadian men's hockey team had won the Olympics. The crowd was yelling, "'Hull sucks, Draper sucks, everybody sucks,' and then Stevie comes off the bus and it's, 'Yay Steve, way to go Stevie!'" Draper laughs. "So that kind of summed up the power of Steve Yzerman."

Even in retirement, Yzerman was humble.

Paul Woods explains, "The thing you appreciate the most is there was no farewell tour, no one knew it was going to be his last game. When it was over he just skated off the ice, he was done, and retires.

That to me is just an example of the character of that person, how strong he is, of course all that he did . . . he's an amazing guy."

In 2010, after four years of tutelage within the Red Wings organization as an executive in the hockey department, Yzerman took over as general manager of the Tampa Bay Lightning. Under first-year head coach Guy Boucher, the team reached the playoffs for the first time in three seasons, and progressed all the way to Game 7 of the 2011 Eastern Conference finals. A franchise that had been down was back up again.

"He's always been a very smart guy, and things haven't changed," states his former teammate and current assistant GM Pat Verbeek.

Not bad for a "fall-back" draft pick who was almost traded twice.

"The best deals are the deals you don't make," says former Wings play-by-play man Dave Strader, repeating an old axiom.

Devellano agrees, saying, "That's for sure. And we know what happened after that. We would go on to win four Stanley Cups; he would go on to play 22 years, get his sweater hung to the rafters, and become a local icon that he still is. And now he's gone to the Tampa Bay Lightning."

Wings radio announcer Ken Kal affirms that Yzerman is one of those performers who's productive at whatever he does.

"There are rare people in the world today that have that quality," says Kal. "He's a leader, he's smart, he's fair, he was a great hockey player, and you can see he's a great general manager. He was an intense competitor out on the ice, soft-spoken, but a guy who you knew whatever he was going to do, he'd be successful at it."

ABOVE LEFT: *Yzerman acknowledges the reaction of the fans at the Joe Louis Arena on January 29, 2004, after his third-period assist moved him into seventh place on the career NHL point scoring list with number 1,702. The point came against New Jersey in a 5–2 win. Teammates (left to right: Brett Hull, Boyd Devereaux, and Henrik Zetterberg. Ex-teammate turned video assistant coach Joe Kocur stands in the suit. Head trainer Piet Van Zant is on the left.*

ABOVE RIGHT: *Yzerman while wearing a visor during his final season, December 1, 2005.*

ABOVE: On January 2, 2007, "The Captain" and his number 19 joined the other legends in the rafters at the Joe Louis Arena.

OPPOSITE: May 1, 2006. Literally, Yzerman's last step as an active NHL player, leaving the ice for the final time in Edmonton after the eighth-seeded Oilers eliminated the top-seeded Red Wings in the first round of the Stanley Cup playoffs four games to two.

Whether or not he returns someday to lead the organization, Steve Yzerman will always be a Red Wing. You can take Yzerman out of the hockey family, but you can't take the hockey family out of Yzerman. Think of the speech he delivered to his fans, which became a challenge to his active Red Wings teammates near the conclusion of his jersey-retirement night.

There was no farewell tour, no one knew it was going to be his last game. When it was over he just skated off the ice, he was done, and retires.

"The reason some of you came here with your grandfathers, some of you came with your fathers, and some of you bring your children now, and wherever we go in the National Hockey League, there's a throng of Red Wings fans in the building . . . there's a nation of Red Wings fans wherever we play. And the reason for this is the gentlemen [living legends] sitting over here to my left. This organization, 'Hockeytown' as it's known now, was built by Gordie Howe, by Alex Delvecchio, by Ted Lindsay, by Terry Sawchuk, by Sid Abel, and by all the tremendous players from the '30s, '40s, '50s, and '60s. The only way I feel, as a player, that I could live up to the expectation and the honor which these players bestowed on the jersey was to play, to play hard, to do everything I possibly could to represent the Red Wings well. These players set a tremendous standard for hockey in Detroit and hockey everywhere. Myself, my teammates, and as I look behind to the present Detroit Red Wings, the only way we can say thank you to these players, the only way we can truly honor them, is to play the way they did, and that is to play with pride, to play hard, and to give everything you have to represent the Red Wing logo, the Red Wings organization, and the City of Detroit just like these gentlemen did."

The Russian Five

> *"That really was the beginning of who we are today, when [coach] Scotty [Bowman] put together the Russian Five."*
>
> — RED WINGS GENERAL MANAGER **Ken Holland**

OPENING SPREAD LEFT: *Sergei Fedorov celebrates a goal against the New York Islanders at Nassau Coliseum in 2003.*

OPENING SPREAD RIGHT: *Shown left to right, Slava Fetisov, Igor Larionov, and Slava Kozlov hoist the Stanley Cup outside the Kremlin in Red Square, Moscow, Russia, on August 17, 1997.*

As a unit, for the better part of two seasons beginning in 1995, forwards Sergei Fedorov, Slava Kozlov, and Igor Larionov, and defensemen Vladimir Konstantinov and Slava Fetisov, bewildered and astonished fellow players, coaches, and fans.

With their game of NHL keep-away at times resembling the Harlem Globetrotters of hockey, the group would completely discombobulate opponents.

"All of a sudden you're sitting there on a nightly basis watching your team, and you've got the puck 60 or 65 percent of the time," remembers Red Wings general manager Ken Holland. "It not only became offense, it became defense. We started to trade, draft, and develop to build our teams really out of the Russian Five. Just watching them, that's really been the basis of who we are from 1995 to 2012."

Puck possession: the hallmark of the old Soviet Red Army teams and similar programs throughout Russia. The Russian Five had upbringing and training in common.

Their magical chemistry was evident from the first night they ever played together, October 27, 1995, in Calgary. TV play-by-play man Dave Strader calls it a night he'll never forget, a night that saw Wings goalie Chris Osgood pick up an eight-save shutout victory.

> *All of a sudden they've got five guys all playing the same game. It was a great feeling to be together, it was unbelievable.*

"Calgary never had the puck," says Strader. "When you first saw these guys play together it was like 'Oh my God.' It was just fascinating."

"In Calgary, the shots were 25 to 8 and our unit scored two goals and we had a three–zero victory," recalls Larionov proudly. "We only had one practice; I had come from San Jose the day before. I had been sitting in San Jose for 10 days waiting for a trade. It was spectacular to be able to control the game and to have the victory. We got to play the game in the NHL like we did as kids, and then like the Red Army team. All of a

sudden they've got five guys all playing the same game. It was a great feeling to be together, it was unbelievable."

"We had the puck the whole night. It was keep-away," Holland says.

Larionov calls the strategy they used that night in the Saddledome "the Russian offense." He remembers waiting to see how Calgary would react.

"Were they [the Flames] going to wait? Were they going to come [at us]?" he wondered that night. "We waited to see what options we were going to have. After that, we went quick, one-touch passes, five or six in a row, and tried to get some speed going in the right direction. We had a group that could see the ice so well and had the skill to make the right pass at the right time in the right area when someone was open. Then we just started to take over the game."

Through the 1995–96 season, the strength of the Russian Five, and of the Red Wings, continued to grow.

"They were incredible," smiles Holland. "They were five guys that thought the same, never dumped it in if they didn't have a play, regrouped in the neutral zone, passed it back to the D, D to D to D, regroup, come at you with speed, come through the neutral zone, and then someone would break in. They had the puck the whole time."

"They would pass around and cycle the puck," confirms mucking winger Kirk Maltby. "And then all of a sudden they'd send someone in on a breakaway or a two-on-one, and it didn't matter if it was a defenseman or a forward . . . I mean, we were the 'Grind Line': dump, chase, and cause havoc. They were definitely the prettier side of the game. It was fun to watch what they could do—they were all on the same page. It was actually pretty incredible what they could do."

Typically, breakaways for NHL defensemen are rare. With the Russian Five it became commonplace.

"The amazing thing is the way they used to play it, the guy they used to free up, sailing in for a scoring chance, was often either Fetisov or more likely Konstantinov," Bowman affirms. "They'd be moving around the neutral zone and then they'd be looking to make passes on the side, and then all of a sudden up the middle came Konstantinov."

Former Wings GM Jimmy Devellano, who was the team's senior vice-president in 1995, gives all the credit to Scotty Bowman for putting the group together.

"We had drafted Fedorov, we had drafted Kozlov and Konstantinov, Scotty inherited them from me, but Scotty gave up a third-round pick for Slava Fetisov to New Jersey and he traded Ray Sheppard to San Jose for Larionov," says Devellano. "They were Scotty Bowman deals and he put them together and it was beautiful."

Devellano suspects that Bowman's experience as a coach playing against the Soviet teams with Montreal and in the Canada Cups had a lot to do with putting together the Russian Five.

"He knew their style of game," he explains, "and I guess he said, 'Holy criminy, this will work.' Fedorov's a world-class player, Larionov knows how to play properly, Kozlov is close to a world-class player, we've got Konstantinov who's a Russian, and it probably clicked and he said, 'I know these guys are going to play well together.' They all had that certain style."

Larionov agrees that Bowman deserves credit, saying, "He knew what he was looking for from all the guys he had at that time. Some wondered if he would put five Russians together for the first time in the NHL, but he knew the skill levels, the strengths and weaknesses of every guy, he knew the units. So he gave it a try."

As Devellano pointed out, it didn't hurt having world-class individuals to put together into the group. By the time the unit was gathered, Fedorov had established himself as one of the greatest players in the world. He was arguably the league's best skater, who had already won a Hart Trophy and Pearson Award as MVP, two Selke Trophies as best defensive forward, and had been a finalist for the Calder Trophy as Rookie of the Year, a finalist for the Selke again, and a finalist for the Lady Byng Trophy for sportsmanship.

"When I started in Detroit we had Fedorov and Kozlov, and we had just brought Kozlov up," remembers Bowman. "He was a hell of a player too. He was a very skillful player. And of course we had Konstantinov already there, and I really think Konstantinov, when I first went there in 1993, he was on par with Lidstrom. They were different kinds of players, but Konstantinov had that edge about him, and he was good offensively, and he was really strong."

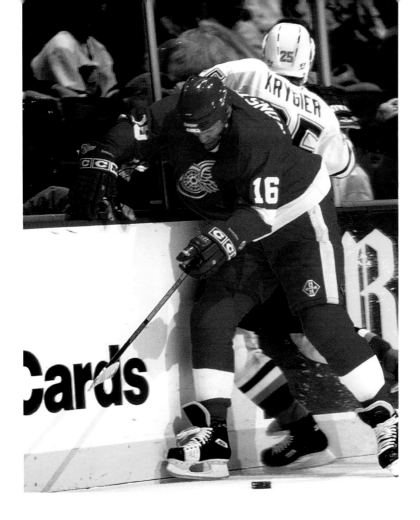

"Konstantinov, for lack of a better term, he was the most Canadian in his style of play of those guys," adds Strader. "He would just do things, like fighting Dirk Graham one night in Chicago, and playing tough, and he was just a fun guy to be around, even with his difficulty with the language. He would have won a Norris Trophy eventually."

In his two seasons with the Russian Five, "the Vladinator" was a plus-60 and a plus-38.

Many argue he should have won the trophy in 1997, when he was runner-up to Brian Leetch of the Rangers. He was as physical and intimidating as any defenseman in the league, with 151 penalty minutes to go with 38 points. In his two seasons with the Russian Five, "the Vladinator" was a plus-60 and a plus-38.

"Vladdie would have had five or ten more years easily, and he was playing his best hockey," adds Larionov. "When he was in the lineup he had an impact like Yzerman, he was part of the core, a key part of the lineup every day."

A limousine accident on Woodward Avenue outside of Detroit six days after the 1997 Stanley Cup championship ended Konstantinov's career and began a lifetime of injury convalescence. It also ended the

OPPOSITE TOP: *Fedorov was paid $28 million in 1997–98, the largest single season pay-out in NHL history. The total came as a result of the Red Wings matching a front-loaded free agent contract offer made by the Carolina Hurricanes.*

OPPOSITE BOTTOM: *Fedorov is the only player in NHL history to win the Hart Trophy (NHL MVP) and the Selke (best defensive forward) Trophy in the same season (1994). He won the Selke again in 1996.*

ABOVE LEFT: *Vladimir Konstantinov, the "Vladinator," crunches Chad Krygier of the Mighty Ducks and takes the puck on February 3, 1995, in Anaheim.*

ABOVE RIGHT: *Konstantinov plasters Scott Niedermayer of the New Jersey Devils at the Joe during Game 2 of the Stanley Cup final on June 20, 1995. The Devils won the game and the series in four straight.*

career of team masseur Sergei Mnatsakanov, who was more seriously injured. The third passenger in the car, teammate Fetisov, escaped with minor injuries.

Bowman remembers keeping vigil at the hospital for several weeks after Konstantinov's accident: "We'd go in and see him, we kept up with him, and we'd meet him, and then when he got out of the hospital it was a big deal. I think most of us, when a guy is in a coma for so long, we wondered if he was ever gonna get out of it."

"I'm not surprised at all that Coach was there [at the hospital every day]," says Larionov. "Many people think of Scotty as tough, or not a players' coach, but at the same time he has so much respect for everyone on the team. The players put their heart and soul into the team, and we won the Cup for the first time in 42 years in Detroit, and I'm not surprised Scotty was there every day. A lot of guys went in to see both of those guys, every day, for a long time, until Vladdie came out of his coma."

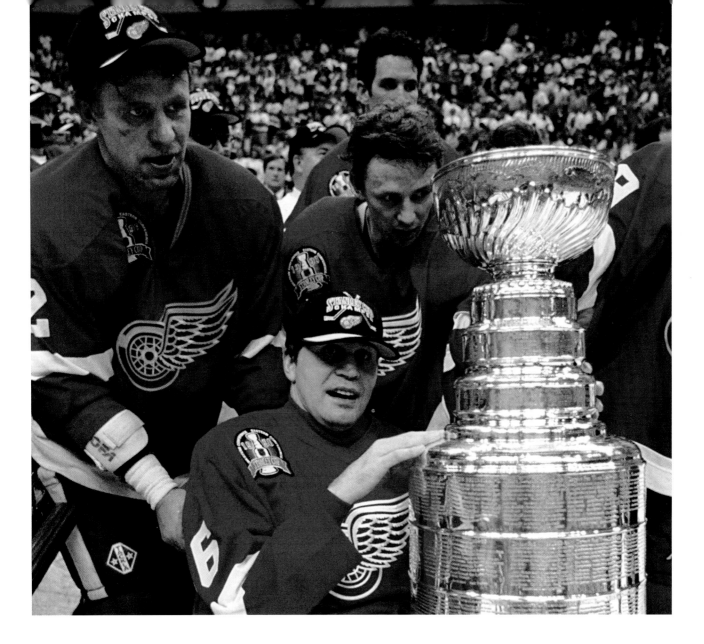

As of spring 2012, the Red Wings of 1997 and 1998 are the last to win back-to-back championships. After winning in '98, they rolled Konstantinov out onto the ice in his wheelchair and placed the Stanley Cup in his lap. "Believe" had been the team's motto all season, and Vladdie had been the inspiration behind their efforts.

Bowman says, "I really think if Konstantinov had not had that terrible accident, he could have challenged Lidstrom in the late '90s, he was that good a player, because he was so powerful."

"He was a tough, top guy, great teammate, and a great defenseman for the Detroit Red Wings," states Larionov.

Meanwhile, at the time of Fetisov's acquisition, the 36-year-old blue-liner was in his sixth NHL season with the Devils, winding down a long international career. Detroit gave him new life.

"Fetisov wasn't really playing with New Jersey, he was just sort of a spare part," explains Bowman. "[New Jersey GM] Lou Lamoriello, I phoned him one day, and he didn't fool us. He said, 'This guy's gonna help you,

ABOVE LEFT: *Slava Fetisov had already played 12 professional seasons in Russia and five more with the New Jersey Devils before he was obtained by the Red Wings during the 1994–95 season. He turned 40 just prior to helping Detroit win the second of back-to-back Cups. Then he retired.*

ABOVE RIGHT: *Fetisov was in the limousine crash in 1997 that seriously injured Konstantinov and team masseur Sergei Mnatsakanov, but he escaped with minor injuries and played the next season. In honor of the injured men, the team wore a patch with their initials and the word "believe" in Russian and English for the 1997–98 season.*

OPPOSITE: *"The Professor" Igor Larionov battles Adam Oates of the Anaheim Mighty Ducks in front of goalie Jean-Sebastien Giguere during the 2002–03 season. Defenseman Sandis Ozolinsh is on the left.*

we've got so many defensemen, he's a wonderful guy.' So we made an amicable trade, he came over, and as soon as he came over we put him together with Vladdie.

"Then we made a trade to get Larionov," continues Bowman. "We had too many right-wingers. We had Lapointe and we had Ciccarelli and Sheppard; we had so many right-wingers, we had an overflow."

Sheppard went out, Larionov came in.

"I think the influence of Larionov and Fetisov being older guys, older Russians, that helped," points out Bowman. "And one of the centers had to move to be a right-winger. It's funny, because Sergei still wanted to play center, so Larionov moved to the wing. I wanted Sergei to move to the wing because he's a bigger guy, but Larionov did it. Sergei was much better on face-offs anyway, so it worked out.

"When we first used them they were so good, I didn't even know how they were playing, they had their own system," Bowman confesses. "I didn't use them all the time because I was concerned that somebody would figure this system out . . . Fedorov didn't embrace the idea at the beginning—he was sort of not as enthused—but we put them together and we used them in the playoffs a lot and they were something. They

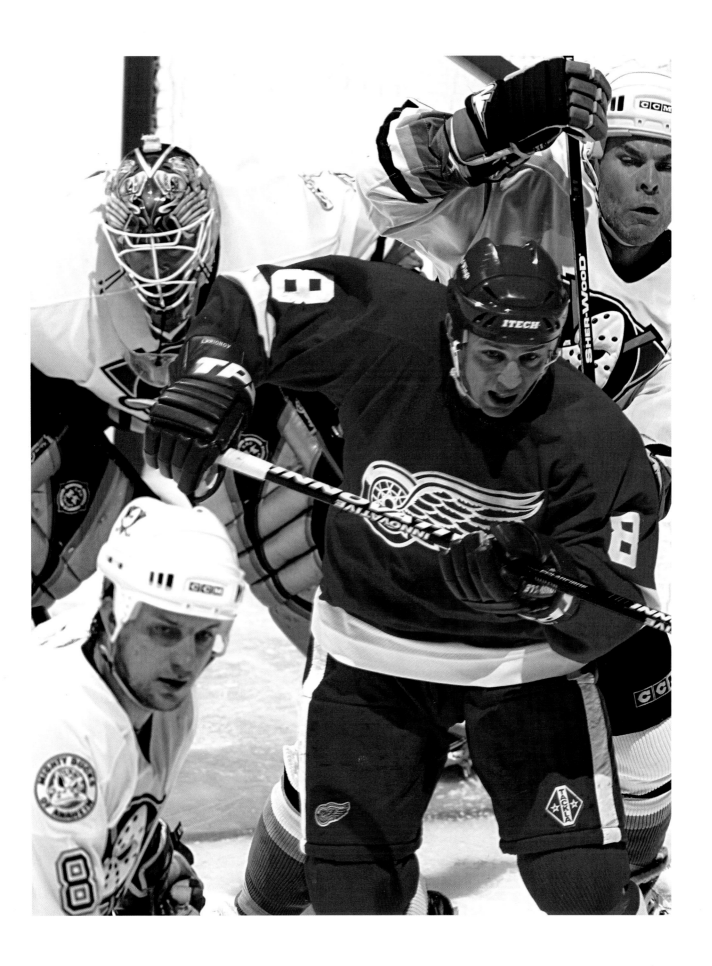

were awesome. I think looking back I probably should have used them more, because I don't think anyone would have figured out how they were playing. It worked also because no one else did it . . . By the time it was all said and done they were pretty proud of their accomplishments."

The limo accident brought the end of the Russian Five, and no lineup of players has come close to duplicating their efforts since. It's highly unlikely that all of the factors—talent, attitude, background, and timing—will ever fall into place again and bring the NHL another unit like this one.

"It's a great question whether this could happen again," Larionov says. "That's the way the game is supposed to be played. Obviously there are different ways to coach and to train, but we had a concept: to play the game the way the Russian Five played, moving the puck, puck possession, the strength of the players, it was like going to the theater. Like a great actor or actress putting on a stage play, in Europe or in Russia or in New York, or reading a nice book and not being able to put it down. That's the way we played the game.

"Today, I don't know if you could have that style of play, the rules have changed and I'm not sure the coaches that are coaching the game today are allowed to teach it that way to young players," he continues. "They are more offensive-minded players . . . I don't know if they could play the same way now. It would be fantastic to have that kind of hockey again."

LEFT: *Kozlov, here running into St. Louis Blues goalie Roman Turek at the Joe on March 28, 2001, was originally drafted by Detroit in the third round in 2000. He played parts of 10 seasons for the Red Wings and was part of the back-to-back Cup titles.*

BELOW: *Kozlov's number 13 was taken over the next season by all-around phenom Pavel Datsyuk, the lone Russian on the Red Wings roster at the end of the 2011–12 season. Here, he scores a shoot-out goal against Boston's Tuukka Rask on November 25, 2011.*

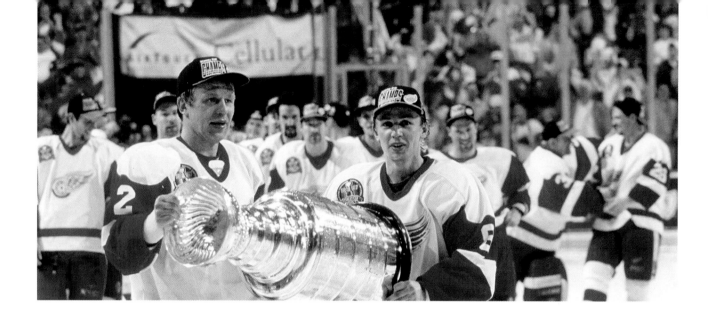

ABOVE: *Fetisov, left, and Larionov with the Stanley Cup at Joe Louis Arena on June 7, 1997.*

OPPOSITE *(clockwise from top left):* *Larionov kisses the Cup on June 13, 2002, after the Red Wings beat the Carolina Hurricanes in the Stanley Cup final four games to one.*

Fetisov hoists the Cup in 1998.

It's five Russians, but it's not the Russian Five. Missing from this 1998 Cup photo is Sergei Fedorov. Back left is defenseman Dmitri Mironov, obtained from Anaheim at the trade deadline (March 24) that year for defenseman Jamie Pushor and a draft pick. His Red Wings career included 11 regular season games, seven playoff games, and a Stanley Cup. Next to him is Kozlov. Front row from left, Fetisov, Konstantinov, and Larionov.

To some extent, as General Manager Holland has pointed out, the general concept endures. The desire to play a puck-possessive style is understood. But the ability to execute this game plan to perfection is gone, because the systems and the players who were taught in such a manner no longer exist. The myopic, dictatorial training programs under the old Communist regime and the Soviet Red Army program fell with the Iron Curtain more than two decades ago.

Red Army or Red Wings, selflessness is an ageless concept and attribute.

"It was the right time, everyone working together in sync, it was a good time for us, to play the game the way we wanted to play it," Larionov notes. "At the same time, you had to play the Red Wings' system, you had to play defense. We had freedom to think offensively, but we had to backcheck and show our skills and take the responsibility to play defense, and we did."

Red Army or Red Wings, selflessness is an ageless concept and attribute in hockey. Harnessing it, and passing it along, is a key to the success of any organization.

"Pavel Datsyuk, when he got here, maybe knew a little more English than he let on—just a bit—but he used to always sit on the bus with Igor, and learned to train from Igor, and Igor set the stage for him," says Ken Daniels. "His puck skills, how he sees the ice; he sat with Igor all the time."

"We did not worry about how much ice time an individual had," Larionov concludes. "We had one goal: to be successful as a team, and to have the unit be successful. And if you did your best as a unit, you could play great hockey. Individual performances and bonuses should stay on the side, because this is about your linemates, no matter who is better, performing as one."

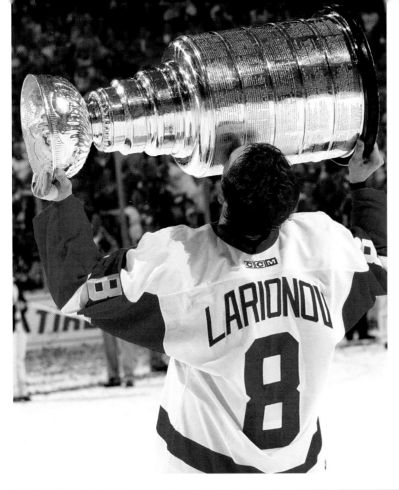

Swedish Silk

"I think there's Orr, and then there's Nick. That's pretty much it."

— HALL OF FAME DEFENSEMAN **Mark Howe**

ABOVE: *On May 31, 2012, after 20 seasons, six as Captain, and four Stanley Cups, Nicklas Lidstrom retired as a Red Wings player.*

OPPOSITE: *For two decades, the name Lidstrom was synonymous with the term "excellence along the blue line."*

NICK LIDSTROM HAS BEEN CALLED the perfect defenseman, and then some.

"They call Nick the perfect human," says Ken Daniels. "And maybe he is the perfect player. As I've said many times, give me a hand and one finger—I've seen him make that many mistakes in his career."

Add quiet leadership and humility. Nick Lidstrom will never boast, regardless of his accomplishments, but "greatest ever," "superstar," and "future Hall of Famer," are all terms that others in his line of work use to describe him.

"He does everything right, he doesn't make it look hard, he's as smooth as they come," states another lock for the Hall, Chris Chelios. "I can't say I ever saw Bobby Orr play, I never saw Doug Harvey, and, I don't know, I can't say that he's better than them, but I can't imagine anyone better than him. It's apples and oranges. But if he doesn't go down as the greatest, he's at least one of the greatest."

He's the best of this generation for sure.

Lidstrom expresses it a different way. During his acceptance speech for his seventh Norris Trophy as the NHL's best defenseman in 2011, which he kept to 43 seconds, Lidstrom said pretty much what he always says: he thanked the Red Wings owners, the GM, his teammates, and the coaching staff. Given his stature in the game, his humble appreciation for the head coach who provided him with an opportunity was remarkable.

". . . and thanks to our coaching staff, Mike Babcock, for still believing in me and giving me a chance to be out there and play."

Seriously?!

"He's the best of this generation for sure," Babcock told reporters at a recent training camp. "To me, he's ahead of anybody that I've seen. Now, Ray Bourque is a heck of a player, and Bobby Orr, obviously. I don't know anyone before that, but Nick's the best. You don't win seven Norris Trophies without doing something right. He's smoother, smarter, and better than everybody else. He's just better, he just doesn't make mistakes. He's risk free, skates unbelievable, sees the ice, good offensively, good defensively, doesn't force anything, great leader."

Some of that leadership was passed down from "the Captain" Steve Yzerman. Lidstrom took over the "C" from Stevie-Y in 2006–07, and a season later became the first European captain to hoist the Stanley Cup.

"He's just quiet and I think when he says something, his teammates know Nick Lidstrom knows what he's talking about," adds Daniels. "And he learned from Steve, he's been around here that long. It's by osmosis, and that's why the culture of the Red Wings has come on the way it has. That leadership is passed on, that's why the core group sticks together and this team, while adding bits and pieces, carries on the tradition."

Lidstrom doesn't mind his behavior being compared to Yzerman's, nor does he mind any theories of him trying to emulate Number 19.

"I try to," Lidstrom laughs. "I'm not an overly vocal guy in the room, either. We have all different kinds of characters in the room so I think we all chip in with our own individual things, but I try to be a leader on the ice and lead by example too."

Lidstrom was a late bloomer in the world of NHL awards. He didn't win his first Norris until 2001, after his 10th season. It was the fifth and final year that he was partnered with Hall of Famer Larry Murphy, who retired after 21 years in the game.

Murphy arrived in Detroit in 1997 with 12 games remaining in the regular season. He was the missing link the Wings needed to capture their first Cup in 42 years. Watching Lidstrom and Murphy work together for a half decade was like watching a well-oiled machine.

Lidstrom took over the "C" from Stevie-Y in 2006–07, and a season later became the first European captain to hoist the Stanley Cup.

When Murphy started with the Red Wings, he knew he would be skating next to one of the top defensemen in the NHL. "But," he says, "I didn't realize until I got to Detroit how this guy does it game in and game out, how great he is. And the opportunity to play with him, for me, just fit right in. I always loved playing with a D-man that liked utilizing his partner. And for him it was the same way, so it was a great opportunity. I always knew where he was going to be, so I was fortunate. It didn't

ABOVE LEFT: *In 2002, Lidstrom became the first European-born or -trained player to win the Conn Smythe Trophy as Stanley Cup playoff most valuable player. In 23 games he had five goals and 16 points and controlled play with D-partner Larry Murphy.*

ABOVE RIGHT: *Lidstrom takes the Stanley Cup for a skate on June 16, 1998, after the Wings swept the Capitals.*

ABOVE: Lidstrom took over for Steve Yzerman as the Captain of the Red Wings in 2006–07. He became the first European to captain an NHL team to a Stanley Cup when Detroit beat Pittsburgh in the final in six games in 2008.

OPPOSITE TOP: Known more for his cool demeanor and smarts, and less for his physical play, Lidstrom would still take care of business near his net when necessary, here clearing out Phoenix Coyotes forward Todd Fedoruk on February 9, 2009. Red Wings goalie Chris Osgood also pictured.

OPPOSITE BOTTOM: Lidstrom seals off countryman Henrik Sedin of the Vancouver Canucks on March 23, 2011, at the Joe Louis Arena.

happen right away, but after a few games I got matched up with him and it went that way for me the whole time in Detroit from that point on."

Lidstrom won three consecutive Norris Trophies over two separate periods: from 2001 to 2003, and then again between 2006 and 2008. He won his seventh three seasons later.

"The thing that amazed me the most about Lidstrom, and still does, is his point total is always so high," says Scotty Bowman. "So you think 'offensive defenseman,' but I don't remember him ever getting caught up the ice and leaving his defense partner to defend a two-on-one or three-on-one. That's how I remember him. No matter who his partner was, and he's had a lot of them through the years, he never left his partner alone."

Lidstrom's ability to make adjustments, short- and long-term, and to communicate instructions to less experienced players, would make him the proverbial "coach on the ice." Before he turned 42 in April of 2012, he was already older than a couple of active NHL head coaches. With age comes wisdom.

According to Babcock, the team approaches Lidstrom often for advice and guidance. The coach says, "I talk to him about players all the time; I talk to him about our travel. We talk to our best players all the time. We call them 'Nick-isms' and 'Pav-isms' [Datsyuk] and 'Z-isms' [Zetterberg], and we steal what they do and turn it into a system play

because they do it better than everyone else. Nick told me something on the penalty kill just a couple of days ago. [Assistant coach] Bill Peters called them in and we were talking PK and he told us something, and I said, 'I've been here seven years with you, Nick, how come it took me seven years to learn this today? I had never thought about that.'"

"He's just one of those special players who never seem to age much," adds Bowman. "People thought that when they changed the game, the format, or rules, he might get a few more penalties. He was so smart when we played in the old system, he'd put his stick out sideways, guys couldn't get by. People said when the game changed he'd get more penalties, he can't do that. He adjusted. I think under the new rules he's probably adjusted so easily because experienced defensemen are so keyed on the blue line. They have so much time and space, and he's so good on the blue line."

The word *unflappable* comes to mind when describing Lidstrom, or the phrase *calm, cool, and collected.* These qualities may simply come from his upbringing in Sweden—the essentials of his nationality.

"Maybe a little bit," agrees Lidstrom. "If you go over there you see all kinds of Swedes, but in general I think we're looked upon as being a little more levelheaded guys and kind of reserved guys. I think I'm like that too, I'm similar to that. Hockey-wise, growing up, I think we're very

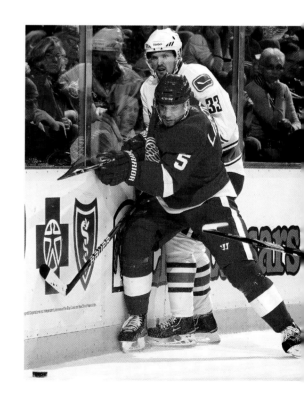

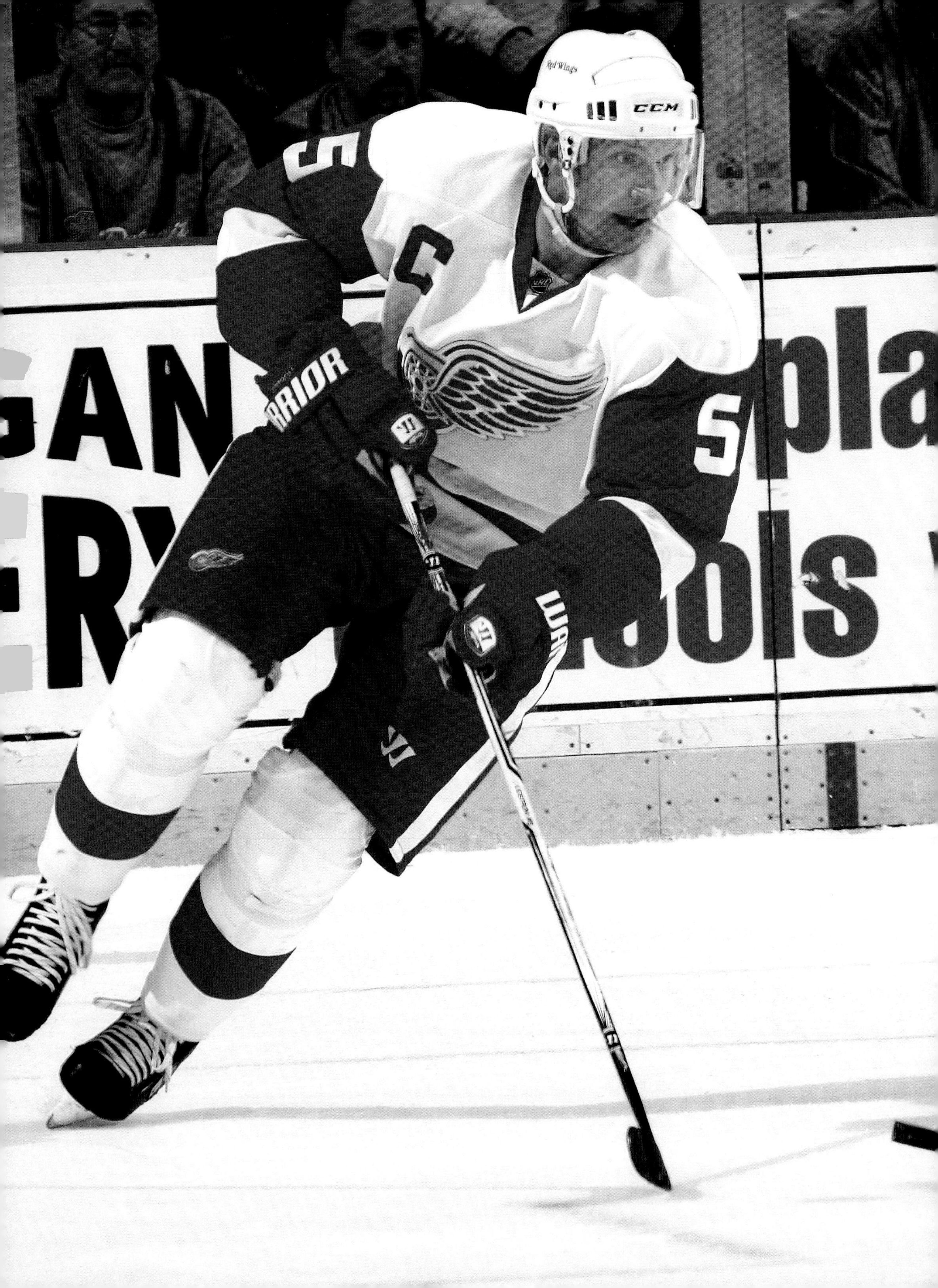
Red Wings
CCM

good at teaching kids at young ages the different tactics, how to play, and how to adapt to systems. From my hockey background I think that's what helped me coming from Sweden, having been taught that at an early age."

Lidstrom was still a young player when the Wings chatted about trading him just a couple of years after he was drafted in the third round in 1989. Christer Rockstrom, the scout who found Lidstrom, former Wings assistant general manager Neil Smith, and assistant coach Colin Campbell had moved on to the Rangers organization in 1990 and 1991.

"I do recall a call from Detroit inquiring about Rangers' 1989 first-round pick Steven Rice, and the people there at the time, not Jimmy D [Devellano], I won't mention names, but the people there at the time were tossing this kid's name around," recalls Campbell. "Steven Rice had great, great upside, he was captain of Team Canada, with [Eric] Lindros there, he was your perfect power winger, and Detroit was trying to pawn off on us at the time this Swedish defenseman who was drafted kind of late. I think his name was Lidstrom," Campbell laughs.

"They weren't going to fool us; there was no way they were going to suck us in," Campbell continues with tongue firmly planted in cheek. "You kidding me? That was discussed, they were trying to fool us, who did they think they were? I don't know how close it was but that was certainly discussed."

Rice went on to tally 125 points in 329 NHL games and retired at age 27. From Detroit's perspective, as with the earlier Yzerman transaction talk, the phrase "some of the best trades are the ones you don't make" comes to mind.

OPPOSITE: *Nick Lidstrom, "the perfect human."*

ABOVE: *A battle between captains: Lidstrom upends Sidney Crosby of the Penguins during Game 3 of the 2008 Stanley Cup final on May 28, 2008, at the Mellon Arena in Pittsburgh.*

ABOVE: *Lidstrom leaves the Red Wings after 1,564 regular season games and 263 playoff matches. He retires as the sixth leading scorer among NHL defenseman in career points with 1,142 tallied in the regular season.*

"It would have been awful having [Sergei] Zubov, [Brian] Leetch, and Lidstrom on the blue line [in New York], wouldn't it?" Campbell jokes again.

It worked out for the Rangers. They packaged Rice in a deal with Edmonton for Mark Messier just before the start of the season in 1991.

Meanwhile, the Red Wings' European influence continued to grow. If the '90s will be remembered for the Russian Five, then the 2000s will definitely be remembered for Detroit's "Team Sweden."

Hakan Andersson, the scout who assumed Rockstrom's role in Detroit in 1990, continued to find gems. The Wings began taking on more of a Scandinavian look, basically in an attempt to find more Lidstroms. By 2006 the Detroit roster featured seven Swedes, and when Sweden won the gold medal in hockey at the 2006 Winter Olympics in Torino, Italy, the victorious Swedish roster featured a five-man Red Wings unit. Defensemen Lidstrom and Niklas Kronwall, and forwards Tomas Holmstrom, Henrik Zetterberg, and Mikael Samuelsson all played together when at full strength.

The Wings' NHL roster also featured Swedes Johan Franzen and Andreas Lilja at the time. Previously, defenseman Fredrik Olausson had been a part of the 2002 Cup win, and more recently another defenseman, Jonathan Ericsson, has been part of the club. Forwards Mattias Ritola, Fabian Brunnstrom, and Gustav Nyquist have also gotten a look.

"For me personally it helped a lot, those guys being here," states Zetterberg. "When I got over here the first time, back then it was just Nick and "Homer" [Holmstrom] on the team. It was a big help for me, not just on the ice but off the ice too. There are a lot of little things, you have to get settled in, and stuff like that, and also we have a lot of fun, all the Swedes. All the sports going on back in Sweden we follow, we always go out to dinner. It's a nice thing and it's not common, to have that many of the same countrymen playing together not in Sweden. It's rare and we're enjoying it."

Unfortunately for Zetterberg, for Detroit's management, and for "Wing Nuts," the opportunity to enjoy Lidstrom's skill on the ice has concluded. Every career must come to an end, and Number 5 officially ended his on May 31, 2012.

For his career, through 20 seasons and almost 1,600 regular-season games, Lidstrom tallied 264 goals, 878 assists, and had a cumulative plus/minus of plus-450.

"The longevity factor is remarkable," asserts Red Wings director of pro scouting Mark Howe. "He's been a Norris-caliber guy for 14 or so seasons—14 seasons!"

Paul Woods points out that there's more to Lidstrom than his exceptional skill: "It's the intelligence, the leadership, the stamina. You know in baseball you say a 'five-tool player,' he would be that guy. He is so good in every aspect of the game, and it's just amazing, when you can do what he has done, play against the opposing team's best players, shift after shift after shift. When you can say you're the best offensive and defensive player on the team at the same time—and very few players in the National Hockey League can say that—you know you're good."

ABOVE: Lidstrom, along with goalie Henrik Lundqvist of the Rangers, helped Team Sweden win Olympic Gold in 2006 at Torino, Italy. Lidstrom scored the gold-medal winning goal in the 3–2 victory over Finland, in a game that featured five Swedish Red Wings.

LEFT: Henrik Zetterberg, another of the Red Wings Swedish gold medalists, along with Tomas Holmstrom, Mikael Samuelsson, and Niklas Kronwall, celebrates Detroit's Stanley Cup win in Pittsburgh on June 4, 2008. With Lidstrom's retirement, Zetterberg, the team's leading scorer in 2010 (shared), 2011, and 2012, stepped to the forefront on and off the ice.

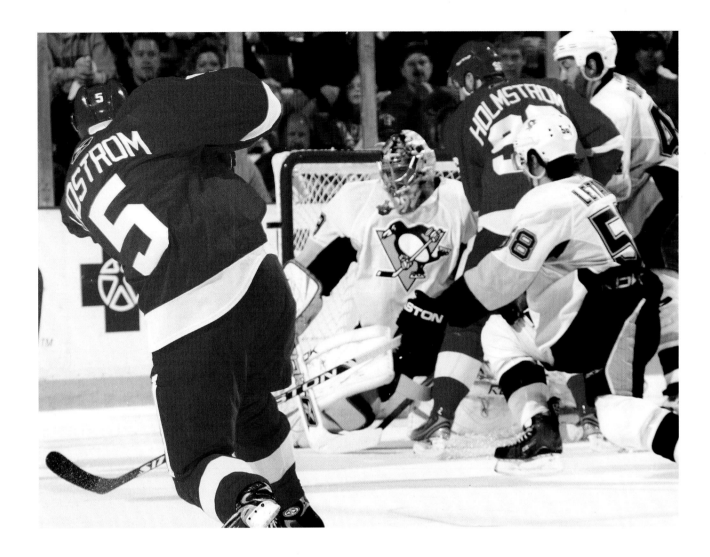

ABOVE: *Swedes in familiar places: Lidstrom rips a shot from the left point as Tomas Holmstrom creates havoc in front of Penguins goalie Marc-Andre Fleury, during Game 1 of the Stanley Cup final in Detroit. Pittsburgh D-men Kris Letang and Brooks Orpik attempt to move number 96, May 24, 2008.*

OPPOSITE TOP: *Post-retirement, Nick, wife Annika and sons Kevin, Adam, Samuel, and Lucas (not shown), planned to return to Sweden to be with grandparents and extended family. Photo from 2008.*

OPPOSITE BOTTOM: *The Red Wings hockey family: Lidstrom taps gloves with the youth-player-of-the-game Wiley Monroe at the Joe on March 23, 2011.*

"The way he plays the point, he doesn't hit guys with the puck, he gets his shot through, and if he has time, the velocity he can put on it and the fact he never gets caught is something," marvels Bowman as part of a Lidstrom dissertation. "He gets the points but he doesn't get them cheating, or staying in, or joining the rush and getting caught. When they changed the rules that didn't allow defensemen to play as physical, it didn't really affect him, he's not a physical defenseman; he's a positional defenseman."

Bowman concludes, saying, "All the great defensemen that I've seen in my day, [Ray] Bourque, [Denis] Potvin, they're all the same. How good were they at the point, how good were they at just knowing when to stay in, when to back out, when not to get caught? That's what Lidstrom does better than anyone I've seen. He never lets a partner get alone covering a rush."

"He's just an amazing guy, and the way he handles himself, and the example he sets for younger players, no one can complain about anything he has done game in and game out," agrees Woods. "For me it's just him and Bobby Orr, and no disrespect to anybody, but to me those two are

the two best defensemen to play in the National Hockey League. At his age, to still be the best, or best two at your position, is amazing."

And like Barry Sanders, or Al Kaline, or Steve Yzerman, or Gordie Howe, for all intents and purposes, Lidstrom belongs solely to Detroit.

He gets the points but he doesn't get them cheating, or staying in, or joining the rush and getting caught.

"It's been special, with one team the whole time I've been over here," reflects Lidstrom. "Just the history, the tradition of the Red Wings, when you walk into our locker room you see the pictures up on the walls, you see the Ted Lindsays, the Gordie Howes, guys that played in the '30s and '40s. Just knowing the tradition of the team, it's been something special for me to be a part of that for so many years."

9 Bench Bosses

"The owner, Bruce Norris, had a phone to the bench. He used to phone down and say, 'How come you're playing so-and-so, and how come you don't play this guy, and why are you doing this?' So I ripped the cord out one night and that was it." — Bill Gadsby, ON COACHING THE WINGS

OPENING SPREAD: *Scotty Bowman oversees activities on the Red Wings bench with assistant coach Barry Smith in 1996. Players include Kris Draper, Doug Brown, Tim Taylor, Slava Kozlov, and Igor Larionov.*

OPPOSITE TOP: *Red Wings head coach Sid Abel on the bench at Maple Leaf Gardens. Sitting in front of him are Floyd Smith (number 17) and Alex Delvecchio (number 10), circa 1963.*

OPPOSITE BOTTOM: *Delvecchio stood up and stepped back, to assume an almost identical vantage point as Detroit head coach at the Olympia a decade later. Forward Bill Collins is sitting in his spot.*

JACK ADAMS CAST A LONG SHADOW. He was the Red Wings' coach and general manager from 1927 to 1947, when he left the bench to focus on management duties alone, a job he kept until 1963. He oversaw the Wings' first seven Stanley Cups, and the National Hockey League has honored its Coach of the Year with the Jack Adams Award since 1974.

Even when he was general manager, Adams had a difficult time leaving the coaching to the current coach. The late Johnny Wilson, former Detroit winger and later head coach, remembered how Adams used to be an overpowering presence.

"One time, when Tommy Ivan was coaching, we were having a tough time in the first period," explained Wilson. "Jack used to sit in the trainers' room on a chair, and on the rubbing table he'd play solitaire. When things didn't go so good he'd come barreling in the dressing room and he'd pick on somebody, or a line, or a defenseman, or whatever. This one night he comes in the dressing room and he looks around and he spots Gordie Howe and says to Gordie, 'You should have paid to get in the rink tonight, like those people out there watching ya!' Gordie blinked a few times, period started, and I don't think anyone else touched the puck after that, second or third period. He was unreal, and we ended up winning the game. Jack got him going."

Ivan, who replaced Adams behind the bench, gave way to Jimmy Skinner, who in turn surrendered the reins to Hall of Fame center turned mentor Sid Abel. Abel took over midway through the 1957–58 season, and kept coaching full time until 1968, while also acquiring the GM duties from Adams.

"Sid was great. He let you play," states former Wings center Peter Mahovlich. "Back then you didn't have video, you didn't have the assistant coaches that you have today. He had to try to do all the jobs, really."

"Detroit just treated us first class, and with Sid Abel in charge there, we really got close together," reflects winger Wayne Connelly. "I really enjoyed playing for Sid, I think we all did. He was team-first all the time and we were a close-knit group. We'd go on the road and we'd arrive somewhere and Sid would say, 'Okay, let's all go to dinner tonight.' We'd get the whole team together all the time and we'd go, and it showed on the ice. He was a pro and we enjoyed playing for him."

ABOVE: *Head coach Ned Harkness (left) with locker room assistant Wally Crossman in 1970. The smiles were misleading, as it's generally believed Harkness's tenure as coach and then general manager ruined the on-ice product for the next decade. The "Darkness with Harkness" led to the "Dead Wings."*

But Abel never coached his way to a Cup. On four separate occasions he lost in the final, the last time in 1966. Two years later he turned his attention to his general manager responsibilities full time, handing the coaching duties over to former teammate Bill Gadsby. After one full season and, oddly, two games into the next, owner Bruce Norris fired the Hall of Fame former defenseman, forcing Abel back to the bench for the final 74 games in 1969–70.

"[Norris] had his arm around me the night before in Chicago," remembers Gadsby, "and he was happy because we beat Chicago and he liked beating them because his brother [James] was involved with them. He said, 'You really have these guys going, Bill.' And I said, 'Yeah Bruce, we're gonna have a good year.' It was noon the next day that he hit me with the news that I was going to be replaced. I couldn't believe it. He's got his arm around you the night before and the next day he tells you he wants a change."

It was the first step toward a slippery slope. After Gadsby was fired and Abel fulfilled his interim duties, Norris and his team director Jim Bishop made a decision that would negatively impact the franchise for at least the next decade. Bishop brought in Ned Harkness, a successful college hockey coach who had won three national championships, including two at Cornell University. His 1970 team, with goaltender Ken Dryden, went undefeated. Harkness was also successful in coaching lacrosse, the sporting thread he shared with Bishop.

Unfortunately, Ned's collegiate success didn't translate at the pro level, and his arrival began an era in Red Wings history known as the "Darkness with Harkness." The college approach in 1971, with a lot of whistles, and meetings, and drills, apparently didn't appeal to the Howes, Delvecchios, or Garry Ungers of the world. These weren't sophomores in need of a micromanaging authoritarian; they were seasoned professionals coming off a productive year.

Unger, then a sleek, young, highly touted scorer, remembers going to lunch with Harkness early in the season. Although the player was suffering from a back injury, Harkness never brought it up.

"He was drawing on a napkin how he wanted my hair cut," Unger says. "I thought, 'Jeez, this is gonna be interesting.'"

"In those days players were not used to having a ton of meetings and sitting down at a blackboard and going over a ton of plays and things like that," recalls Wayne Connelly. "It started to get to the players a little bit about Ned's way of operating a hockey team. We ended up having a players' meeting one day when we were in Buffalo, and we decided we had to do something about it. Our team was falling apart. Bruce McGregor was our player rep, and he got a couple of guys together and went to ownership and asked if something could be done, because it really wasn't working out."

"Harkness wasn't ready for prime time, so to speak," adds Nick Libett. "I think Sid wanted to fire him at one point but Jim Bishop had Norris's ear at the time and I think that's why Sid quit. He basically resigned because he couldn't fire Ned and that was the start right there."

Ned's collegiate success didn't translate at the pro level, and his arrival began an era in Red Wings history known as the "Darkness with Harkness."

Once Sid Abel left the team, Harkness became general manager for the Red Wings after 38 games and a 12–22–4 record. Connelly laughs in exasperation, remembering the situation: "[Harkness] actually had the last laugh. He started moving guys."

"Earlier, we had all signed a piece of paper saying we weren't going to play for him," remembers Unger. "Somehow he got the list, they made him general manager instead of coach, and with that list he traded guys. The only guys that made it through were Gordie and Alex and Nick Libett."

The veteran crew from a resurgent and successful 1969–70 team (40–21–15) under Abel was dispersed. The gutting began a period of futility that opened a revolving door to the head coaching position.

Libett can easily enumerate the coaches that passed through Detroit at the time: "Sid was here, then there was Billy Dea, Doug Barkley, Harkness, Teddy Garvin, Johnny Wilson. That's six [in no particular order]. Bobby Kromm—that's seven—Larry Wilson, Alex Delvecchio would be what, nine? That's a lot of people in my 12 years in Detroit. Not too much longevity."

ABOVE: *Former Red Wings defenseman Doug Barkley coached the team during three different seasons for a grand total of 77 games. That's Red Berenson behind him at practice.*

Earlier, Libett had also played for Gadsby.

The constant changes were not only symptomatic of the club's problems, but also contributed to them.

Former Wings defenseman Doug Barkley coached the team for stints during three different seasons. After 11 games in 1971–72, he was replaced by another former Detroit player, affable storyteller Johnny Wilson.

"One night, we're playing the Maple Leafs, and we're losing four-nothing at the end of the first period," said Wilson. He recalled trying to channel his inner Jack Adams, and he picked Mickey Redmond, one of Detroit's key players at the time, to single out.

Wilson said to Redmond, "The way you're playing, you're making me dizzy, you're making the team dizzy, and you're making the fans watching you dizzy. Quit doing circles; your job is to go up and down the wing and shoot pucks at the net."

He mentioned that goalie Al Smith didn't get let off the hook, either.

"I said . . . 'You've got guys standing in your crease. You've gotta get those guys out of there, so use your stick.' In the old days the goalie would crack guys in the ankles."

The way you're playing, you're making me dizzy, you're making the team dizzy, and you're making the fans watching you dizzy. Quit doing circles; your job is to go up and down the wing and shoot pucks at the net.

After his speech, things started heating up: "The second period starts, I'm watching from the bench, and all of a sudden behind the play there's a roar from the crowd. Don't you know, I see Al Smith fighting with one of the Leafs. Fans got all excited. Meantime, I fired up Mickey Redmond—he scored three goals. We ended up tying the game at the end of the second period and went on to win it five-four. I figured that's the way to straighten 'em out."

Wilson coached 145 games before being replaced by Ted Garvin, who lasted 12.

"Ted Garvin had a very successful International Hockey League career," remembers Libett. "Harkness hired him. He came right from Port Huron, the Flags of the IHL, and I think he lasted 10 games. He was a nice guy but just an awful coach. He just didn't understand the game at that level, but was very successful at the minor-league level. Something happens—not everyone can coach at that level, even in those days. There are good coaches and there are bad coaches, and unfortunately we had a bunch of bad coaches."

Of the next three bosses, Alex Delvecchio, Billy Dea, and Larry Wilson, Wilson had it the worst. Like his older brother Johnny, with whom he won a Cup in Detroit as a player in 1950, Larry took over the job with enthusiasm and optimism. His pedigree didn't help. His team went 3–29–4 to finish the 1976–77 season.

RIGHT *(clockwise from top left):* Ted Lindsay, an interim coach for 20 games in 1980; Wayne Maxner, who took over for Lindsay; Nick Polano, who took over for Maxner; and Billy Dea, who coached exactly 100 games for Detroit over two different stints.

"I think he was a pretty good guy. I think he was put in a situation he wasn't ready for," speculates former Wings scorer Danny Grant. "It was tough. At best we had a fifth- or sixth-place club if everything went well. Then you had injuries like Redmond—Mickey's back went out on him. He had a couple of 50-goal seasons, then he got hurt, rarely played, and was never really himself again. I was only there one year and I got hurt really bad and missed a year and a half. Larry was put in a situation where there was no way he could win."

"It was old-school then. What played at the rink stayed at the rink," remembers Larry's son Ron, a longtime NHL head coach with Washington, San Jose, and Toronto. He explains that his father "didn't really share too much about what was going on with the team, or talk about details."

Larry passed away of a heart attack while jogging in August 1979, two years after coaching the Wings.

"My greatest memory of him coaching with Detroit was actually the year after he was with the Wings. He was coaching their farm club in Kansas City," reminisces Ron. "It was preseason in 1977, I was [a center] with the Leafs in the minors, and I found out last minute I was going to play in a preseason game in Detroit against the Wings. He [Larry] was there as part of the staff. We didn't have cell phones or anything like that then, so I couldn't really get word to him last minute that I was playing. I skated onto the ice at the Olympia and he was there standing on the bench as one of the assistants for the game. I banged my stick on the boards as I skated by to get his attention. It was the only time he saw me play for an NHL team live in person."

Wholesale changes followed Wilson's dismissal in 1977. The tide temporarily turned with the hiring of "Terrible" Ted Lindsay.

"I was general manager for three years and then I was coach for five games, six games, whatever it was before I got fired," says Lindsay. "The first year [as GM] was wonderful. Bobby Kromm was the coach of the year and I was the manager of the year. I was thinking, 'Jeez, this is the life,'" he laughs.

That season, in the spring of 1978, Detroit swept Atlanta in the preliminary round, and even beat the Canadiens in the second game of the quarterfinals in Montreal. But the Habs ultimately dominated the series four games to one, and the Wings were quickly out of the running.

Gradually the Red Wings went back to sleep. Kromm gave way to figurehead Marcel Pronovost, who gave way to Lindsay, who gave way to Wayne Maxner, who coached from the end of one season into the next in 1981.

"Wayne just didn't jell with the team that was there," remembers former winger Errol Thompson. "I can't speak for anyone else; I just don't think he was well respected. When Bobby Kromm was coaching, Wayne was coaching Windsor, I think, and he was always around the dressing room after their games and after our games. The general perception was the guys didn't think too much of that, because he showed up after Bobby was let go."

Nick Polano was next on the merry-go-round. Hired by the team's new GM Jim Devellano, Polano actually lasted three full seasons. At the time, however, Polano knew that coaches in his position rarely lasted long.

Polano remembers how Jim Devellano reassured him of a place with the team, even if coaching didn't work out: "[Devellano] said, 'If something happens and Mr. Ilitch doesn't want you to coach, you can still be the assistant GM, or you'll be free to go and look for another coaching job.' We had made the playoffs two years in a row but never advanced. Mr. Ilitch wanted more, and he thought bringing in a different coach might be good. So I just moved up into my office upstairs and did that for another seven years before I went to Calgary."

Again the franchise took a dip. Another roster overhaul made for more changes behind the bench. Harry Neale came over from Vancouver where he had been coach and general manager.

"Harry is one of my favorite people. I think he's awesome," says former Wings goalie Greg Stefan. "He was in a bad situation. It had nothing to do with his coaching ability; it was just a mess here."

Just as messy was the way Neale learned of his dismissal. After landing in Windsor on the team charter after a game in New York, Neale was driving with assistant coach Danny Belisle into Michigan from Ontario when the story broke. "And just as we were entering into the tunnel, the

ABOVE: *Harry Neale stepped in for the first 35 games of the 1985–86 season before getting fired. He was the victim of some bad free agent signings. Neale is a well-known TV commentator across Canada and in Buffalo where he analyzes Sabres games.*

news came on the radio and the sportscaster, I don't remember who it was, the rumor was Detroit is going to make a coaching change very soon," Neale explains. "Soon as we heard that, we went into the tunnel and lost the sportscast, and when we came out the other side it was over."

Neale was fired the next morning, just after Christmas, after 35 games.

"Jimmy D tried to go at it a different way with Harry Neale," remembers Colin Campbell, a Wings defenseman at the time, "and signed a bunch of players that summer that didn't jell from a free-agent binge, like Adam Oates, and Ray Staszak and Tim Friday and a couple other players—Harold Snepsts and Warren Young—who had a good year with Mario [Lemieux]. It just blew up. Brad Park then found his way back there, he convinced some people he could do the job and it only got worse. Then Jimmy brought in Jacques Demers."

Demers, a boisterous French Canadian, had guided St. Louis to the playoffs the previous three seasons.

"Jacques wasn't a big *x*'s and *o*'s guy, he was just a 'go play, have fun, and work hard' guy," says ex-Detroit-winger Gerard Gallant. "[Assistant coaches] Colin Campbell, Dave Lewis, and Donnie MacAdam at that time were the guys who put a lot of structure into our game, and Jacques was just a players' coach: good on the bench, good person, and a good personality for our team."

Joining the franchise in 1986, the energetic Demers was the perfect complement to the resurgent Wings, who featured the "Bruise Brothers" (Joe Kocur and Bob Probert) and a young Steve Yzerman.

"It was fun working with Jacques," remembers Red Wings public relations man Bill Jamieson. "Jacques Demers is one of my favorite people, and I would say that if he was my mailman or my butcher, forget the fact he was a hockey coach, he was just one of my favorite people ever. Very fun to work with, he was a very generous man, really cared about people. He was as much at home with the vendors at the arena as

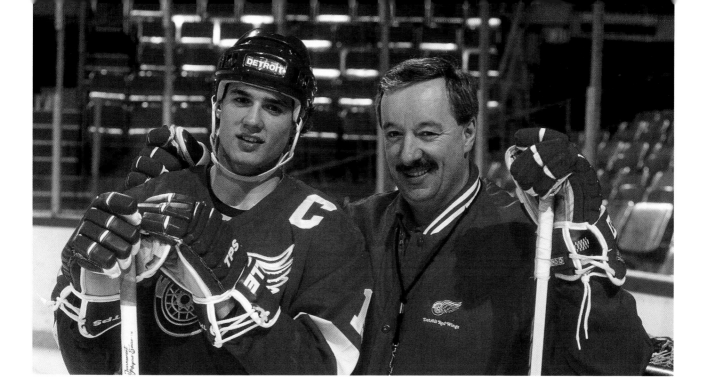

he was with Mr. Ilitch. He did a lot to help out charities, a lot of secret stuff. He knew this nun that worked with a lot of poor in the city and the suburbs, and he used to take a lot of his own money, or money from team fines, and give it to me to give to Sister Helen."

Demers's magic wore off in 1989, and the Red Wings swooned. Owner Mike Ilitch decided to replace his coach, who was fired, and his general manager, who was promoted, with one man.

Joining the franchise in 1986, the energetic Demers was the perfect complement to the resurgent Wings, who featured the "Bruise Brothers" (Joe Kocur and Bob Probert) and a young Steve Yzerman.

Moving forward into the 1990s, Ilitch and Jimmy D decided to go with veteran hockey coach Bryan Murray to fill both positions. For the next three seasons, Murray had regular-season success followed by postseason disappointment.

"It was disappointing [to be fired] because I thought we had turned the corner with the organization," reflects Murray. "I think just being around some of the players I had there, and the level of play they brought to the table every night. Having Steve Yzerman as a younger player, and 'Probie' played for me, and during the stage he was with me he was pretty well behaved, good man, and a really good contributor to the team. We were on the verge, talent-wise, of getting the core that they ended up getting."

But the next step for hockey executive Devellano was paramount. He brought in Scotty Bowman.

ABOVE: *Head Coach Scotty Bowman drinks from the Stanley Cup on June 13, 2002, after the Red Wings defeated the Carolina Hurricanes in Game 5 of the final 3–1. Bowman won three Cups as coach in Detroit, following five championships with Montreal and another with Pittsburgh. One of his two Jack Adams Awards as NHL coach-of-the-year came with Detroit in 1996.*

"I signed a two-year contract—I wasn't planning on staying more than a couple years—but the team was good and I just kept on going," says Bowman. "I had a couple spots where I had to miss, I had a [heart] stent put in, but I did that in the off-season."

The man many consider to be the greatest bench boss in league history stuck around for nine years as head coach, and six more as a team executive. He took over a team that couldn't get over the hump, and attended to the franchise as it won Stanley Cup numbers eight, nine, ten, and eleven.

"We struggled for a couple years trying to get a number-one goalie," Bowman points out. "The team was okay during the regular season, it was an offensive team, could score goals, but it wasn't really . . . it couldn't stop the other team from scoring. I saw a high-scoring team that couldn't keep it out of its own net. It wasn't Stanley Cup caliber yet."

Bowman gradually found goaltending combinations that worked, turned Steve Yzerman into a complete two-way player, managed a number of incoming superstars, and seemed to push all the right buttons.

Jamieson says, "The thing I really enjoyed about Scotty was how he could sit on a plane and recount games like you wouldn't believe. He'd be in the playoffs in May and remember that someone lost a face-off to someone else back in November, and he'd probably send another guy out for the face-off, that's the way he was. The players were astounded sometimes by his memory and his knowledge of the game, how he knew the game."

"Scotty had his quirks, his idiosyncrasies in everything he did, in coaching, obviously, as players and other coaches can tell you," states Wings communications executive John Hahn. "We'd have a lineup in the morning for practice, then we'd have a lineup for pregame skate, then right before the puck drop he'd move everyone around. Scotty treated everyone the same. You never knew who you were playing with, you never knew if you were in the game or out of the game, whose shift was next. He was the same with everyone including the PR people—you never really knew which Scotty you were gonna get each day."

"Scotty could get distracted," points out longtime Wings TV play-by-play man Dave Strader. Strader remembers a story that he heard former coach Dave Lewis tell on several occasions. It was Game 3 of the 1997 final against Philadelphia, and Detroit had won the first two games in Philly.

"Game 3 starts, and Philadelphia just puts on the full press, with the puck down in the Red Wings zone, and it's just a mad scramble. So Lewis and Barry Smith and Scotty are on the bench, and Louie is looking at the D, thinking about a change if possible, and he looks up, and Scotty isn't looking down at the end where all the action is, he's looking straight across the ice. And Scotty goes, 'Is that Gordie Howe?' Louie goes, 'What?!' 'Is that Gordie Howe?' Scotty asked again. 'How did he end up in those seats?' That was his question first shift into Game 3 of the Stanley Cup final. And then boom! Scotty was focused and right back into it."

ABOVE: *One of Bowman's assistants during his successful run in Detroit was Dave Lewis, who took over as head man in 2002–03. Like Murray a decade prior, Lewis had regular season success followed by playoff failures. He coached for two seasons. Joe Kocur is his assistant on the left. Players from left, Darren McCarty, Sergei Fedorov, and Boyd Devereaux.*

When Bowman moved to upper management, Lewis took over as coach. It was sort of a Bryan Murray do-over, in that the Wings would produce in the regular season, only to flounder in the post.

After two seasons with "Louie," the reins were handed to Mike Babcock in 2005. "Babs," with a stern, level-headed approach, had led the Anaheim Ducks to the Stanley Cup final in 2003 in his first season as an NHL coach.

Aside from the obvious, a Stanley Cup win in 2008, Babcock's success in Detroit is reflected in the ongoing success of his championship assistants. Paul MacLean went on to take over the head job in Ottawa, and Todd McLellan did the same in San Jose.

During the 2011 playoff series between his new team, the Sharks, and his former, McLellan reflected back on first arriving in Detroit to work for the Wings

He said, "I had the opportunity to walk in this building, and as a coach that hadn't experienced the NHL before, and have Mr. Lindsay, Mr. Howe, Mr. and Mrs. Ilitch around, Kenny Holland and all of his staff, Steve Yzerman—I could go on and on—you see all the names up on the wall. That doesn't happen around the league, that's not an every place, everyday thing. I was very lucky to come into the organization at a very good time, with Mike and Paul, and try to absorb as much as I could, and hopefully that pays off for us down the road."

Meanwhile, Babcock believes in what he calls the "Red Wings way" and he attempts on a consistent basis to perpetuate its themes: humble, hard working, consistent excellence.

Jack Adams would be proud.

Coaches whose Detroit tenures included or began after 1962–63, a half century ago.

RED WINGS REGULAR SEASON STATISTICS	GC	W	L	T/OTL	WIN%
SID ABEL 1957–1968, 1969–1970 Took over in 1957, also became GM for six-plus seasons	811	340	339	132	.501
MIKE BABCOCK 2005–2012 Won Stanley Cup in third season as coach	574	352	154	68	.731
DOUG BARKLEY 1970–1972, 1975–1976 Former player, worked with Wings PR before coaching	77	20	46	11	.303
SCOTTY BOWMAN 1993–2002 Won three of his nine coaching Cups with Detroit	701	410	195	96	.678
BILLY DEA 1975–1977, 1982 Uncle of current NHL D-man James Wisniewski	100	32	57	11	.360
ALEX DELVECCHIO 1973–1976 Had Billy Dea work a number of his games behind the bench	155	53	81	21	.396
JACQUES DEMERS 1986–1990 Now a Canadian Senator	320	137	136	47	.502
BILL GADSBY 1968–1969 Preceded and succeeded by Sid Abel	78	35	31	12	.530
TED GARVIN 1973 Success as IHL coach, two Turner Cups; didn't translate to NHL success	12	2	9	1	.182
NED HARKNESS 1970–1971 Won national championships as college lacrosse and hockey coach	38	12	22	4	.353
BOBBY KROMM 1977–1980 Coach when GM Lindsay declared "Aggressive hockey is back in town"	231	79	111	41	.416
DAVE LEWIS 2002–2004 Former assistant, didn't possess Bowman's savvy in the postseason	164	96	41	27	.701
TED LINDSAY 1980 Brief attempt at head coaching after run as GM	20	3	14	3	.176
WAYNE MAXNER 1980–1982 Had previously coached the Windsor Spitfires	129	34	68	27	.333
BRYAN MURRAY 1990–1993 Solid regular seasons followed by playoff failures	244	124	91	29	.577
HARRY NEALE 1985–1986 Went on to have a long, clever career in broadcasting	35	8	23	4	.258
BRAD PARK 1985–1986 Gave it a whirl; not so good	45	9	34	2	.209
NICK POLANO 1982–1985 First coach under owner Mike Ilitch; now scouts for Ottawa	240	79	127	34	.383
MARCEL PRONOVOST 1980 Wasn't officially head coach; went behind bench for Ted Lindsay	9	2	7	0	.222
JOHNNY WILSON 1971–1973 Passed away 12/'11. His little brother Larry died of a heart attack in 1979	145	67	56	22	.545
LARRY WILSON 1976–1977 His son Ron has coached Washington, San Jose, and Toronto	36	3	29	4	.094

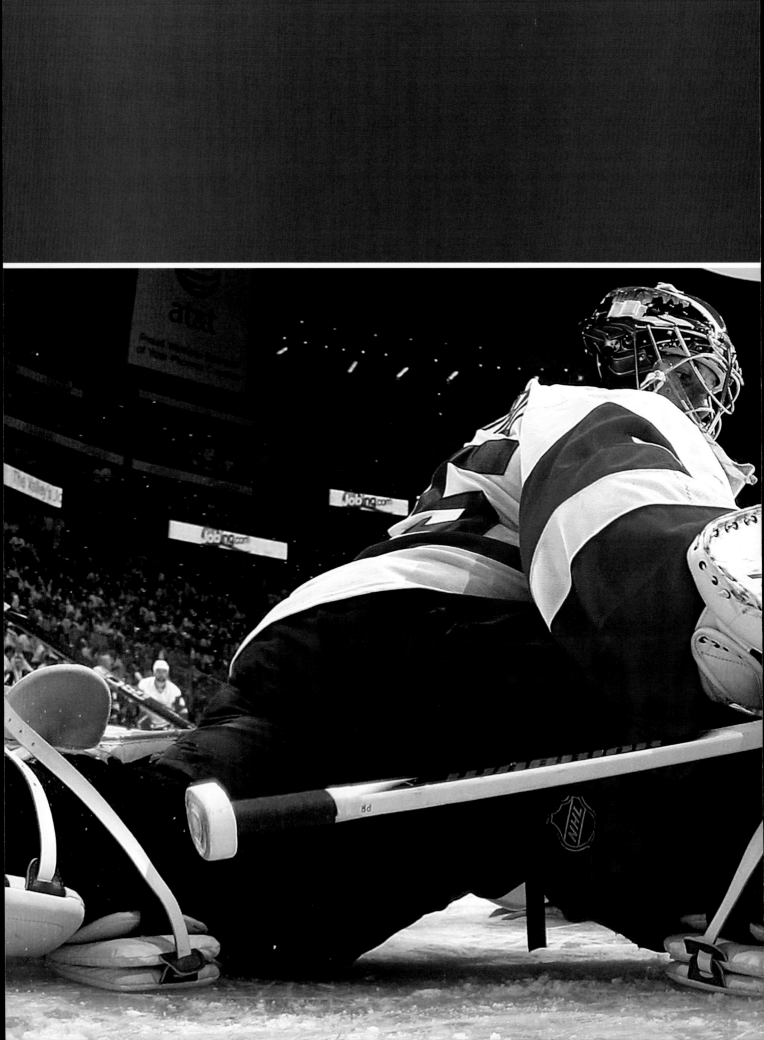

10 | Masked Men

> *"Jimmy Howard's last two seasons have been remarkable, and he's been very durable. Knock on wood, I hope that keeps up and he's always raring and ready to go."* — DETROIT GOALIE COACH **Jim Bedard**

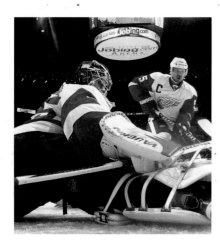

ABOVE: *Jimmy Howard, here with Lidstrom, is the Red Wings latest number-one goalie as of the spring of 2012. After three and a half seasons patiently developing with Grand Rapids in the American Hockey League, Howard finally got a full-time crack at it in Detroit in 2009–10.*

NETMINDING HAS NOT DEFINED the Detroit Red Wings. Since Terry Sawchuk in the 1950s, Detroit hasn't had a Ken Dryden, a Bernie Parent, a Patrick Roy, a Martin Brodeur, or even a Henrik Lundqvist. There have been great goalies in Detroit, and great goaltending moments, but for the most part it's been greatness by committee.

There's absolutely nothing wrong with this phenomenon. In fact, it points to the balance and consistency the organization has usually exhibited: strong or weak talent spread evenly across the roster in good times and bad. No goaltender has transcended the team during two decades of dominance, just as no one man was able to pull the Wings from the abyss in the days of less delight.

Red Wings goalies have been team-first in that, for the most part, they've simply been part of the team.

The closest the Red Wings have been to having an NHL "brand-name" goaltender in the last five decades is Dominik Hasek. He won two Cups with the Wings, one as a playoff starter and the other as backup, but most fans would still more closely associate him with the Buffalo Sabres or even the Chicago Blackhawks. Hasek was truly remarkable and his career legendary, but the "Dominator" brand was long established before he arrived in Detroit.

"When you got to see him every day, you realized Dom wasn't really making it up as he went along, he just had an incredible flexibility and competitiveness," explains longtime Detroit goaltending coach Jim Bedard. "If you saw him just in sweats, cruising around, you might think he couldn't skate. But when you got him in the crease, he's one of the best skaters I've ever seen going lateral, up to the top, back to posts, and up and challenging. Plus, he had really long arms and legs, almost octopus-like, which is appropriate for Detroit, and when you saw him every day, you'd get to realize the amount of preparation he'd do."

Before arriving in Detroit, Hasek was a back-to-back Hart Trophy (MVP) winner, a six-time Vezina Trophy winner, and an Olympic champion. He was an NHL First-Team postseason All-Star six times, all before coming to Motown.

It was with the Red Wings, of course, that he finally got his Cup.

"He was a perfectionist," adds Bedard. "He didn't want to leave the ice until he had it right. He'd ask for more practice, have me set up more

situations. Sometimes he'd be so buckled over, going to the boards to leave the ice, he'd actually miss the gate and bounce back because his head was down. Then he'd skate forward, try again, and find it. He'd have slobber on his mouth like a St. Bernard because he'd give you every single thing in his body. He just gave it. That's why he's played so long, bouncing around, still playing, having fun. He's a very, very unique individual."

Unique enough to win his Cup, retire, come back, get hurt, sign with Ottawa, return to Detroit, and win another Cup. It was a four-year span that seemed to last much longer.

Meanwhile, the goalie most closely associated with the Red Wings during those years, and in recent times, is Chris Osgood. In 1997, after his second full NHL season, he won a Cup in Detroit as Mike Vernon's backup. A year later he became the playoff starter and won it all again. In 2008, a full decade later, at 35 years of age, he again backstopped the Wings to a title.

Why is a man with these credentials "arguably" a future Hall of Famer, when anywhere else he'd probably be a lock for the honor? Because some would argue that in Detroit he was just one man in an incredible cast.

"I was happy with the career I had, whether or not that gets me in [the Hall], I'm not sure it will or won't," says Osgood. "To me, I knew

ABOVE: When he arrived in Detroit in 2001, Dominik Hasek had pretty much done it all in the National Hockey League except for winning the Stanley Cup. Within a year he'd do it, and he'd win another as the Red Wings backup goalie six years later. That's Colorado Avalanche center Joe Sakic to the left and Nick Lidstrom.

what it took, how hard it is to win, what it takes to win, so for me I do think I belong in there. But again, some people think differently than I would. It's tough to win in the NHL these days, and it always has been."

Add to that the expectations in Hockeytown.

"Detroit's a tough place to play," states Bedard. "It's in a big-time hockey belt and people are very in tune with what goes on on the ice, and people either play the game themselves or take young ones to the rink, and they know what they like and what they don't like. There are not a lot of places to hide in the net. So Ozzie [Osgood] might be of diminutive stature, but he played very big in the net for a long time in Detroit."

Since Osgood's retirement, that responsibility—or opportunity, or burden—has belonged to Jimmy Howard, who patiently played and waited in the minor leagues to get his shot. After four full seasons in the American Hockey League in Grand Rapids, with nine NHL appearances sprinkled in along the way, Howard finally got his crack at full-time in 2009. He signed a two-year contract extension in 2011.

Of becoming part of the Detroit Red Wings, Howard says, "It means a lot. They've had such great goaltenders throughout the years. I'm very fortunate that I've gotten to learn from a couple of the best. I've watched Dom [Hasek], and have become really good friends with Ozzie."

Howard's rookie year was exemplary, with 37 wins and a 2.26 goals against average—numbers reminiscent of one of the finest rookie goaltending campaigns of all time.

Roger Crozier's rookie numbers for Detroit in 1964–65 were only slightly different than Howard's, with 40 wins and a 2.42 goals against average. But there were also a couple of huge differences. Crozier, just

five foot eight and 160 pounds, started all 70 games on the schedule that season and was one of only six number-one goalies on the planet. Given the elite competitiveness of the league at the time, Crozier was a true phenomenon, and the deserved winner of the NHL's Calder Trophy as Rookie of the Year.

There are not a lot of places to hide in the net. So Ozzie might be of diminutive stature, but he played very big in the net for a long time in Detroit.

After the following season, Crozier became the first player from a non-Stanley-Cup-winning team to win the Conn Smythe Trophy as playoff MVP. He almost literally stood on his head to carry the Wings past Chicago in six games in the semifinals and through to overtime of Game Six of the final against Montreal. There, Henri Richard's series winner proved controversial to say the least, as it appeared "The Pocket Rocket" fell and pushed the puck in with his body and hand. There was no video replay back then, and the protests were for naught: the Habs were Cup champs while Crozier was awarded the impressive consolation prize.

"He wasn't very big, but he was unbelievably quick and had great reflexes," states his teammate Norm Ullman. "He just seemed to read the play pretty good, he was always a jump ahead of most guys. He had an amazing series."

ABOVE: *While Hasek is a lock for the Hall of Fame, Chris Osgood finds himself on the bubble. This, despite Stanley Cup championships as a starter a decade apart (1998, 2008). He also won as Mike Vernon's backup in 1997. The Wings third-round pick in 1991 played 17 NHL seasons, won 401 regular season games and 74 more in the playoffs.*

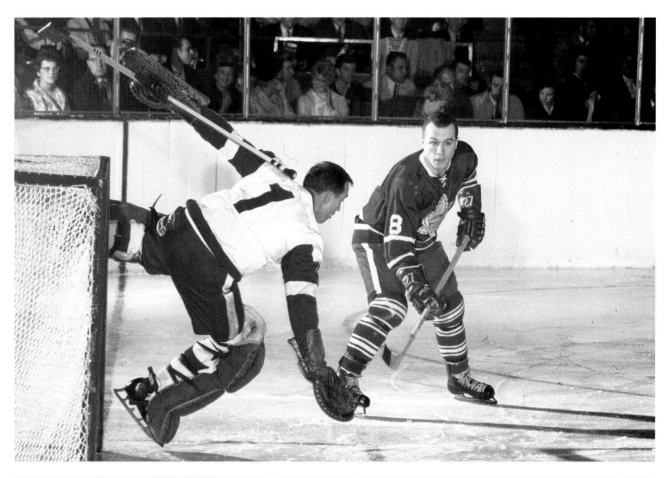

If Terry Sawchuk was the main man in net for the Wings in the '50s and early '60s, and Crozier the bridge to the next decade, then it is Jimmy Rutherford's face—or mask—that best represents the Red Wings during the difficult decade of the '70s. The Wings first-round pick in 1969 played 29 games as a rookie for Detroit in 1970–71, but with veteran Roy Edwards holding down the number-one spot, the Wings left Rutherford unprotected in the intra-league draft in 1971 when he was taken by Pittsburgh. After two and a half seasons with the Penguins, he was re-acquired by Detroit in January of 1974.

Crozier, just five foot eight and 160 pounds, started all 70 games on the schedule that season and was one of only six number-one goalies on the planet.

"It was really special for me because my first year in the league I played with Howe, Mahovlich, Delvecchio, and those guys," remembers Rutherford, a general manager in the NHL with Carolina. "The Red Wings have great tradition and an Original Six team, and it was really special."

Unfortunately for Rutherford, the man with stylish Red Wing–painted eye sockets on his otherwise all-white mask, the cast of characters in front of him wasn't very good. Despite being fourth all-time on Detroit's appearances list for goalies, proving his longevity, talent, and durability, Rutherford managed a grand total of only 97 wins. His one reward

OPPOSITE TOP: *Goalie Roger Crozier, the first player from a losing team (1966 vs. Montreal) to win the Conn Smythe Trophy as playoff MVP, performs some acrobatics while Toronto's Ron Ellis looks on. Crozier also won the Calder Trophy as Rookie of the Year that season with 40 wins.*

OPPOSITE BOTTOM LEFT: *Roy Edwards was a stalwart for six seasons during two different Detroit stints.*

OPPOSITE BOTTOM RIGHT: *Roy Edwards, pre-ugly mask, makes a kick save while Wings defenseman Gary Bergman ties up Maple Leaf Bob Pulford.*

ABOVE LEFT: *Jim Rutherford picked a bad time to be the Red Wings goalie: the 1970s. Fourth on the club in all-time appearances, he lost 68 games more than he won.*

ABOVE RIGHT: *Ron Low backed-up Jim Rutherford during the Wings resurgent 1977–78 season. He went on to a long career in coaching.*

ABOVE LEFT: *If Rutherford was the goalie of the 1970s, then the hot-tempered Greg Stefan was the Red Wings goalie of the '80s, leading the team in starts for seven seasons. Stefan finished his career with 200 penalty minutes.*

ABOVE RIGHT: *Corrado Micalef shared the net with Stefan. The little goalie, five foot eight, 170 pounds, played parts of five seasons in Detroit after an impressive career in the Quebec Major Junior League.*

came in 1977–78, when his youthful, upstart group of teammates briefly became NHL postseason darlings.

"We had a decent year," recalls Rutherford. "Not a great year during the regular season, but we beat Atlanta in the first round and we beat Montreal in a game on the road in the second. It may have been the only game that Montreal lost that year on the way to the Stanley Cup. It created a lot of excitement around Detroit—we hadn't had much for a number of years, so it was pretty exciting."

But the team's effectiveness, and the excitement, quickly dissipated. It would be six years before another playoff berth. By that time the main goaltender of the next decade had started to take over: a little-known fifth-round draft pick from Brantford, Ontario, named Greg Stefan.

"The cupboard was bare, so I was fortunate to get a look, being a low pick. It was good," reflects Stefan. "Having the down years early on, and then Mr. Ilitch coming on, and then Jacques Demers as coach came in and we started to turn things around.

"I played my junior hockey in the 'Motor City,' which [in Canada] is Oshawa. And I played my NHL career in the 'Motor City' in Detroit," points out Stefan. "It worked out quite well."

Stefan played right through to 1990, with a number of backups—or partners, or goalies-on-audition—along the way. One of them was none other than Ken Holland, who later became the franchise's longtime, very successful general manager. As a goalie: not so much. Following a hearty self-deprecating laugh, Holland recalls in great detail a good portion of his three-game stint with the Wings in 1984.

ABOVE: *Ty Conklin reaches to make a save on February 25, 2009, at the Joe Louis Arena, as defenseman Andreas Lilja cuts off San Jose Sharks forward Joe Pavelski.*

MIDDLE: *Bumped by young goalie prospect John Davidson, Rangers legend Ed Giacomin was waived by New York on Halloween, 1975. The Red Wings snatched up the future Hall of Famer, and two nights later he was back in Manhattan to play against his former team. In a surreal environment, with the New York fans chanting his name and cheering for the Red Wings, Detroit won the game 6–4.*

BOTTOM: *Norm Maracle starts to move across the crease in an attempt to stop Maple Leaf Sergei Berezin.*

ABOVE LEFT: *Bob Essensa played for six different NHL teams after winning an NCAA championship at Michigan State. His 13-game Red Wing career was less than stellar. He won a Stanley Cup with Boston as goalie coach in 2011.*

ABOVE RIGHT: *Well-traveled veteran Joey MacDonald makes a glove save against the Florida Panthers on the road on February 18, 2011.*

"We had a big goalie rotation then," he says. "I remember Corrado Micalef and I were playing in the minors, and they had Greg Stefan and Eddie Mio."

On February 1, Holland made his first appearance.

"So I end up getting called up," he recalls. "It's Wednesday night, I'm in and we're playing the Hartford Whalers and we're up 6–3 with about eight minutes to go, and they end up scoring three goals in the last five minutes to tie us . . . so that was 6–6."

The next game Detroit played was against Toronto. Holland says, "Stefan started. Seven minutes into the game it's two–nothing Toronto. Next thing I know Stefan is down at the end of the bench, he's sick, he's throwing up; he's out. I go in and we lost 6–3."

Holland traveled to Boston for a game against the Bruins the next day, only to have his stint, or "cup of coffee," cut short.

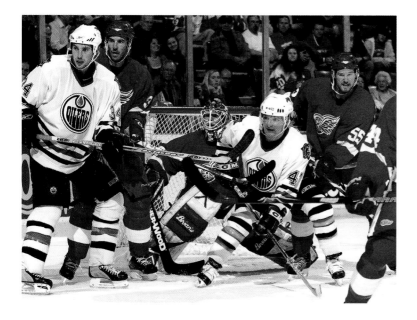

"The red light on my phone in the [hotel] room was blinking," he remembers, "and the message was, 'Call Nick Polano,' and I knew the jig was up. I was going back to Adirondack."

Stefan, meanwhile, became known as a modern-day Billy Smith, a goaltender with a short fuse and a quick stick.

"I had a temper about getting beat or getting embarrassed," Stefan explains. "I don't know if I was a good team guy, or more of a hothead, but if someone was beating us good and rubbing it in, I didn't like that so I guess I got frustrated a little bit. I had a little bit of a hot temper."

On six separate occasions Stefan finished a season with more than 23 penalty minutes, including one campaign with 41. Four of those seasons his PIM total ended in an odd number, meaning there had to have been at least one five-minute major.

"Me and Willi Plett had a few run-ins," Stefan recalls. "I had a fight with Al Secord, which wasn't really smart. I liked to get involved, but back then the forwards would [run you], you were fair game in the crease, and I liked to keep my area a little clean."

After Stefan and his supporting cast of netminders left the team, the Wings saw an elongated goaltending transition. A familiar face or two popped up, including collegiate national champion Bob Essensa.

Essensa says, "For me it was fun because I played up the road there at Michigan State. But my time there with Detroit was short and sweet."

Maybe it was the expectations, or maybe it was being a part of an unexpected first-round playoff ouster in 1994, but the former Michigan State Spartan lasted a total of only 13 regular-season and two playoff games.

"Hockey-wise, being part of that environment was fun, but I wasn't there very long I was there for a cup of coffee," reflects Essensa. "There are certain cities, and Philly might be another, where it's tough for goalies to get a foothold, and for me it was a tough one there."

ABOVE LEFT: *On April 11, 2006, Wings goalie Manny Legace tries to follow the puck through traffic, left to right, Oiler Fernando Pisani, Wings D-man Andreas Lilja, Oiler Marc-Andre Bergeron, Wing D-man Niklas Kronwall, and forward Mark Mowers.*

ABOVE RIGHT: *Mike Vernon back-stopped the Red Wings to their first Stanley Cup in 42 years. In the 1997 postseason, he had 16 wins against four losses, a save percentage of .927, and a goals-against-average of 1.76.*

TOP: *A meeting of the minds between Kevin Hodson (left) and Chris Osgood.*

BOTTOM: *Glen Hanlon recovers from a save behind defenseman Gilbert Delorme.*

It was the same season, 1993–94, as Chris Osgood's first appearance.

"To be honest, when I grew up, I had only seen Detroit play once until I went there," remembers Osgood, a Peace River, Alberta, native. "I didn't really watch or see a lot of them, but I learned what it was all about quickly. When I went there, especially because I got there about the height [of the team's rise in popularity], we were selling out every game and the crowd was crazy and we were working toward that first Cup. We had a couple of tough points but the popularity of the team really took off."

Regardless of celebrity, longevity, or demeanor, most Red Wings goalies eventually share one common trait: an appreciation for the emblem on their chest and the meaning behind it.

"I didn't appreciate the tradition until I got a couple years into my career and I got a chance to meet Gordie and Ted and Alex, and then Sid Abel, who I got to become good friends with," Stefan remembers. "We would carpool together when we went on road trips. I got some great memories with [then-broadcaster] Sid. We used to go over to their house; they lived down the way, got to know [his wife] Gloria. That's when I really took in the tradition of the Red Wings and really respected it for what they had done. I appreciated it more as my career went on."

Red Wings goaltender is one of the more unique, wonderful, yet sometimes thankless job titles in the world. Whether manning the position leads to disappointment or glory, the just rewards are rarely earmarked for the masked man alone. The all-important goaltender is simply the Winged Wheel's last line of defense.

Goalies whose Detroit careers included or began after 1962-1963, a half century ago.

RED WINGS REGULAR SEASON STATISTICS	GP	W	L	T/OT	GAA	SO
HANK BASSEN—Calgary, AB	99	34	39	19	2.99	3
#1, 25, 30 / 1960–1964, 1965–1967 / Part of Lindsay deal; Crozier's backup in 1965–66						
ALLAN BESTER—Hamilton, ON	4	0	3	0	4.31	0
#35 / 1990–1992 / Little "Ernie" had a quick glove with the Leafs						
ANDY BROWN—Hamilton, ON	17	6	6	3	3.80	0
#31 / 1971–1973 / Last NHL goalie to play without a mask						
BOB CHAMPOUX—Ste. Hilaire, QC	0	0	0	0	.000	0
#22 / 1964 / Appeared in one playoff game, 4 goals allowed in 55 minutes						
TIM CHEVELDAE—Melville, SK	264	128	93	30	3.39	9
#31, 32 / 1988–1994 / Led NHL in starts and wins in 1991–92						
ALAIN CHEVRIER—Cornwall, ON	3	0	3	0	6.11	0
#31 / 1990–1991 / Briefly gave Detroit two "Chevys"						
TY CONKLIN—Anchorage, AK	55	30	17	3	2.71	7
#29 / 2008–2009, 2011–2012 / Started first three NHL regular-season outdoor games						
ROGER CROZIER—Bracebridge, ON	310	130	119	43	2.94	20
#22, 1, 30 / 1963–1970 / Calder Trophy 1965, Smythe in 1966; died of cancer in 1996						
JOE DALEY—Winnipeg, MB	29	11	10	5	3.15	0
#1 / 1971–1972 / Goalie for Winnipeg Jets during their entire WHA existence						
DENIS DEJORDY—Saint-Hyacinthe, QC	25	8	12	3	3.86	1
#30, 27 / 1972–1974 / AHL MVP and Calder Cup champ with Buffalo Bisons in 1963						
ROY EDWARDS—Seneca Township, ON	221	95	74	34	2.94	14
#1, 30 / 1967–1971, 1972–1974 / Led NHL in shutouts (6) as a 36-year-old in 1972–73						
DARREN ELIOT—Hamilton, ON	3	0	0	1	5.57	0
#31 / 1987–1988 / Played with fellow NHL goalie & TV guy Brian Hayward at Cornell						
BOB ESSENSA—Toronto, ON	13	4	7	2	2.62	1
#35 / 1993–1994 / Longtime goaltending coach in Boston						
DAVE GAGNON—Windsor, ON	2	0	1	0	10.29	0
#35 / 1990–1991 / Won ECHL Kelly Cup and playoff MVP for Toledo Storm in 1994						
GEORGE GARDNER—Lachine, QC	24	7	7	3	3.59	0
#25, 30 / 1965–1968 / The Vancouver Canucks' first goalie						
ED GIACOMIN—Sudbury, ON	71	23	37	7	3.47	6
#31 / 1975–1978 / Hall of Famer's return to NYC with Wings in Nov. 1975 was a classic						
GILLES GILBERT—Saint-Esprit, QC	95	21	48	16	4.18	0
#30, 1 / 1980–1983 / Cheevers's longtime sidekick in Boston played in one All-Star Game						
DOUG GRANT—Corner Brook, NL	46	17	22	2	4.33	1
#30, 31 / 1973–1976 / Played five seasons in Newfie Senior League before NHL backup						
GERRY GRAY—Brantford, ON	7	1	4	1	4.73	0
#30 / 1970–1971 / Traded to Islanders in 1972 where he played one more NHL game						
HARRISON GRAY—Calgary, AB	1	0	1	0	7.50	0
#22 / 1963 / 2nd period injury replacement for Sawchuk on Nov. 28, gave up 5 in loss						
GLEN HANLON—Brandon, MB	186	65	71	26	3.47	7
#1 / 1986–1991 / Alexander Ovechkin's first NHL head coach						
DOMINIK HASEK—Pardubice, Czechoslovakia	176	114	39	10	2.13	20
#39 / 2001–2002, 2003–2004, 2006–2008 / Hall of Famer finished career in Russia						

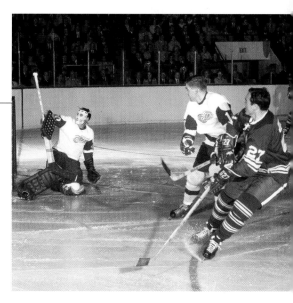

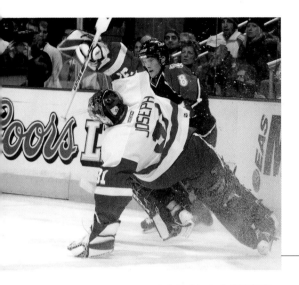

OPPOSITE: *Jimmy Howard is crushed by teammate Brad Stuart and Blackhawk Viktor Stalberg on February 21, 2012.*

GOALIES

RED WINGS REGULAR SEASON STATISTICS	GP	W	L	T/OT	GAA	SO
KEVIN HODSON—Winnipeg, MB	35	13	7	4	2.37	4
#31, 37 / 1995–1999 / 21 regular season, and one playoff appearance to earn Cup in '98						
KEN HOLLAND—Vernon, BC	3	0	1	1	4.11	0
#35 / 1983–1984 / Had a substantially better career as Red Wings GM						
JIMMY HOWARD—Syracuse, NY	192	110	54	19	2.41	11
#35 / 2005–2012 / Bided time in Grand Rapids to develop as Wings number-one in 2009						
PETER ING—Toronto, ON	3	1	2	0	5.29	0
#31 / 1993–1994 / Big goalie; earned brief, early accolades as rookie with Toronto						
AL JENSEN—Hamilton, ON	1	0	1	0	7.00	0
#31 / 1980–1981 / Went on to win a Jennings Trophy with Pat Riggin in Washington						
CURTIS JOSEPH—Keswick, ON	92	50	29	9	2.46	7
#31 / 2002–2004 / Fourth most wins and tied for most losses in NHL history						
SCOTT KING—Thunder Bay, ON	2	0	0	0	2.95	0
#38, 31 / 1990–1992 / Star at U of Maine; won an ECHL title with Toledo in 1993						
MARK LAFOREST—Welland, ON	33	6	22	0	4.71	0
#31 / 1985–1987 / "Trees" wasn't that tall (5'11"); made stops with four NHL clubs						
MARC LAMOTHE—New Liskeard, ON	2	1	0	1	1.44	0
#35 / 2003–2004 / Most recently played in Russia, Finland, and Germany						
MANNY LEGACE—Toronto, ON	180	112	37	16	2.18	13
#34 / 1999–2006 / Hasek's backup for 2002 Cup win						
CLAUDE LEGRIS—Verdun, QC	4	0	1	1	2.66	0
#31 / 1980–1982 / Fan favorite and IHL best goals against in Kalamazoo in 1980–81						
RON LOW—Birtle, MB	32	9	12	9	3.37	1
#30 / 1977–1978 / Head coach in Edmonton and New York (Rangers); two Cups as asst.						
LARRY LOZINSKI—Hudson Bay, SK	30	6	11	7	4.32	0
#31 / 1980–1981 / Preceded Legris in Kalamazoo and also had IHL's lowest GAA						
JOEY MACDONALD—Pictou, NS	37	14	15	13	2.38	1
#31 / 2006–2007, 2010–2012 / Boston, New York Islanders, and Toronto in between						
NORM MARACLE—Belleville, ON	20	10	7	2	2.22	0
#34, 38 / 1997–1999 / Led major juniors with 41 wins with Saskatoon in 1993–94						
PETE MCDUFFE—Milton, ON	4	0	3	1	5.50	0
#30 / 1975–1976 / Came to Detroit from Kansas City in Gary Bergman's departure deal						
BILL MCKENZIE—St. Thomas, ON	26	5	13	6	4.16	0
#1, 30 / 1973–1975 / With Bergman to Kansas City; moved with franchise to Colorado						
DON MCLEOD—Trail, BC	14	3	7	0	5.15	0
#1, 30 / 1970–1971 / "Smokey" played for the Michigan Stags in the WHA						
CORRADO MICALEF—Montreal, QC	113	26	59	15	4.23	2
#30, 31, 1 / 1981–1986 / Once attacked Stan Smyl, claiming the Canuck spit on him						
GREG MILLEN—Toronto, ON	10	3	2	3	2.71	0
#34 / 1991–1992 / Led NHL in shutouts (six) with St. Louis in 1988–89; TV guy on CBC						
EDDIE MIO—Windsor, ON	49	10	20	5	5.00	1
#41 / 1983–1986 / Eight NHL goalies had three-letter surnames, three have played for Detroit						
CHRIS OSGOOD—Peace River, AB	565	317	149	75	2.49	39
#30 / 1994–2001, 2005–2012 / Cup starter and winner in 1998 and again a decade later						
CHRIS PUSEY—Brantford, ON	1	0	0	0	4.50	0
#31 / 1985–1986 / Played two periods of one NHL game, three goals against						
BILL RANFORD—Brandon, MB	4	3	0	1	1.97	0
#40 / 1998–1999 / Brief stop after long career and two Cups in Edmonton						

GOALIES

RED WINGS REGULAR SEASON STATISTICS	GP	W	L	T/OT	GAA	SO
TERRY RICHARDSON—Powell River, BC	19	3	10	0	5.31	0
#1, 30 / 1973–1977 / Never able to match minor-league prowess						
VINCENT RIENDEAU—St. Hyacinthe, QC	32	17	8	2	3.28	0
#37 / 1991–1994 / Came from St. Louis for defenseman Rick Zombo in 1991						
DENNIS RIGGIN—Kincardine, ON	18	5	9	2	3.27	1
#1 / 1959–1960, 1962–1963 / Eye injury in Western league game in '61 led to career end						
PAT RUPP—Detroit, MI	1	0	1	0	4.00	0
#22 / 1963–1964 / Only one NHL game, but twice a Team USA goalie at the Olympics						
JIMMY RUTHERFORD—Beeton, ON	314	97	165	43	3.68	10
#30, 1, 27 / 1970–1971, 1973–1981, 1982–1983 / Winged eye sockets: coolest mask ever						
SAM ST. LAURENT—Arvida, QC	30	5	11	4	3.76	0
#34, 32, 35 / 1986–1990 / Adirondack's Calder Cup–champion goalie in 1989						
BOB SAUVE—Ste. Genevieve, QC	41	11	25	4	4.19	0
#31 / 1981–1982 / Brother Jean Francois a center in NHL, son Philippe 32 NHL GP in net						
TERRY SAWCHUK—Winnipeg, MB	734	352	244	130	2.46	85
#1, 29 / 1950–1955, 1957–1964, 1968–1969 / Died May 31, 1970; into Hall of Fame 1971						
AL SMITH—Toronto, ON	43	18	20	4	3.24	4
#30 / 1971–1972 / Journeyman, "The Bear," started career with hometown Leafs						
GREG STEFAN—Brantford, ON	299	115	127	30	3.92	5
#29, 30 / 1981–1990 / Knee injury ended hot-tempered goalie's all–Red Wing NHL career						
ROGIE VACHON—Palmarolle, QC	109	30	57	19	3.74	4
#40, 30 / 1978–1980 / Three Cups in Montreal, then LA, then expensive free agent signee						
MIKE VERNON—Calgary, AB	95	53	24	14	2.40	4
#29 / 1995–1997 / Starter for Cup in Calgary and then again eight years later in Detroit						
CARL WETZEL—Detroit, MI	2	0	1	0	8.00	0
#22 / 1964–1965 / Spare goalie in San Francisco of Western league while in the army						
KEN WREGGET—Brandon, MB	29	14	10	2	2.66	0
#31 / 1999–2000 / Longtime Leaf, Flyer, and Penguin won Cup as Pitt backup in 1992						

11 | Blueliners

"They retired my jersey, but I was still in it."

— FORMER DEFENSEMAN Colin Campbell

ABOVE: *To be "Kronwalled" is to get buried by one of Niklas's open-ice hits. In this case, Kronwall collides along the boards with Nashville Predator forward Jerred Smithson on January 17, 2006.*

THE LAST HALF CENTURY BEGAN WITH a couple of Hall of Famers on the Detroit blue line, Bill Gadsby and Marcel Pronovost, and ended with the presence of another, Nicklas Lidstrom. In between there have been other legends, and a fair share of characters manning the defensive zone for the Red Wings, from hip-checkers, to big shots, to utter flops.

Big D became the key in the NHL in the late 1970s and early 1980s, and Barry Melrose briefly fit the bill. At 6-foot, 205 pounds, and actually more of an enforcer, Melrose manned the Detroit blue line for the equivalent of just a half-a-season. He'd later become much better known for his coaching, his TV exploits, and his mullet.

"I was there when Mr. Ilitch just bought the team, and Jimmy Devellano just took over running it," remembers Melrose, the ESPN personality and analyst. "It was a hodgepodge, a mishmash of guys from other organizations, guys that they brought in. Danny Gare was the captain, a real good guy, a real gutsy guy . . . just a parade of players in and out."

Jim "Schony" Schoenfeld, current Rangers assistant general manager, was an even bigger man on the Red Wings blue line in the early '80s.

"We didn't perform very well as a team. As you look back, maybe we weren't very good players," Schony says with a smile. "The next year Ilitch bought the team and the handwriting was on the wall, and they were gonna go with younger players and they should. Had to rebuild, had to start somewhere."

The former All-Star Schoenfeld came over late in his career in a trade from Buffalo with Danny Gare, and suffered through injuries in Detroit, with a bad knee one year and banged-up ribs the next. It didn't curb his appreciation for Motown.

He says, "All hockey players, especially from our era—maybe not so much the kids today—for us, the Original Six teams had an allure because that's what you grew up watching. Howe, Delvecchio, Abel, these are names that every kid from my era knew everything about. To be part of that organization with all that history certainly was special.

"They treated all the players—even though we weren't performing that well—like we were special players and special people. My memory in Detroit is a good one," he concludes.

Defenseman Bryan "Bugsy" Watson feels the same way. He came through Detroit twice, first in the mid-1960s, and again a decade later.

ABOVE: *Hall of Fame defenseman Marcel Pronovost races ahead of Toronto's Red Kelly for a loose puck behind Detroit goalie Terry Sawchuk, while D-partner Pete Goegan keeps watch.*

"It didn't take me very long to realize that the Olympia was very, very special and the crowds and the whole way, the American way, was tremendous," recalls the Bancroft, Ontario, native. "I just thrived on it and I thrived in Detroit. I had more damn fun than anyone there. We loved to go to practice, and the friendships have lasted forever."

Watson played close to 900 NHL games with a total of six different teams. He wasn't a Hall of Famer, but he's legendary because of his face: one only a mother could love. Bugsy played the epitome of "old-time hockey" and he proudly displayed his many stitches and broken bones because, ultimately for him, he had no choice.

"If you're on my team I would protect you with my life. And if you left my team, you were one of the dirtiest son-of-a-bitches in the world," states Bugsy. "I was all about team, I was all about winning, and I agree with Ted Lindsay that winning is the only thing. My philosophy was that it was a war out there."

Watson is not unlike countless other Detroit players, past and present, who regard their time with the Wings as something unique and extraordinary.

"I had a tremendous time and experience," he says of his 16 seasons in the NHL, "and I'm very proud of the fact that I played six or seven

ABOVE: *Hall of Fame defenseman Bill Gadsby untangles with Montreal winger Dick Duff in a shot from the 1965–66 season.*

OPPOSITE: *Lock Hall of Fame defenseman Chris Chelios won a Stanley Cup his third year in the league (1986) with the Montreal Canadiens. After seven years with the Habs, and nine years with Chicago, "Cheli" began a decade with the Red Wings, with whom he'd win two more Cups (2002, 2008). Playing pro hockey until age 47, he's considered one of the most physically fit players in NHL history.*

years in a league that only had six teams, and I was one of 120 of the best players in the world. I think about that now that I'm older; then, I never really thought about it."

Gadsby echoes the sentiment.

"I played '46 to '66, I got 20 years in. It was a great life," he states. After spending most of his career in Chicago and New York, Gadsby's last five seasons were with the Red Wings. This "Original Sixer" is proof that regardless of the number of teams in the league, and regardless of how strong one is as a player, a Stanley Cup win is elusive. The Hall of Famer never won a championship in his career, including losses in the final with Detroit in 1963, '64, and '66.

Decades later, a similarly gritty Hall of Fame defenseman, Chris Chelios, finished his career (except for seven games in Atlanta) in Detroit, also after successful runs in two other Original Six cities. The two differences from Gadsby being, one, due to fantastic modern conditioning, "Cheli" stretched his 20 seasons into 25, with a brief attempt at 26, and two, Cheli won championships.

Chelios won a Cup with Montreal in 1986, after his third year in the league, and played seven seasons with the Habs. Then during nine seasons in Chicago, his Blackhawks always fell short of the big prize. He joined Detroit at the trade deadline in 1999 in exchange for two first-round draft picks and a former first-round pick, defenseman Anders Eriksson. With nine-plus seasons in Detroit, Chelios helped the Red Wings twice win Lord Stanley's chalice.

"I'm all about history and tradition, and seeing the legends like Howe and Lindsay and Delvecchio," states Chelios. "With those guys

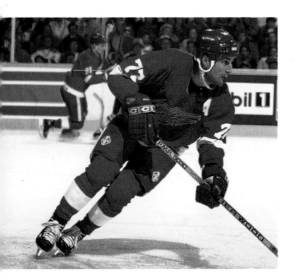

still around, and wonderful owners with the Ilitches, and the success they've had the last little while with the team, it's been a great ride."

Cheli's Motown career overlapped with that of another hockey great, Larry Murphy, one of the more low-key, overlooked Hall of Famers of all time. He offered great consistency and longevity.

"There was nothing flashy that you would identify with, but that's the way I played the game," states Murphy. "I wasn't out there with the hardest shot or was going to run anybody over, but I just wanted to be as effective as I could be and I take great pride that I was."

Larry Murphy, one of the more understated, overlooked Hall of Famers of all time.

For whatever reason, Murphy had been the whipping boy for the fans in Toronto during his two-year stay there, despite tallying 61 points and finishing with just a minus-two on a bad team his first year as a Leaf. A season later at the trade deadline, the Red Wings snatched him up.

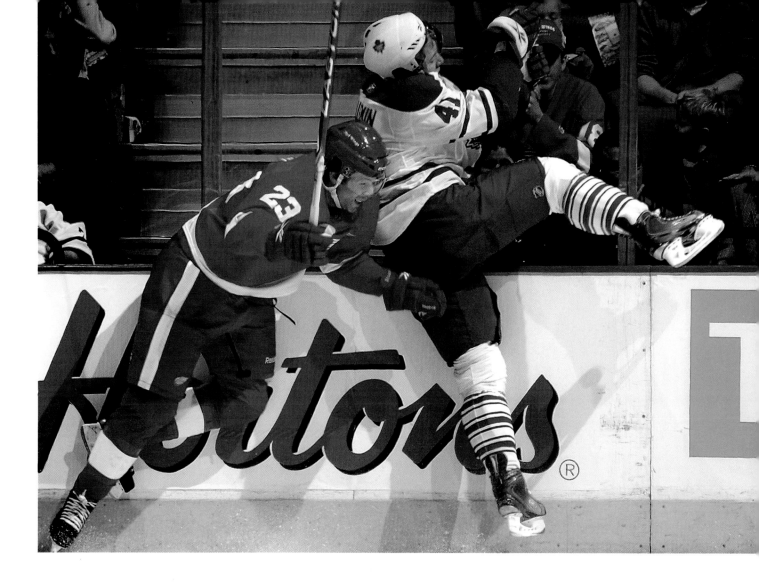

With a smile, Murphy adds, "I wasn't looking to jump ship. I had a no-trade clause, but I had an opportunity to go to a team and win a Cup, and it didn't take me very long to decide on that situation."

Murphy actually added two Cups to the two he had won earlier in his career in Pittsburgh. After 21 seasons, he retired in 2001 and was inducted into the Hall three years later with fellow defensemen Ray Bourque and Paul Coffey, also a one-time Red Wing.

Coffey's time in Detroit was unfortunately marked by frustration. The three-time Cup winner in Edmonton, who added another in Pittsburgh, played three and a half seasons in Detroit. Season two culminated in a loss to New Jersey in the Stanley Cup final, and the following year ended with a loss to the eventual champions, the Colorado Avalanche, in the Western Conference finals. By the time all the pieces were put together in Detroit for their 1997 win, Coffey was no longer part of the team.

A more recent Hall of Fame inductee, Mark Howe, never won a Cup in Detroit either. In fact, he never won a Cup at all, but his play was exemplary, and his bloodlines off the charts. Howe played 22 professional seasons, won two championships during six years in the World Hockey Association with his dad, Gordie, and brother, Marty, and ended his

OPPOSITE TOP: *Larry Murphy, another Hall of Famer, duels with Maple Leaf Dmitry Yushkevich, while teammate Stacy Roest looks on. Murphy played 21 seasons, won two Cups in Pittsburgh, and two more in Detroit.*

OPPOSITE BOTTOM: *Paul Coffey was with Murphy for a Stanley Cup win in Pittsburgh in 1991, after winning three previously in Edmonton. Unfortunately the Hall of Famer's three and a half seasons in Detroit ended in frustration; the team losing in the final against New Jersey in 1995 and in the Western Conference finals against Colorado the next season.*

ABOVE: *Wings D-man Brad Stuart crunches Toronto Maple Leaf Nikolai Kulemin at the Air Canada Centre on November 7, 2009.*

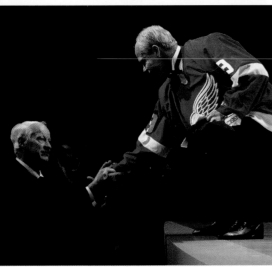

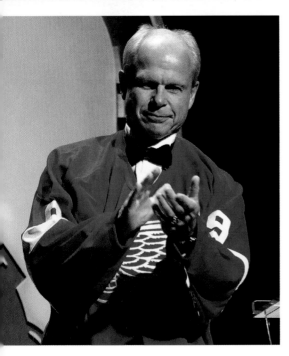

16-year NHL career after two and a half seasons in Detroit in 1994–95. He overcame serious knee and back injuries along the way.

Howe says that sporting a Wings jersey seemed pretty natural to him after seeing his father wearing the sweater for so many years.

"I grew up basically being a stick boy every once in a while," he explains. "I grew up with it, lived it and died it my whole life, so when I got a chance to finish my career there [in Detroit] it was good. If I had tried to play for that team when I was 20 years of age, I think the pressure might have been too much. By the time I went there I was 37, so I was used to the pressure by then and it was a great organization, and a great chance for me to get back and play in that uniform."

As a teenager, when the Wings were on the road, Howe would skate for hours by himself on the Olympia ice—just one of the many privileges enjoyed when your father is the greatest player in the world.

"My dad always used to sit between Normy Ullman and Alex Delvecchio, so I spent a lot of time with those guys," recalls Mark. "For any young kid that's in a room trying to steal sticks off the rack, Lefty Wilson, who was the trainer, he was great to me too."

> *I grew up with it, lived it and died it my whole life, so when I got a chance to finish my career there it was good.*

Mark played for the old Junior Red Wings before joining the WHA with his family as an 18-year-old and winning Rookie of the Year.

Six seasons later, in 1979, Mark became an NHL "rookie" after his Hartford Whalers and three other WHA teams were absorbed by the mainstay league. On January 12, 1980, Gordie, Mark, and Marty all started and played together against the Red Wings in Detroit. Marty, normally a defenseman, moved up to the left wing, Gordie was at center, and Mark played on the right. The Howes relished their memorable return.

"I have a nice picture of it at home. It was a proud moment for us, but it was a great, proud moment for Dad."

Both brothers had actually moved up for the opening face-off. While Marty had always been a D-man, Mark had just months before moved from wing to the back end. The smooth-skating ex-winger quickly became a blue-line stalwart in the NHL.

At Mark's 2011 Hall of Fame induction, this great hockey family's journey came full circle. At the end of the speech, Mark recalled the following: "Dad, I remember just after I retired, key word there, *after* I retired, 16 years ago, you mentioned you would have liked to have seen me wear your sweater, at least for one game. Your timing was pretty bad. You've never asked me for anything in your lifetime, so I'd like to honor your request at this time, on a much bigger stage."

With that, Howe reached down, pulled his father's Red Wings number 9 out of a bag, and donned it onstage.

"Dad, I love you," Howe said to a standing ovation. "Thank you."

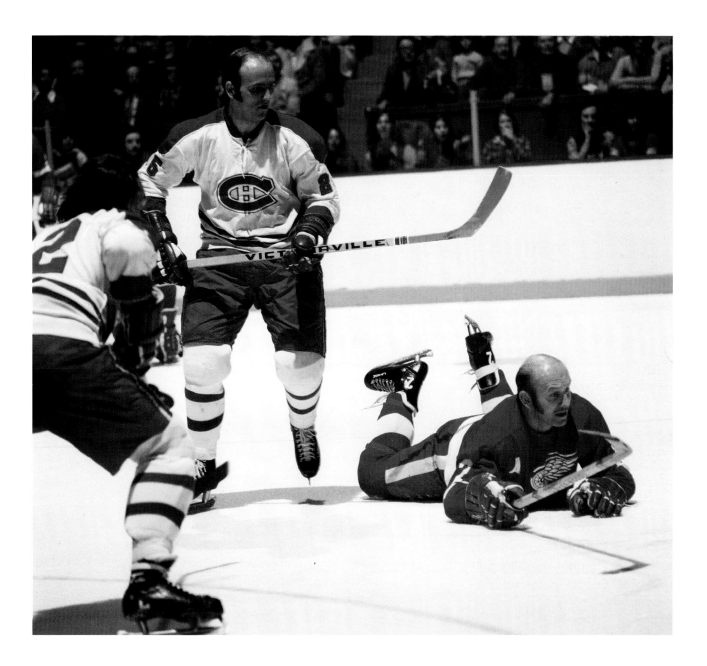

Among the legions of other Red Wings defensemen from the past half century, there have been many who have left a lasting impression. Gary Bergman played most of his 12-year career in Detroit, and was easily recognizable because of his bald head. Many of the teams he played on struggled mightily, but Bergman, wearing number 2, was a solid mainstay, talented enough to play in all eight games for Team Canada against Russia in the famous 1972 Summit Series.

What Bergman's Detroit blue-line crew lacked in the early 1970s was a true offensive defenseman, a puck mover. The Wings tried big Ron Stackhouse, who later went on to have a 71-point season in Pittsburgh, and they tried the Swede Thommie Bergman, whose output was injury plagued and wildly inconsistent.

OPPOSITE TOP TO BOTTOM:

Mark Howe at his Hall of Fame induction in November 2011, surprising his dad by donning Gordie's Red Wing number 9, thanking his father, and then joining the standing ovation.

ABOVE: *Gary Bergman was a stalwart on the Detroit blue line from 1964 to 1975. Here, Bergman falls in front of Canadiens Jacques Lemaire (number 25) and Jacques Laperriere.*

Finally, the year after Gary Bergman left Detroit, 1976, the Wings drafted Reed Larson out of the University of Minnesota. With his mobility and his frightening slapshot from the point, Larson averaged 63 points a season for nine years beginning in 1977.

But Larson also didn't get a whole lot of help from his fellow defensemen. Only three of his teams made the playoffs, and the last two, in 1984 and 1985, were both ousted in the first round.

Soon after, "offense by committee" finally began to take shape along the blue line. In 1987–88, a season in which Detroit surprisingly reached the Clarence Campbell (what would become the Western) Conference final for a second year in a row, Darren Veitch, Jeff Sharples, Lee Norwood, and Doug Halward combined for 132 points.

Of the four, only Sharples was a Detroit draft choice, as the Wings tried to fill the gaps along the blue line via trade and free agency. Only five of the thirteen D-men who saw action that season were "home-grown," the others being Rick Zombo, Joe Kocur (who actually became a forward), Steve Chiasson, and Doug Houda.

"It meant a lot [starting my career there]" states Houda, who went on to win a Stanley Cup in 2011 as an assistant coach in Boston. "I was drafted by Detroit in '84 and I played with a lot of great players: Steve Yzerman, Kocur and Probert, and Fedorov. I was very fortunate to spend some time there. Jimmy Nill, Ken Holland, and Jimmy Devellano were super people, and it gave me roots. It was a great place, and the start for my whole career; so many good people back then to help me out and show me the right way."

And despite only playing 77 of his 561 career NHL games with Detroit, Houda is part of the historical fabric of the franchise, especially by wearing a low digit: number 3.

For the most part, from the origins of the NHL through the 1970s, there were no number 66s, or 87s, or 91s. Goalies wore 1, 30, or 31, and skaters wore sweaters numbers 2 through 29. Modern players, like Houda, who pick low numbers, share a common historical thread.

In the '50s and '60s, it was Hall of Famer Marcel Pronovost who wore the number. After four Cups and 16 seasons in Detroit, he was traded to Toronto in 1965.

In the late '70s, number 3 belonged to Perry Miller, who perfected his devastating hip-check while growing up on the outdoor rinks of Winnipeg, Manitoba.

Chiasson donned number 3 for eight seasons into the early '90s, while Bob Rouse then wore it for four seasons and helped the Wings win two Cups.

Pick any sweater number and one finds a terrific history: a cross section of the hockey world, and a microcosm of the talented variety of individuals who have battled along the blue line while wearing the Winged Wheel.

ABOVE: *University of Michigan product Aaron Ward won two Cups with Detroit and another in Carolina. Here, he battles Islander Ziggy Palffy on Long Island. "To be a Red Wing was almost euphoric in a way, that every day the Wings were on the minds of everyone in the city or state, it's such a huge component to who people are around there," Ward said in 2011.*

OPPOSITE TOP LEFT: *Doug Houda, who won a Cup with Boston as an assistant coach in 2011.*

OPPOSITE TOP RIGHT: *All-Star defenseman and rifleman Reed Larson.*

Defensemen whose careers included or began after 1962–1963, a half century ago.

A handful of defensemen have been moved to the enforcer list.

RED WINGS REGULAR SEASON STATISTICS	GP	G	A	PTS	PIM
DOUG BARKLEY—Lethbridge, AB **#5 / 1962–1966** / Suffered career-ending eye injury against Black Hawks in January 1966	247	24	80	104	380
JOHN BARRETT—Ottawa, ON **#2, 3 / 1980–1986** / Comeback with Minny failed after broken kneecap ended career with Caps	418	18	75	93	548
BOB BAUN—Lanigan, SK **#4 / 1968–1971** / Four Cups in Toronto, including win over Detroit in '64 on broken foot	158	5	37	42	257
SERGEI BAUTIN—Rogachev, Russia **#29 / 1993–1994** / Former Jets first rounder went back to Europe	1	0	0	0	0
MARC BERGEVIN—Montreal, QC **#27 / 1995–1996** / Eight NHL teams as player; front office Cup win with Hawks in 2010	70	1	9	10	33
GARY BERGMAN—Kenora, ON **#18, 23, 3, 2 / 1964–1973, 1974–1975** / Fan favorite on mostly bad teams died in 2000	706	60	243	303	1,101
THOMMIE BERGMAN—Munkfors, Sweden **#4 / 1972–1975, 1977–1980** / Early NHL Swede; like Borje Salming, put up with thugs	246	21	44	65	243

DEFENSEMEN

RED WINGS REGULAR SEASON STATISTICS	GP	G	A	PTS	PIM
TOM BLADON—Edmonton, AB	2	0	0	0	2
#4 / 1980–1981 / First NHL defenseman to have an eight-point game (Philly vs. Cleveland)					
JOHN BLUM—Detroit, MI	6	0	0	0	8
#33 / 1988–1989 / Played at Notre Dame HS and then four years at Michigan					
PATRICK BOILEAU—Montreal, QC	25	2	6	8	14
#27 / 2002–2003 / Major juniors scholastic honoree, lost in two Memorial Cups with Laval					
LEO BOIVIN—Prescott, ON	85	4	22	26	94
#24, 4 / 1965–1967 / Longtime Bruin went from Detroit to Pitt in 1967 expansion draft					
CARL BREWER—Toronto, ON	70	2	37	39	0
#5 / 1969–1970 / Three Cups; died in 2001; helped put ex-NHLPA boss Alan Eagleson in jail					
ARNIE BROWN—Oshawa, ON	104	4	29	33	114
#4 / 1970–1972 / Mostly a Ranger; won Memorial Cup with St. Michael's Majors in 1961					
LARRY BROWN—Brandon, MB	33	1	4	5	8
#4 / 1970–1971 / Expansion draft Oiler, never played for them; never a basketball coach					
DMITRY BYKOV—Izhevsk, Russia	71	2	10	12	43
#55 / 2002–2003 / Played in Russia's top league before and after stint with Wings					
AL CAMERON—Edmonton, AB	190	7	31	38	263
#26 / 1975–1979 / Claimed by Winnipeg Jets in 1979 expansion draft					
COLIN CAMPBELL—London, ON	178	5	16	21	306
#4 / 1982–1985 / Cup win as assistant coach with NYR; longtime head of NHL hockey ops					
TERRY CARKNER—Smiths Falls, ON	88	2	8	10	151
#2 / 1993–1995 / Stalwart on Florida team that lost Cup final to Colorado in 1996					
DWIGHT CARRUTHERS—Lashburn, SK	1	0	0	0	0
#2 / 1964 / Philly snagged him from Detroit in 1967 expansion draft					
MILAN CHALUPA—Oudolen, Czech	14	0	5	5	6
#7 / 1984–1985 / 11 years in Czech league, then Wings, then seven years in German league					
CHRIS CHELIOS—Chicago, IL	578	21	131	152	613
#24 / 1998–2009 / Hall of Famer won three Cups; second-oldest NHL player ever behind Howe					
STEVE CHIASSON—Barrie, ON	471	67	205	272	886
#3 / 1987–1994 / Died after rolling his truck following a Canes season-ending party in '99					
PAUL COFFEY—Weston, ON	231	46	193	239	295
#77 / 1992–1996 / Nine NHL teams; four Cups: three in Edmonton, one in Pitt; Hall of Fame 2004					
BART CRASHLEY—Toronto, ON	109	4	29	33	34
#24, 15, 8, 4 / 1965–1969, 1974–1975 / Maybe the coolest name ever; to LA with Dionne					
CORY CROSS—Lloydminster, AB	16	1	1	2	15
#4 / 2005–2006 / Former University of Alberta star now coaching in Canadian colleges					
DOUG CROSSMAN—Peterborough, ON	43	3	12	15	31
#39, 29 / 1990–1992 / 900-plus NHL games; best effort was 1987 playoffs in Philly					
IAN CUSHENAN—Hamilton, ON	5	0	0	0	4
#18 / 1963–1964 / Played in NHL All-Star Game in 1958; Cup with Montreal in 1959					
MATHIEU DANDENAULT—Sherbrooke, QC	616	48	101	149	342
#11 / 1995–2004 / Three Cups in Detroit, finished career with four seasons in Montreal					
GILBERT DELORME—Boucherville, QC	121	5	14	19	165
#35, 29 / 1987–1989 / Played for Montreal in Roller Hockey International in 1996					
PETER DINEEN—Kingston, ON	2	0	0	0	5
#5 / 1989–1990 / Older brother of Kevin and Gord and son of Bill could drop the mitts					
PER DJOOS—Mora, Sweden	26	0	12	12	16
#36 / 1990–1991 / Preferred the Olympic-size ice in Sweden (and Switzerland)					

DEFENSEMEN

RED WINGS REGULAR SEASON STATISTICS	GP	G	A	PTS	PIM
GARY DOAK—Goderich, ON	48	0	5	5	63
#24, 19 / 1965–1966, 1972–1973 / Longtime Bruin still active in B's charitable events					
BOBBY DOLLAS—Montreal, QC	89	6	6	12	42
#8 / 1990–1993 / Played with three of four former WHA teams and with Ducks when "Mighty"					
KENT DOUGLAS—Cobalt, ON	105	9	39	48	143
#5 / 1967–1969 / Rookie of the Year in 1963; three All-Star Games and Cups with Leafs					
STEVE DUCHESNE—Sept-Iles, QC	197	19	65	84	118
#28 / 1999–2002 / Former Cup winner and All-Star owns Central League team in Texas					
JONATHAN ERICSSON—Stockholm, Sweden	232	10	34	44	197
#52 / 2007–2012 / Given ring in 2008 for eight regular-season games but name not on Cup					
ANDERS ERIKSSON—Bolinas, Sweden	151	9	30	39	78
#34, 26, 44 / 1995–1999 / "Butsy" went to Chicago in deal for Chris Chelios in 1999					
CHRIS EVANS—Toronto, ON	23	0	2	2	2
#11 / 1973–1974 / To Detroit from St. Louis with Bugsy Watson and Jean Hamel in 1974					
BOB FALKENBERG—Stettler, AB	54	1	5	6	26
#5, 3, 22 / 1966–1969, 1970–1972 / Detroit was "Steady Bob's" only NHL team					

ABOVE: *A second-round pick of the Red Wings in 1994, Mathieu Dandenault could play forward or defense. He spent almost all of his time in Detroit on the blue line and won Stanley Cups in 1997, 1998, and 2002, before moving on to play for his hometown Montreal Canadiens.*

ABOVE: *The start of the next wave of Swedes? Jonathan Ericsson was called up and played eight regular season games in 2007–08, not enough to earn Stanley Cup recognition with the champs at the end of the playoffs. Since then, he's been a six-foot-four, 220-pound NHL regular on the blue line.*

DEFENSEMEN

RED WINGS REGULAR SEASON STATISTICS	GP	G	A	PTS	PIM
MARK FERNER—Regina, SK	3	0	0	0	0
#27, 21 / 1995 / On Kamloops Western league champ in 1984, ended career in WCHL					
VIACHESLAV FETISOV—Moscow, Russia	205	17	81	98	246
#44, 2 / 1995–1998 / Slava, a Hall of Famer, became a member of Russia's legislature					
JIRI FISCHER—Horovice, Czech	305	11	49	60	295
#2, 8 / 1999–2005 / Playing career ended after collapsing on bench with heart condition					
TIM FRIDAY—Burbank, CA	23	0	3	3	6
#4 / 1985–1986 / Won national title with Rensselaer Polytechnic Institute (RPI) in 1985					
BILL GADSBY—Calgary, AB	323	18	94	112	478
#4 / 1961–1966 / One of the all-time greats never to win a Cup; Hall of Fame in 1970					
TODD GILL—Cardinal, ON	104	7	16	23	79
#15, 29, 23 / 1998–1999, 2000–2001 / Head coach of Kingston in the OHL					
LARRY GIROUX—Weyburn, SK	56	3	24	27	91
#22, 3, 4 / 1974–1978 / His nickname was "Buffalo Head"					
LORRY GLOECKNER—Kindersley, SK	13	0	2	2	6
#11 / 1978–1979 / Boston draftee, sat out in contract dispute with Harry Sinden; bad idea					
WARREN GODFREY—Toronto, ON	528	23	77	100	527
#11, 23, 25, 2, 18, 3, 21 / 1955–1962, 1963–1968 / Big boy; from Boston to Detroit twice					

DEFENSEMEN

RED WINGS REGULAR SEASON STATISTICS	GP	G	A	PTS	PIM
PETE GOEGAN—Fort William, ON	330	18	63	81	329
#2, 22, 23 / 1957–1967 / Half his time in the AHL, mostly with the Pittsburgh Hornets					
YAN GOLUBOVSKY—Novosibirsk, Russia	50	1	5	6	30
#28, 15, 44 / 1997–2000 / Traded to Florida for Igor Larionov in December 2000					
RICK GREEN—Belleville, ON	65	2	14	16	24
#5 / 1990–1991 / Caps made him first-overall pick in 1976; won Cup with Montreal in '86					
DOUG HALWARD—Toronto, ON	99	5	25	30	185
#7 / 1986–1989 / "Hawk" came for a sixth-round pick, left for a 12th rounder					
JEAN HAMEL—Asbestos, QC	451	19	62	81	574
#19, 5 / 1973–1981 / Much younger brother Gilles played for nine NHL seasons					
TERRY HARPER—Regina, SK	252	14	56	70	230
#2 / 1975–1979 / Previously won five Stanley Cups with the Canadiens					
RON HARRIS—Verdun, QC	252	8	51	59	342
#18, 4, 16 / 1962–1964, 1968–1972 / Back to Detroit with Bob Baun from Oakland in '68					
TED HARRIS—Winnipeg, MB	41	0	11	11	66
#14, 19 / 1973–1974 / Four Cups with Montreal and five All-Star Games					
DOUG HARVEY—Montreal, QC	2	0	0	0	0
#5 / 1967 / Six-time Cup winner, seven Norrises in Montreal; Hall of Fame in 1973					
DERIAN HATCHER—Sterling Heights, MI	15	0	4	4	8
#2 / 2003–2004 / 16 NHL seasons; kid brother of Kevin went into U.S. Hockey Hall in 2010					
DOUG HOUDA—Blairmore, AB	172	5	26	31	231
#22, 33, 27, 3 / 1985–1986, 1987–1991, 1998–1999 / Asst. coach with Bruins since 2006					
MARK HOWE—Detroit, MI	122	8	56	64	40
#4 / 1992–1995 / Started NHL career in Hartford with dad Gordie and brother Marty					
WILLIE HUBER—Strasskirchen, Germany	372	68	140	208	612
#7 / 1978–1983 / Part of six-player deal with Rangers in 1983. Died of heart attack in 2010					
BRENT HUGHES—Bowmanville, ON	69	1	21	22	92
#24 / 1973–1974 / Claimed by the Kansas City Scouts in the expansion draft					
RON INGRAM—Toronto, ON	50	3	6	9	50
#2 / 1963–1964 / Played eight AHL years with Buffalo Bisons and three with Baltimore Clippers					
DOUG JANIK—Agawam, MA	29	0	3	3	31
#37 / 2009–2012 / Won national title with Maine in 1999 under the late Shawn Walsh					
LARRY JOHNSTON—Kitchener, ON	203	7	44	51	419
#3 / 1971–1974 / Became a Colorado Rockie when the Kansas City Scouts moved					
GREG JOLY—Calgary, AB	267	12	52	64	178
#24, 22 / 1976–1983 / 1974 Memorial Cup MVP was NHL first-overall pick of Capitals					
JAKUB KINDL—Sumperk, Czech	106	3	14	17	61
#46 / 2010–2012 / Wings first-round pick (19th overall) in 2005					
STEVE KONROYD—Scarborough, ON	25	0	1	1	14
#8 / 1992–1994 / Began and ended stellar NHL career with Calgary					
VLADIMIR KONSTANTINOV—Murmansk, RU	446	47	128	175	838
#16 / 1991–1997 / Limousine accident after '97 Cup ended his playing career					
CHRIS KOTSOPOULOS—Scarborough, ON	2	0	0	0	2
#29 / 1989–1990 / After juniors, played university hockey at Acadia, in Nova Scotia					
NIKLAS KRONWALL—Stockholm, Sweden	467	49	168	217	298
#55 / 2003–2012 / When he crushes unsuspecting opponents, they get "Kronwalled"					
UWE KRUPP—Cologne, W. Germany	30	3	3	6	14
#4 / 1998–1999, 2001–2002 / Sat out two years with bad knee; sued team on treatment					

DEFENSEMEN

RED WINGS REGULAR SEASON STATISTICS	GP	G	A	PTS	PIM
GORD KRUPPKE—Slave Lake, AB	23	0	0	0	32
#40, 8, 44 / 1990–1991, 1992–1994 / His hometown devastated by May 2011 fire					
MAXIM KUZNETSOV—Pavlodor, Russia	117	2	7	9	117
#32 / 2000–2002 / First-round pick of Wings in '95; earned ring but name left off Cup in '02					
RANDY LADOUCEUR—Brockville, ON	290	14	67	81	448
#19, 29 / 1982–1987 / Last Wings player to wear number 19 before Steve Yzerman					
ROGER LAFRENIERE—Montreal, QC	3	0	0	0	4
#17 / 1962–1963 / His son Jason played 146 NHL games for Quebec, NYR, and Tampa					
SERGE LAJEUNESSE—Montreal, QC	97	1	4	5	101
#5, 21, 25 / 1970–1973 / The 12th-overall pick of the Wings in 1970					
AL LANGLOIS—Magog, QC	82	2	18	20	120
#2 / 1963–1965 / "Junior" won three Cups in Montreal and played in two All-Star Games					
RICK LAPOINTE—Victoria, BC	129	12	34	46	175
#4 / 1975–1977 / "Jumbo" was Detroit's first-rounder, fifth overall in 1975					
REED LARSON—Minneapolis, MN	708	188	382	570	1,127
#28 / 1976–1986 / Scary high hard slap shot went well with his Fu Manchu facial hair					
JIM LEAVINS—Dinsmore, SK	37	2	11	13	26
#4 / 1985–1986 / Later played in Finland, Sweden, and Italy					
BRETT LEBDA—Buffalo Grove, IL	326	18	50	68	201
#22 / 2005–2010 / Went to Ann Arbor Pioneer but played USA U-18, then Fighting Irish					
DAVE LEWIS—Kindersley, SK	64	2	5	7	84
#52, 25 / 1986–1988 / Red Wings assistant coach for three Stanley Cups					
NICKLAS LIDSTROM—Vasteras, Sweden	1,564	264	878	1,142	514
#5 / 1991–2012 / 1st European to win Conn Smythe (2002) and to captain a Cup winner (2008)					
ANDREAS LILJA—Helsingborg, Sweden	298	7	40	47	315
#3 / 2005–2010 / One of nine Swedish Red Wings to win Stanley Cup in 2008					
BARRY LONG—Brantford, ON	80	0	17	17	38
#2 / 1979–1980 / Head coach of Winnipeg Jets just two years after retiring from team					
DAVE LUCAS—Downeyville, ON	1	0	0	0	0
#18 / 1962 / Played 11 seasons with the Johnstown Jets in the Eastern league					
CHRIS LUONGO—Detroit, MI	4	0	1	1	4
#37 / 1990–1991 / 1986 national championship with Michigan State					
JACK LYNCH—Toronto, ON	85	5	24	29	73
#21, 3 / 1973–1975 / Came to Detroit with Jim Rutherford from Pittsburgh in 1974					
JAMIE MACOUN—Newmarket, ON	76	1	10	11	38
#34 / 1997–1999 / Cup in Calgary and then Detroit nine seasons later					
RANDY MANERY—Leamington, ON	3	0	0	0	0
#24, 12 / 1970–1972 / Younger brother Kris played for Barons, North Stars, Canucks, Jets					
BOB MANNO—Niagara Falls, ON	136	19	35	54	92
#33, 23 / 1983–1985 / Played some LW in Detroit, finished his career in Italy					
LOU MARCON—Fort William, ON	60	0	4	4	42
#21 / 1958–1960, 1962–1963 / 18-years in minors, made book with one game in 1962–63					
DANNY MARKOV—Moscow, Russia	66	4	12	16	59
#95 / 2006–2007 / "Elvis" for the way he dressed, scored 10,000th goal in Flyers history					
BRAD MARSH—London, ON	75	4	7	11	69
#20 / 1990–1992 / Was Atlanta Flames first-round pick in 1978					
BERT MARSHALL—Kamloops, BC	155	1	34	35	169
#3, 5 / 1965–1968 / Six-year Islanders career ended the year before their first Cup					

DEFENSEMEN

RED WINGS REGULAR SEASON STATISTICS	GP	G	A	PTS	PIM
BOB MCCORD—Matheson, ON	26	1	4	5	45
#2, 25, 24, 3 / 1965–1968 / Played nine seasons for Eddie Shore in Springfield					
BRAD MCCRIMMON—Dodsland, SK	203	8	49	57	270
#2 / 1990–1993 / Died in plane crash as head coach of Lokomotiv (KHL) in 2011					
MIKE MCEWEN—Hornepayne, ON	29	0	10	10	16
#7 / 1985–1986 / Three Cups on Long Island					
AL MCLEOD—Medicine Hat, AB	26	2	2	4	24
#2 / 1973–1974 / "Moose" played three seasons at Michigan Tech					
MIKE MCMAHON—Quebec City, QC	2	0	0	0	0
#21 / 1969 / Jumped to the WHA in 1972 and played there four seasons					
DEREK MEECH—Winnipeg, MB	128	4	12	16	43
#36, 14 / 2006–2010 / D-partner of Dion Phaneuf in Red Deer; name on the Cup in 2008					
TOM MELLOR—Cranston, RI	26	2	4	6	25
#24, 25 / 1973–1974 / Boston College NHLer long before the many BC NHLers					
PERRY MILLER—Winnipeg, MB	217	10	51	61	387
#3 / 1977–1981 / Known for his tremendous hip-check					
DMITRI MIRONOV—Moscow, Russia	11	2	5	7	4
#51, 15 / 1998 / Trade deadline pickup got his name on the Cup					
JOHN MISZUK—Naliboki, Poland	42	0	2	2	30
#18, 5 / 1963–1964 / Played for the Michigan Stags in the WHA					
BILL MITCHELL—Port Dalhousie, ON	1	0	0	0	0
#3 / 1964 / Played for the Toledo Mercurys, Toledo Blades, and coached the U of Toledo					
JOHN MOKOSAK—Edmonton, AB	41	0	2	2	96
#5, 37 / 1989–1990 / Older brother Carl played 83 NHL games between five teams					
DEAN MORTON—Peterborough, ON	1	1	0	1	2
#5 / 1989 / One of only four players to score a goal in their only NHL game					
WAYNE MULOIN—Dryden, ON	3	0	1	1	2
#19 / 1963 / Played for Providence Reds and Rhode Island Reds eight years apart					
LARRY MURPHY—Scarborough, ON	312	35	136	171	136
#55 / 1997–2001 / Trade deadline add from Toronto helped win two Cups					
KEN MURRAY—Toronto, ON	31	1	1	2	36
#24 / 1972–1973 / Kansas City Scouts snagged him in expansion draft in 1974					
TERRY MURRAY—Shawville, QC	23	0	7	7	10
#4 / 1976–1977 / Longtime NHL coach now head coach in Los Angeles					
ANDERS MYRVOLD—Lorenskog, Norway	8	0	1	1	2
#22 / 2003–2004 / Playing in native land despite drug issues and an off-ice assault injury					
JIM NAHRGANG—Millbank, ON	57	5	12	17	34
#3, 24 / 1974–1977 / On Michigan Tech team that lost national title to Minnesota					
RICK NEWELL—Winnipeg, MB	6	0	0	0	0
#23, 25 / 1972–1974 / Acquired from Rangers with Gary Doak in 1972 trade					
JIM NIEKAMP—Detroit, MI	29	0	2	2	37
#20, 3 / 1970–1972 / Michigan Stags' (WHA) property in 1974 but never played for them					
LEE NORWOOD—Oakland, CA	259	36	96	132	539
#23 / 1986–1991 / Severe ankle injury in 1993 with Flames against Wings ended career					
MIKE O'CONNELL—Chicago, IL	270	17	75	92	187
#2 / 1986–1990 / Traded from Boston for Reed Larson; Boston GM who traded Thornton					
GERRY ODROWSKI—Trout Creek, ON	138	2	10	12	69
#22 / 1960–1962 / Played one game in the 1962–63 season to make this book					

DEFENSEMEN

RED WINGS REGULAR SEASON STATISTICS	GP	G	A	PTS	PIM
FREDRIK OLAUSSON—Dadesjo, Sweden	47	2	13	15	22
#27 / 2001–2002 / Popular Jet for seven-plus seasons; won Cup in his penultimate NHL year					
BRAD PARK—Toronto, ON	147	18	83	101	138
#22 / 1983–1985 / End of a Hall of Fame career for a five-time First Team All-Star					
ROBERT PICARD—Montreal, QC	20	0	3	3	20
#7 / 1989–1990 / Brawler and All-Star in Quebec juniors; played two NHL All-Star Games					
POUL POPIEL—Sollested, Denmark	94	2	17	19	111
#3 / 1968–1970 / Played four seasons with the Howes in Houston of WHA					
MARCEL PRONOVOST—Lac-de-Tortue, QC	983	80	217	297	717
#3 / 1950–1965 / Four Cups with Detroit and one with Toronto					
JAMIE PUSHOR—Lethbridge, AB	134	6	13	19	217
#4 / 1995–1998 / Heavyweight in juniors drafted by Detroit and won Cup in 1997					
KYLE QUINCEY—Kitchener, ON	31	3	1	4	33
#45, 4, 27 / 2005–2008, 2011–2012 / Wings to Kings to Avalanche to Wings; concussion in 2010					
YVES RACINE—Matane, QC	231	22	102	124	230
#33 / 1989–1993 / Wings first-rounder, 11th overall in 1987					
BRIAN RAFALSKI—Dearborn, MI	292	35	169	204	78
#28 / 2007–2011 / Two Cups in New Jersey, one in Detroit; three Olympics for Team USA					
MIKE RAMSAY—Minneapolis, MN	82	3	6	9	58
#15, 23 / 1994–1996 / On "Miracle" Team USA from 1980 Olympics					
MATT RAVLICH—Sault Ste. Marie, ON	46	0	6	6	33
#18 / 1969–1970 / Traded to Kings in February 1970 in six-player deal					
JAMIE RIVERS—Ottawa, ON	65	3	5	8	53
#4 / 2003–2004, 2005–2006 / Seven NHL teams and stops in three other countries					
MIKE ROBITAILLE—Midland, ON	23	4	8	12	22
#21 / 1970–1971 / Longtime Sabres TV-man at ice level and in studio					
DALE ROLFE—Timmins, ON	66	5	18	23	60
#18, 3 / 1969–1971 / As Ranger, got pummeled by Dave Schultz in a playoff game					
BOB ROUSE—Surrey, BC	247	6	33	39	199
#3 / 1994–1998 / Steady veteran on '97 and '98 Cup winners					
RUSLAN SALEI—Minsk, Belarus	75	2	8	10	48
#24 / 2010–2011 / 14 international tournaments for Belarus; died in Lokomotiv plane crash					
BORJE SALMING—Kiruna, Sweden	49	2	17	19	52
#21 / 1989–1990 / Hall of Famer spent all but this one season with Leafs					
BARRY SALOVAARA—Cooksville, ON	90	2	13	15	70
#19, 28 / 1974–1976 / Headed to Austria and Finland after NHL stint					
ULF SAMUELSSON—Fagersta, Sweden	4	0	0	0	6
#2 / 1990 / Wings gave up a second- and third-rounder to Rangers for aging pest					
MATHIEU SCHNEIDER—New York, NY	231	48	116	164	224
#23 / 2002–2007 / 10 NHL teams; one Cup in Montreal; now working for NHLPA					
JIM SCHOENFELD—Galt, ON	96	6	19	25	87
#2 / 1981–1983 / Lengthy tenure with New York Rangers management/coaching staff					
DWIGHT SCHOFIELD—Waltham, MA	3	1	0	1	2
#20 / 1976–1977 / In IHL, played for K-Zoo, Fort Wayne, Dayton, Milwaukee, Toledo					
JEFF SHARPLES—Terrace, BC	105	14	35	49	70
#32, 34, 4 / 1987–1989 / With Klima, Murphy, and Graves in bad deal with Oilers in '89					
STEVE SHORT—Roseville, MN	1	0	0	0	0
#26 / 1978–1979 / Came from LA for the rights to a Hanson Brother (Steve Carlson)					

DEFENSEMEN

RED WINGS REGULAR SEASON STATISTICS	GP	G	A	PTS	PIM
JIRI SLEGR—Jihlava, Czech Rep	8	0	1	1	8
#71 / 2001–2002 / This and one playoff game, enough for a Cup in 2002					
BRENDAN SMITH—Toronto, ON	14	1	6	7	13
#2 / 2011–2012 / Scored his first NHL goal on Josh Harding of the Minnesota Wild					
GREG SMITH—Ponoka, AB	352	24	105	129	467
#5 / 1981–1986 / Went with Golden Seals to Cleveland and later to Minnesota in merger					
RICK SMITH—Kingston, ON	11	0	2	2	6
#2 / 1980 / Two stints with Boston, won a Cup in 1970					
IRV SPENCER—Sudbury, ON	30	3	1	4	12
#11, 15, 21 / 1963–1966, 1967–1968 / 1965 and '66, only played playoff games for Wings					
RON STACKHOUSE—Haliburton, ON	185	12	68	80	198
#21 / 1971–1974 / Future All-Star went to Pitt for Jim Rutherford and Jack Lynch in 1974					
GARRETT STAFFORD—Los Angeles, CA	2	0	0	0	0
#36 / 2007–2008 / Assaulted by Alex Perezhogin; led to longest suspension ever in AHL					
BRAD STUART—Rocky Mountain House, AB	306	16	62	78	119
#23 / 2007–2012 / Third-overall pick in 1998 NHL draft (San Jose) from Regina Pats					
JOHN TAFT—Minneapolis, MN	15	0	2	2	4
#11 / 1978–1979 / Two National Championships at Wisconsin and 1976 Olympic team					
JEAN-GUY TALBOT—Cap-de-la-Madeleine, QC	32	0	3	3	10
#3 / 1967–1968 / Seven-time Cup winner with the Canadiens					
LARRY TRADER—Barry's Bay, ON	55	3	9	12	45
#26, 2, 24 / 1983, 1984–1985 / Enjoyed Austrian and Italian leagues after North America					
RICK VASKO—St. Catharines, ON	31	3	7	10	29
#4, 3 / 1977–1978, 1979–1981 / Nicknamed "The Moose" but no relation to Moose Vasko					
DARREN VEITCH—Saskatoon, SK	153	20	83	103	99
#5 / 1986–1988 / Fifth-overall pick in 1980 won a WCHL title late in career in Phoenix					
BOB WALL—Richmond Hill, ON	85	5	7	12	43
#23, 16, 4, 5, 19 / 1965–1967, 1971–1972 / LA claimed him in expansion draft					
JESSE WALLIN—Saskatoon, SK	49	0	2	2	34
#3 / 2000–2003 / A Cup, a concussion, and now coaching Red Deer, his WHL alma mater					
AARON WARD—Windsor, ON	276	16	27	43	238
#29, 8, 39, 27, 14 / 1993–2001 / Minus player every full season in Detroit					
JIM WATSON—Malartic, QC	77	0	4	4	97
#2, 11, 24, 18, 3, 21 / 1963–1966, 1967–1970 / Not the Jim Watson with Cups in Philly					
IAN WHITE—Steinbach, MB	77	7	25	32	22
#18 / 2011–2012 / Part of a seven-player deal between Calgary and Toronto in 2010					
BOB WILKIE—Calgary, AB	8	1	2	3	2
#28 / 1990–1991 / Memorial Cup winner with Swift Current in 1989					
RICK WILSON—Prince Albert, SK	77	3	13	16	56
#19 / 1976–1977 / Won Stanley Cup as an assistant coach with Dallas					
MURRAY WING—Thunder Bay, ON	1	0	1	1	0
#3 / 1973–1974 / The "player to be named later" part of Gary Doak deal with Boston					
JASON WOOLLEY—Toronto, ON	170	11	50	61	78
#15 / 2002–2006 / Former Spartan was on Sabres team that lost Cup final to Dallas					
JASON YORK—Nepean, ON	19	2	4	6	4
#38, 27, 40 / 1992–1995 / Traded to Anaheim with Mike Sillinger for Stu Grimson, others					
RICK ZOMBO—Des Plaines, IL	353	14	78	92	442
#11, 23, 4 / 1984–1991 / Fifth-to-last name on the NHL's all-time name registry					

"Mr. Ilitch saved that franchise. I played under Bruce Norris and this thing was going down." — HALL OF FAME CENTER **Marcel Dionne**

ABOVE: *Henrik Zetterberg finishes against Pascal Leclaire of the Columbus Blue Jackets on November 28, 2008, at the Joe. "Z" is just short of being a point-a-game man in his nine-season career with the Red Wings.*

IT STILL SURPRISES SOME PEOPLE to learn that Gordie Howe never scored 50 goals in a single NHL season; the most he had was 49 in 1952–53. Frank Mahovlich had 49 for the Wings as well in 1968–69. The first to hit the magic number for Detroit was right-winger Mickey Redmond, who tallied 52 goals in a 76-game schedule in 1972–73, the franchise's 47th season. Mick did it again the following year with 51.

"One of them [50-goal season] I got in Toronto against Ron Low with my parents in the stands, so that was very special, and I remember getting two [goals] that night," says Redmond. "The other one I got at home against the Rangers and Eddie Giacomin. I think the first time I did it was on the road because I remember a little disappointment that I didn't get it at home in front of the home fans. The Toronto goal was a deflection off a shot from Gary Bergman, and the second [50th] was a giveaway, I picked off the puck and scored."

The subsequent year, with Redmond ailing from a bad back that would eventually cut his career short, fellow right-wing Danny Grant took advantage of the extra ice time and tallied his 50th goal of the season on April 2, 1975.

"It was home in Detroit," recalls Grant. "It was against Washington, I think Ronnie Low was the goaltender. I was playing on a line at that time with Phil Roberto and Marcel Dionne. Marcel dumped the puck in the right-hand corner, Phil went in, threw it in behind the net, I went in behind the net to get it with the intent to pass it out in front to Marcel, he was covered, there was an opening, so I just stepped out in front and backhanded it inside the far post."

Along with the remarkable goaltending coincidence, with Ron Low giving up a 50th to both Redmond and Grant, the two men also shared misfortune. Grant too would suffer a career-debilitating injury, in his case a ruptured thigh muscle, the very next season. In limited games playing for Detroit and Los Angeles over the next five years he'd never score more than 10 goals in a campaign, and instead of retiring well recognized, he'd go down as the unlikely answer to a goal-scoring trivia question. Surrounded on the list by names like Bobby Hull, Phil Esposito, and Rick MacLeish, Grant was the 12th NHLer in history to score 50 goals in a season.

Meanwhile, his prolific linemate Dionne became infamous in Detroit. His six 50-goal seasons all came with the Los Angeles Kings after he fled

the Red Wings—known at the time as the "Dead Things"—via early free agency. Officially, the league intervened and arranged a trade so that the Wings wouldn't lose the eventual Hall of Famer for nothing, but most Wings fans never forgave him.

"It was for the money," Dionne admits, "but you have to be secure in it. There are other players who left and did more things than I did. I was one of the first players to elevate the salaries and I was rejected by it [disliked for it]. Now if a guy makes that kind of money he's a hero. So it's changed. Mickey Redmond, very special for me, he said at the time, '[Hey, the] money is there.'"

Dionne says that he really enjoyed his time with Detroit: "I turned pro with them. Going back to the press conference and meeting Gordie and being at the Olympia, starting training camp with Mickey Redmond who was key then. It was just a tough situation. Gordie retired and I was not the savior of anything, but I got caught up in that situation."

A number of gifted young scorers came and went during the turbulent '70s, often-times with a splash. Garry Unger was a prospect who came to Detroit in a trade from Toronto in 1968 along with future Hall of Famer and Leafs legend Frank Mahovlich, Pete Stemkowski, and Carl Brewer. Toronto traded them in exchange for future Hall of Famer

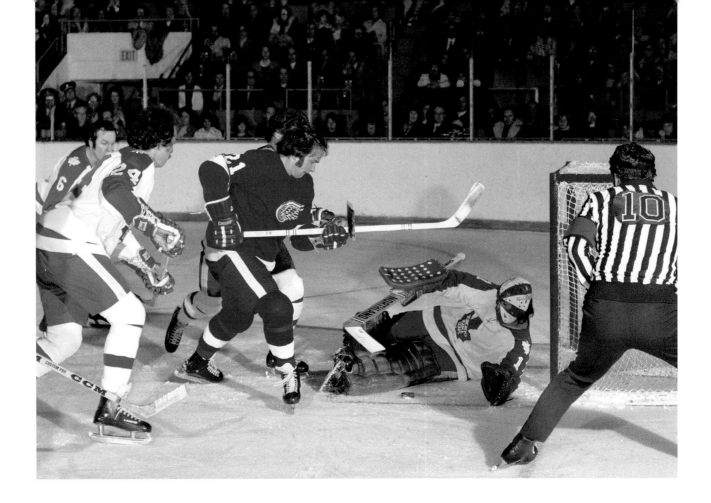

Norm Ullman, eventual 1972 Team Canada Summit Series hero Paul Henderson, and two others. Just 35 months and 84 goals later, Unger was sent packing to St. Louis with Wayne Connelly. An injury suffered while horseback riding in the off-season likely didn't help his cause.

Surrounded on the list by names like Bobby Hull, Phil Esposito, and Rick MacLeish, Grant was the 12th NHLer in history to score 50 goals in a season.

"Ned Harkness called me in a bit after Christmas. There were a lot of rumors that I was going to be traded, everywhere we went, so I thought, okay, this is it," remembers Unger. "He sat me down and he said, 'You know, Alex Delvecchio is going to be retiring soon, and I want you to be my next captain.' I thought that was great. I loved Detroit, I wanted to stay there, I was getting back in shape [after the injury] and was ready to play. And three weeks later he traded me."

Center Red Berenson and winger Tim Ecclestone came the other way in the deal.

"I was captain of the Blues team, I was Players' Association representative, kind of making a niche in St. Louis in my career, so when I was traded, we had four kids, it wasn't a happy time," explains Berenson.

 "I was glad I was going to the Red Wings for a lot of reasons though, because I had gone to school at Michigan and I still had a lot of friends in Ann Arbor, and I was a Red Wings fan of sorts because we watched them in school and we loved Gordie Howe. I really respected the fact that they were an Original Six team with a great history, and when we went there I got to play with Howe and Delvecchio, but the team was in an upheaval."

Berenson remembers the power struggle that ensued when Ned Harkness took over.

"We had as many players living in the motel where we were staying as we did living in town. They were bringing in some good players, they got Mickey Redmond, and they got Marcel Dionne in the draft. You could see they were going in the right direction, but it was hard to believe in Detroit, after watching the team for the previous 20 years, that they weren't a playoff team, not a playoff contender."

Connelly, whose NHL career would come to an end a full season later, after he jumped to the World Hockey Association, was as upset as anyone to make the move from Motown.

"Unger was my centerman," points out the right-winger, "But a lot of what had to do with me having such a good year was that I played the point on the power play. We had the big line with Howe, Delvecchio, and Mahovlich, and I was at the right point most of the time with Carl Brewer. That's where I ended up getting a lot of my points. I had 35 goals one year in Minnesota, but I think my best year was in Detroit, my full year

TOP RIGHT: *After Gordie Howe retired in 1971, heaps of pressure was piled on 1971 second overall NHL draft choice Marcel Dionne to revive the Red Wings. After four excellent years with a struggling Detroit club, Dionne bolted for Los Angeles, where he spent the bulk of his Hall of Fame career.*

BOTTOM RIGHT: *Garry Unger had a promising start to his career as well, before an off-season horseback riding injury and a run-in with GM Ned Harkness ended his time in Detroit prematurely. In 1970 he finished with 42 goals, then the next year just 13, and he was shipped to St. Louis.*

with the Red Wings [1969-70]. I played steadier and I think it was my best year in the NHL."

Reflecting on Unger's trade to St. Louis, Berenson adds, "Unger was a popular player in Detroit, a young up-and-coming star, and I was an older player, so there were a lot of questions about the trade. They were trying to build the team a little different in Detroit. I think we went through four coaches during my time, and I eventually ended up back in St. Louis."

Berenson would later return to Michigan to take over the hockey program at his alma mater.

Throughout the '70s there seemed to be only one constant: left-winger Nick Libett.

"I was the only guy left on that playoff team [1978], basically from the early-'70s team," states Libett, who played close to 900 games with the Wings. "I was fortunate to play here, it was good for business later and I loved the area, but it was tough all that time for hockey, for seven, eight, nine years. I thought for sure I was traded a number of times, but it never came about. 'Dead Wings,' all those terms, nobody likes those, that's for sure."

Libett doesn't appreciate that terminology, just like many of the young fans from that time period don't appreciate it. Bad, yes, but it was Detroit's hockey team, and Libett, partly because of his reliability, a fan favorite.

"They respected the way I played and my ability and all that kind of stuff, and that makes you feel good," reflects Libett. "And you've got to pick the good out of a bad situation."

For many of the players at the time, that good meant building camaraderie and relationships—hockey friendships that lasted a lifetime.

"We actually had some good players on that team and we were close," says Walt McKechnie, a centerman in Detroit for two and a half seasons beginning in 1975. "I'm still close with a bunch of the guys now, have stayed in contact. Dan Maloney and Dennis Polonich, Dennis Hextall. A lot of the guys have stayed in touch."

"I loved Detroit, I really did, it was a great, great city," states Errol Thompson, a Detroit winger from the 1978 trade deadline to 1981. "Great memories. My son was born there, and had I not been traded from Detroit, I probably would have spent the next couple years fulfilling my contract. And nothing against Pittsburgh, mind you, but the time came and I didn't want to uproot my family, and as a result I retired. I guess I was more brokenhearted when I left Detroit than when I left Toronto [to join the Wings]."

After drafting defenseman Reed Larson in the second round in 1976, and center Dale McCourt first overall in 1977, the Wings actually did start to play better, finally earning a playoff berth again in the spring of 1978. Drama unfolded in the first round as Detroit eliminated Atlanta on an unforgettable goal by winger Bill Lochead, who had two in the series. Lochead drew the Flames goalie out of position, got him to sprawl into the right face-off circle, and tucked the puck into the gaping net.

"We thought he was gonna go back in behind the net and wrap it from the other side but he just sort of reached his stick out and stretched," remembers linemate Paul Woods. "Billy was a really underrated player, skill-wise. He was a really good junior with the Oshawa Generals, and he

ABOVE: *Nick Libett, upended by St. Louis Blue Bob Plager, suffered through the toughest of Red Wing eras; the '70s. On and off the trading block, like much of the team throughout the time period, Libett survived 12 seasons in Detroit before finishing his career in Pittsburgh.*

BELOW: *John Ogrodnick scored 55 goals for Detroit during the 1984–85 season.*

ABOVE: *Paul Woods and Bill Lochead celebrate the latter's goal against the Atlanta Flames in Game 2 of the 1978 best-of-three preliminary round playoff series. The Wings swept, winning 5–3 and 3–2, with Lochead getting the series-winning goal. Teammate Dale McCourt is behind Flame D-man Dick Redmond (Mickey's brother) and a dejected Bill Clement is on the far left.*

RIGHT: *Danny Gare, longtime Buffalo Sabre, was the last Red Wings captain before Steve Yzerman.*

could really handle the puck and make plays and shoot it. He had a lot of talent. He fooled everybody. Dan Bouchard was the goaltender and I think Dick Redmond was the D on that side, but it was just a great play."

It was the biggest goal of the decade, and probably the biggest for the next half-dozen years after that as well, before the Ilitch ownership and Yzerman captaincy began to solidify and the team made the playoffs again in 1984. In the interim, more trades, more tweaking, more free-agent legal wrangling. After three 30-goal seasons, McCourt went to Buffalo in December of 1981 with scorer Mike Foligno and popular grinder Brent Peterson. Defenseman Jim Schoenfeld, forward Derek Smith, and veteran scorer Danny Gare, the last man to captain the Wings prior to Yzerman, came the other way.

"There was a lot of turmoil for me at that time when I was traded from Buffalo," explains Gare. "My dad had just passed away, I had a change-out with my agent, and I was just getting married. Then going to a team that was going through change, the Ilitches came in; it was tough there for a bit."

Gare departed in 1986, just about the time the organization was going through a wholehearted transformation, this time for the better. The team was poised to win, the fans were back in earnest, and attitudes were changing.

For Paul Ysebaert, a former American Hockey League MVP who arrived in a deal in 1990 from New Jersey with 21 NHL games under his belt, the Wings organization itself had always been top-notch.

He says, "It made you feel like part of history when you were there. That not only has to do with being an Original Six team, but the guys that were there at the time. I had a locker right between Stevie Y and Gerard Gallant, so you kind of learned to bleed Red Wing."

When Ysebaert was traded away during the supplemental draft three years later, he was devastated: "I guess I didn't realize the business of the game until that moment. I always thought I'd be a Red Wing . . . I was coming off a couple good seasons. But you just learned to be a Red Wing, and everything that surrounded it, the players, the management, the owners, the city, it was just one big family, and still is today as I'm part of the Red Wings alumni. I go back quite a bit for functions and it's still a family."

This sense of belonging and togetherness, and the pride and the wins that stem from it, drew a new generation of elite scorers to Detroit. Possessing a hefty payroll before the implementation of the salary cap didn't hurt either. With Mr. Ilitch willing to spend the big bucks on free agents, the 2002 Cup champions featured the biggest payroll in hockey history, one that peaked in 2003–04 at just under $78 million. An annual hunk of that total went to one of the team's key components: Brendan Shanahan, a benchmark acquisition from 1996.

Coach Scotty Bowman calls the acquisition of Shanahan "a good move." It's a massive understatement.

"We were really good at center," Bowman explains. "We had Yzerman and Fedorov, and Draper was just starting. And we had [Keith] Primeau. He wasn't very happy, he wasn't going to stay as a third-line center forever, and he was a real big holdout, pretty stubborn. Mr. Ilitch really

ABOVE: *NHL executive and lock Hall-of-Famer Brendan Shanahan scored 656 regular season NHL goals and had just short of 2,500 penalty minutes over a 21-year career with five different franchises. His longest run came in Detroit, nine seasons, where he helped win three Stanley Cups. Here, he slugs Maple Leafs defenseman Bryan McCabe.*

ABOVE LEFT: *Dino Ciccarelli played four seasons in Detroit, from 1992 to 1996, almost duplicating the time spent by defenseman Paul Coffey. Both Hall-of-Famers fell short of a Cup in Detroit; in fact, Ciccarelli failed to win one at all during his 19-season NHL career, despite tallying 600-plus goals and earning almost 1,500 penalty minutes. Undersized and constantly abused by much bigger defenseman, he was one of the great crease/slot battlers in history. Here he is set-up in front of Patrick Roy of the Montreal Canadiens.*

ABOVE RIGHT: *Pavel "Planet" Datsyuk operates in his own little world. He's not just a great scorer, but is considered by many of his peers to be the best all-around player in the game in 2012. Datsyuk will often embarrass opponents with his puck-stealing and stick-handling skills. Here, he twists LA King defenseman Drew Doughty into a face plant.*

liked Primeau and he was upset that he was not signing, and was not gonna let him get traded. We were fortunate Shanahan's name came into the picture."

"I definitely consider myself a Red Wing," states Shanahan, who also spent time in New Jersey, St. Louis, Hartford, and New York. "I was lucky to play in some great cities but my [nine] years in Detroit were by far the best. Mr. and Mrs. Ilitch are the kind of owners you dream about. They made it so personal for you. They did little things that no one knew about, and still do. The organization represents selflessness and winning, plain and simple."

The two homegrown players, Datsyuk, a sixth-round pick in 1998, and Zetterberg, a seventh rounder in 1999, currently sport the mantle of Detroit's elite scorers.

The Red Wings roster has featured a number of other current and future Hall of Fame scorers who spent plenty of time elsewhere or who aren't necessarily associated first and foremost with Detroit. Brett Hull, Luc Robitaille, and Dino Ciccarelli all come to mind. Some helped the Red Wings win it all, others fell just short.

"Ciccarelli could dive with the best of 'em," states longtime NHL player, coach, and executive Colin Campbell. "He was great at drawing penalties in front, but, boy, he would also take a beating to score a goal.

He was a pretty good hockey player when it came to that. Holmstrom does a pretty good job, but I'm not sure anyone did a better job than Cicarelli in front of the net."

Three years after scoring a controversial Cup winner for Dallas in 1999, Brett Hull arrived in Detroit just in time to win another Cup and add to his whopping NHL goal total of 741, the third highest of all time. He stayed in Hockeytown for three seasons.

John Hahn remembers the night after Hull had played his last game with the Wings. They were on a plane telling stories, "And I said, 'I'm really going to miss you.' Which may sound strange because he was a little bit of a bear sometimes with the media, and tough to deal with, but he was such a great guy and a character. You miss people like that."

While in Detroit, Hull referred to himself as the "old goat" on a line with two kids, Boyd Devereaux and Pavel Datsyuk. One wonders if he realized the star potential of "Planet Datsyuk" at that time.

"Pavel has his own little world that he goes into once in a while," states teammate Henrik Zetterberg. "He's amazing. It's fun and it's been an honor to have been playing for almost nine years with him now, and hopefully we'll have many more together as well."

Datsyuk the Russian feels the same way about "Z" the Swede, a two-man European mutual-admiration society.

"He's a natural," declares Datsyuk, "and he's a nice person off the ice and in the locker room. He has the skill and he is competitive on every inch of the ice. I've always liked him."

The two homegrown players, Datsyuk, a sixth-round pick in 1998, and Zetterberg, a seventh rounder in 1999, currently sport the mantle of

ABOVE LEFT: *Jordan Staal is going one direction, while Datsyuk and the puck are heading the other, on December 13, 2011, in Pittsburgh. Nick Lidstrom watches from the point.*

ABOVE RIGHT: *Datsyuk curls to the net against fallen Nashville Predators defenseman Dan Hamhuis in an opening-round playoff game on April 20, 2008. Wings teammate Tomas Holmstrom heads to the net expecting a pass. Detroit won this game 2–0 to finish the series in six games.*

Detroit's elite scorers and career-long wearers of the Winged Wheel. Along with Nick Lidstrom, they're the poster boys for the current generation of Detroit's hockey family.

Over the years, one member of this clan has seen it all, or called it all: 50-goal scorer turned Hall of Fame broadcaster Mickey Redmond. Only fellow Foster Hewitt Memorial Award honoree Budd Lynch has been around longer. Mick has been a constant for much of the last half century.

Dave Strader says that he'll never forget his first year broadcasting with Redmond and the Wings in 1985.

"We were in Minnesota, 20 minutes to air, and I'm getting ready to do my first NHL telecast, and the Wings are probably 1–8–1 at that point. And Mickey takes his headset off and taps me on the shoulder and says, 'I want to talk to you for a second.'"

According to Strader, Redmond warned him that the team wasn't great, saying, "There's a good chance they're going to lose every game we televise."

Over the years, one member of this clan has seen it all, or called it all: 50-goal scorer turned Hall of Fame broadcaster Mickey Redmond.

"And I'm looking at him thinking, 'Boy, what a pep talk this is,'" Strader continues. "But he pointed out that there was another team on the ice, it didn't have to be 100 percent the Red Wings' point of view, the other team might have interesting stuff, la dee dah. Three hours later the final score of my first telecast was 10–1 Minnesota. The only goal for Detroit was Ron Duguay. [Redmond] said, 'That's the way it's going to be.' In our telecasts I think the Wings record was 1–13–1, and the average score was like 8–3. So he knew what he was talking about. He was the perfect guy to bring me along in a lot of aspects of broadcasting, and the history of the game, and the respect."

Redmond was simply passing on knowledge acquired from hockey life experience.

Redmond. "They weren't very good, and I was struggling with that. He said, 'You've gotta look harder some nights for the good in the game, it's always there. Turn over some more rocks, you'll always find it. The great game of hockey is always there to be found, because that's exactly what it is: a great game.'"

Scorers and playmakers whose careers included or began after 1962–1963, a half century ago.

RED WINGS REGULAR SEASON STATISTICS	GP	G	A	PTS	PIM
GREG C. ADAMS (LW)—Duncan, BC	28	3	7	10	16
#20 / 1962–1966 / Wings last of seven teams over a 10-year career					
BRENT ASHTON (LW)—Saskatoon, SK	108	41	31	72	72
#33, 14 / 1987–1988 / Listed as a grinder with Boston in book *Black and Gold*					
PIERRE AUBRY (LW)—Cap-de-la-Madeleine, QC	39	6	3	9	41
#27, 24 / 1984–1985 / Scored 85 goals his last season in the Quebec league					
ANDY BATHGATE (RW)—Winnipeg, MB	130	23	55	78	49
#21 / 1965–1967 / Hall of Famer's number 9 was retired by the New York Rangers					
GORDON "RED" BERENSON (C)—Regina, SK	283	73	128	201	64
#7 / 1971–1974 / Head coach of Michigan, his alma mater, since 1984					
MICHEL BERGERON (RW)—Chicoutimi, QC	174	64	46	110	156
#16 / 1974–1977 / Not the former head coach of the Nordiques and Rangers					
FRED BERRY (C)—Stony Plain, AB	3	0	0	0	0
#29 / 1976–1977 / Minor-league scoring prowess not enough in the big show					
TOM BISSETT (C)—Seattle, WA	5	0	0	0	0
#7 / 1990–1991 / During call-up season, had 44 Goals in 73 games in Adirondack					
MIKE BLAISDELL (RW)—Moose Jaw, SK	192	44	61	105	80
#14, 21 / 1980–1983 / Wings first-rounder (11th overall) in 1980, part of big trade to NYR					
IVAN BOLDIREV (C)—Zrenjanin, Serbia	183	67	95	162	50
#19, 12 / 1982–1985 / Once part of an eight-player deal between Atlanta and Chicago					
MEL BRIDGMAN (C/LW)—Trenton, ON	70	8	13	21	61
#15 / 1986–1988 / Six 20-goal seasons while in Philly and New Jersey					
FABIAN BRUNNSTROM (LW)—Jonstorp, Sweden	5	0	1	1	4
#76 / 2011–2012 / Prolific scoring in Sweden hasn't translated to North America					
SHAWN BURR (LW)—Sarnia, ON	659	148	214	362	765
#11 / 1984–1995 / Detroit's first-rounder (seventh overall) in 1984					
JIMMY CARSON (C)—Southfield, MI	240	100	102	202	84
#10, 12 / 1989–1993 / Went from LA to Edmonton as part of the Gretzky deal in 1988					
FRANTISEK CERNIK (LW)—Novy Jicin, Czech	49	5	4	9	13
#21 / 1984–1985 / "Frank" gave NHL a crack after point-a-game prowess in Czech league					
JOHN CHABOT (C)—Summerside, PEI	226	29	99	128	44
#16 / 1987–1991 / Surprise 19 points in 16 games in team's 1988 run to Conference final					
GUY CHARRON (C)—Verdun, QC	265	61	78	139	57
#23, 8 / 1971–1974 / Holds record: 734 regular season NHL games with no playoff games					
DINO CICCARELLI (RW)—Sarnia, ON	254	107	133	240	292
#22 / 1992–1996 / Inducted into the Hockey Hall of Fame in 2010					
WENDEL CLARK (LW)—Kelvington, SK	12	4	2	6	2
#7 / 1999 / Leafs legend was a trade-deadline pickup to provide playoff boost					
DAN CLEARY (RW/LW)—Harbour Grace, NL	492	110	140	250	212
#11 / 2005–2012 / Former first-rounder took a while to reflect his junior scoring proficiency					
ROLAND CLOUTIER (C)—Rouyn, QC	20	6	6	12	2
#21, 19, 23 / 1977–1979 / Played last seven years of his pro career in France					
WAYNE CONNELLY (RW)—Rouyn, QC	146	35	58	93	22
#17 / 1969–1971 / Had 35-goal season with Minnesota in 1968–69					

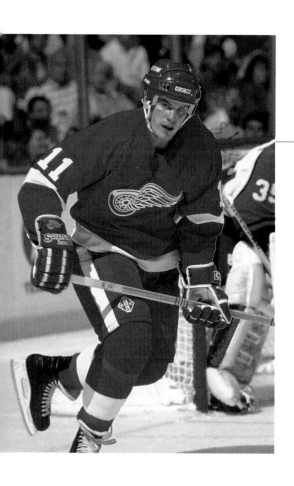

OPPOSITE TOP: *Swede Johan Franzen has been battling and lighting the lamp for the Wings since 2005. Here, he bears down on Nashville Predators goaltender Pekka Rinne on February 17, 2012, at the Joe.*

SCORERS

RED WINGS REGULAR SEASON STATISTICS	GP	G	A	PTS	PIM
MURRAY CRAVEN (LW)—Medicine Hat, AB	46	4	11	15	12
#22, 11, 24 / 1982–1984 / Scoring picked up after he went to Philly for Darryl Sittler					
BOBBY CRAWFORD (RW)—Long Island, NY	1	0	0	0	0
#17 / 1982–1983 / Undersized scorer headed overseas					
RAY CULLEN (C)—Ottawa, ON	27	8	8	16	8
#15 / 1966–1967 / Leading scorer for St. Catharines Teepees that won '60 Memorial Cup					
PAVEL DATSYUK (C)—Sverdlovsk, Russia	732	240	478	718	186
#13 / 2001–2012 / Two Cups, three Selkes, and four Byngs; not bad for a 171st-overall pick					
MAL DAVIS (LW)—Lockport, NS	11	2	0	2	0
#18, 14, 19 / 1978–1979, 1980–1981 / American Hockey League's MVP in 1983–84					
ALEX DELVECCHIO (C)—Fort William, ON	1,549	456	825	1,281	383
#17, 15, 10 / 1951–1974 / NHL record for most games played by a single-franchise player					
MARCEL DIONNE (C)—Drummondville, QC	309	139	227	366	59
#5, 12 / 1971–1975 / Superstar the Wings couldn't keep; Hall of Fame inductee in 1992					
RENE DROLET (RW)—Quebec City, QC	1	0	0	0	0
#24 / 1974–1975 / Great hands, too little for the big show					
RON DUGUAY (C/RW)—Sudbury, ON	227	90	127	217	111
#10 / 1983–1986 / Cheryl Tiegs and Farrah Fawcett; we'll leave it at that					
BLAKE DUNLOP (C)—Hamilton, ON	57	6	14	20	20
#11 / 1983–1984 / Led Ottawa and Ontario league in scoring 1973; Minny's first-rounder					
BRUCE EAKIN (C)—Winnipeg, MB	4	0	1	1	0
#32 / 1985–1986 / Played final 13 years of his career in Europe					
BERNIE FEDERKO (C)—Foam Lake, SK	73	17	40	57	24
#42 / 1989–1990 / Last year of a Hall of Fame career spent with Blues					
SERGEI FEDOROV (C)—Pskov, Russia	908	400	554	954	587
#91 / 1990–2003 / A Selke, a Hart, three Cups, the Hall of Fame awaits					

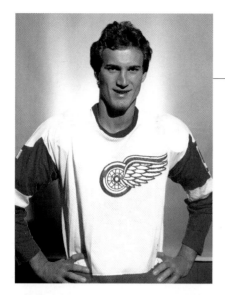

SCORERS

RED WINGS REGULAR SEASON STATISTICS	GP	G	A	PTS	PIM
MIKE FOLIGNO (RW)—Sudbury, ON	186	77	83	160	347
#17 / 1979–1981 / Finished NHL career with 355 goals and 2,049 penalty minutes					
LEN FONTAINE (RW)—Quebec City, QC	46	8	11	19	10
#18, 11 / 1972–1974 / IHL MVP and leading scorer in 1975–76; played for WHA Stags					
DWIGHT FOSTER (RW)—Toronto, ON	215	48	62	110	212
#20 / 1982–1986 / Led Ontario league in scoring in 1976–77; Boston's first-round pick					
BOBBY FRANCIS (C)—North Battleford, SK	14	2	0	2	0
#16 / 1982–1983 / More successful as coach; son of Emile, won Jack Adams in 2002					
JOHAN FRANZEN (C/LW)—Vetlanda, Sweden	472	150	125	275	288
#39, 93 / 2005–2012 / The "Mule" more of a scorer in North America than in Sweden					
MIROSLAV FRYCER (RW)—Ostrava, Czech	23	7	8	15	47
#14 / 1988–1989 / Came from Leafs for defenseman Darren Veitch in summer of 1988					
ROBBIE FTOREK (C)—Needham, MA	15	2	5	7	4
#23, 15 / 1972–1974 / Undrafted, undersized, WHA MVP in 1977, USA Hockey HOF					
DANNY GARE (RW)—Nelson, BC	306	86	95	181	593
#18 / 1981–1986 / Last captain before Yzerman; played with pneumonia, mono', and a bad eye					
DANNY GRANT (RW)—Fredericton, NB	174	64	62	126	58
#21 / 1974–1978 / Consecutive-games run of 566 stopped with thigh injury in Dec. '75					
ADAM GRAVES (C)—Toronto, ON	78	7	7	14	81
#12 / 1988–1989 / Wings career bridged three seasons; Cup wins in Edmonton and New York					
GALEN HEAD (RW)—Grande Prairie, AB	1	0	0	0	0
#15 / 1967–1968 / As Johnstown Jet had non-speaking hockey playing role in *Slap Shot*					
PAUL HENDERSON (RW)—Kincardine, ON	269	67	79	146	132
#22, 19 / 1962–1968 / Famous for 3 Summit Series game winners for Canada vs. USSR in 1972					
MARIAN HOSSA (RW/LW)—Stara Lubovna, Czech	74	40	31	71	63
#81 / 2008–2009 / Lost Cup final with Pens to Wings, then Cup final with Wings to Pens					
GORDIE HOWE (RW)—Floral, SK	1,687	786	1,023	1,809	1,643
#17, 9 / 1946–1971 / Had a 102 point season as a 47-year-old for Houston in WHA					
BRETT HULL (RW)—Belleville, ON	245	92	115	207	69
#17 / 2001–2004 / "The Golden Brett" inducted into the Hockey Hall of Fame in 2009					
DENNIS HULL (LW)—Pointe Anne, ON	55	5	9	14	6
#19 / 1977–1978 / End of career after 13 seasons in Chicago; brother of Bobby, uncle to Brett					
PIERRE JARRY (LW)—Montreal, QC	91	23	36	59	21
#17 / 1973–1975 / Led the Central League (Omaha) in goals and points in 1970–71					
KELLY KISIO (C)—Peace River, AB	236	68	129	197	175
#16 / 1983–1986 / Went on to become the last Captain of the Rangers before Messier					
PETR KLIMA (LW/RW)—Chomutov, Czech	306	130	93	223	158
#85 / 1985–1989, 1998–1999 / First Czech to defect to an American-based team					
SLAVA KOZLOV (LW/C)—Voskresensk, Russia	607	202	213	415	376
#13 / 1991–2001 / Finished his 20-year career in the KHL (Russia) in 2010–11					
DAN LABRAATEN (LW)—Leksand, Sweden	198	52	54	106	28
#21 / 1978–1981 / "Rusty" went on to lead the Swedish league in scoring in 1983–84					
ROBERT LANG (C)—Teplice, Czech	159	40	79	119	138
#20 / 2004–2007 / Member of 1998 Czech Olympic Gold Medal team in Nagano, Japan					
IGOR LARIONOV (C)—Voskresensk, Russia	539	87	298	385	302
#8 / 1995–2003 / Three-Cup run interrupted by 26 GP with FLA in 2000, 2008 Hockey HOF					
REGGIE LEACH (RW)—Riverton, MB	78	15	17	32	13
#27 / 1982–1983 / "The Riverton Rifle," third-overall pick of B's in '70, Cup win in Philly					

SCORERS

RED WINGS REGULAR SEASON STATISTICS	GP	G	A	PTS	PIM
FERN LEBLANC (C)—Gaspesie, QC	34	5	6	11	0
#18 / 1976–1979 / Undersized, dominant scorer in Switzerland the last seven years of career					
NICK LIBETT (LW)—Stratford, ON	861	217	250	467	454
#22, 14 / 1967–1979 / Crowd favorite on bad teams; finished career with two seasons in Pitt					
TED LINDSAY (LW)—Renfrew, ON	862	335	393	728	1,423
#7, 15 / 1944–1957, 1964–1965 / "Terrible Ted" did all, feared no one, Hall of Fame 1966					
BILL LOCHEAD (RW/LW)—Forest, ON	296	65	60	125	162
#23 / 1974–1979 / Scored series-winning goal vs. Atlanta in first round in 1978					
MARK LOFTHOUSE (RW/C)—New Westminster, BC	40	11	8	19	31
#10, 17 / 1981–1983 / Six goals in six games for New Westminster in '77 Memorial Cup win					
DON LUCE (C)—London, ON	58	3	11	14	18
#11 / 1970–1971 / Tall pivot had 200-plus goals and 500-plus points over 10 seasons in Buffalo					
TORD LUNDSTROM (LW)—Kiruna, Sweden	11	1	1	2	0
#23 / 1973–1974 / Gentlemanly, torrid scorer in 20 seasons in Sweden; not much in NHL					
GEORGE LYLE (LW)—North Vancouver, BC	69	18	20	38	34
#18 / 1979–1981 / "Sparky" won a NCAA championship with Michigan Tech in 1975					
PARKER MACDONALD (LW/C)—Sydney, NS	361	94	122	216	135
#20, 14 / 1960–1965, 1965–1967 / To B's in a six-player deal, dealt back after for Pit Martin					
BRUCE MACGREGOR (RW)—Edmonton, AB	673	151	184	335	173
#16, 12 / 1961–1971 / "The Redheaded Rocket" behind Howe for a decade on depth chart					
DON MACLEAN (C)—Sydney, NS	3	1	1	2	0
#42 / 2005–2006 / Had 56 goals the same season in Grand Rapids; now playing in Russia					
PAUL MACLEAN (RW)—Grostenquin, France	76	36	35	71	118
#15 / 1988–1989 / Mike Babcock's asst. coach; first Frenchman with name on the Cup					
RICK MACLEISH (LW)—Lindsay, ON	25	2	8	10	4
#23 / 1984 / Ended career with Wings; first Flyer with 50-goal season; won two Cups					
FRANK MAHOVLICH (LW)—Timmins, ON	198	108	88	196	129
#27 / 1986–1971 / "The Big M" won four Cups in Toronto and two more in Montreal					
PETE MAHOVLICH (C)—Timmins, ON	186	26	64	90	145
#24, 11, 21 / 1966–1969, 1979–1981 / Four Cups in Mont., plus '72 Summit Series with bro					
STEVE MALTAIS (LW)—Arvida, QC	4	0	1	1	0
#34 / 1993–1994 / NHL numbers belie prowess; led IHL in goal scoring for five seasons					
PIT MARTIN (C)—Noranda, QC	119	18	23	41	60
#12, 8 / 1962, 1963–1965 / Memorial Cup winner in Hamilton flourished in Chicago					
DALE MCCOURT (C)—Falconbridge, ON	341	134	203	337	92
#10 / 1977–1981 / First-overall pick had 33 goals as rookie, led brief "Dead Wings" respite					
AL MCDONOUGH (RW)—Hamilton, ON	13	2	2	4	4
#17 / 1977–1978 / Played in WHA for Cleveland Crusaders and Minnesota Fighting Saints					
BILL MCDOUGALL (C)—Mississauga, ON	2	0	1	1	0
#43 / 1990–1991 / Scored 80 goals in 57 ECHL games in 1989–90 for Erie Panthers					
WALT MCKECHNIE (C)—London, ON	321	89	167	256	218
#11 / 1975–1977, 1981–1983 / Sixth-overall pick of Toronto in '63 played for eight NHL teams					
TONY MCKEGNEY (LW)—Montreal, QC	14	2	1	3	8
#7 / 1989 / First black player to have significant impact and lengthy career in NHL					
DON MCKENNEY (C)—Smiths Falls, ON	24	1	6	7	0
#20 / 1965–1966 / Eight and a half seasons with Boston, won a Cup with Toronto					
ANDREW MCKIM (C)—St. John, NB	2	0	0	0	2
#14 / 1994–1995 / Undersized, not physical; four NHL teams gave him shot as free agent					

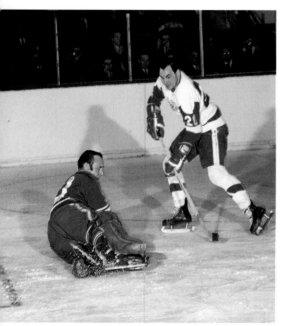

RIGHT: *A shot goes wide and Red Wing Floyd Smith slams on the brakes in front of Leafs goalie Johnny Bower.*

SCORERS

RED WINGS REGULAR SEASON STATISTICS	GP	G	A	PTS	PIM
GLENN MERKOSKY (C)—Edmonton, AB	20	0	2	2	0
#22, 44 / 1985–1986, 1989–1990 / 1986 Calder Cup with Adirondack; now Wings scout					
DON MURDOCH (RW)—Cranbrook, BC	49	9	13	22	23
#14 / 1981–1982 / Former NYR sixth-overall; kid brother of Robert Lovell (Bob) Murdoch					
JOE MURPHY (RW)—London, ON	90	14	18	32	71
#10 / 1986–1989 / First-overall pick flopped in Detroit, won Cup after trade to Edmonton					
VACLAV NEDOMANSKY (RW)—Lany, Czech	364	108	139	247	86
#20 / 1977–1982 / Trail blazer, defected from Czechoslovakia at age 30, six NHL seasons					
GUSTAV NYQUIST (C)—Halmstad, Sweden	18	1	6	7	2
#14 / 2011–2012 / Hobey Baker Award finalist led the NCAA in scoring in 2009–10					
ADAM OATES (C)—Weston, ON	246	54	145	199	65
#12, 21 / 1985–1989 / Undrafted signee after winning national title with RPI in 1985					
JOHN OGRODNICK (LW)—Ottawa, ON	558	265	281	534	150
#25, 18 / 1979–1987, 1992–1993 / Team record 55 goals in 1985–86 stood for four seasons					
MARK OSBORNE (LW)—Toronto, ON	160	45	65	110	144
#23 / 1981–1983 / "Ozzie" helped Leafs to two Conference finals, now Leafs TV analyst					
BUTCH PAUL (C)—Rocky Mountain House, AB	3	0	0	0	0
#22, 14 / 1964–1965 / Died in car accident, age 22 in '66; same home town as Brad Stuart					
DEAN PRENTICE (LW)—Schumacher, ON	230	60	89	149	86
#20 / 1966–1969 / Listed in *100 Ranger Greats* as the 37th-greatest all-time NYR					
KEITH PRIMEAU (C)—Toronto, ON	363	97	133	230	781
#55 / 1990–1996 / Big, tough scorer part of deal that brought Shanahan from Hartford					
MICKEY REDMOND (RW)—Kirkland Lake, ON	317	177	133	310	107
#20 / 1971–1976 / Known to fans for TV work; first Red Wing to have 50-goal season					
BOB RITCHIE (LW)—Laverlochere, QC	28	8	4	12	10
#27 / 1977–1978 / Bridged two seasons; part of six-player deal with Flyers in February of '77					
NATHAN ROBINSON (C)—Scarborough, ON	5	0	0	0	2
#38 / 2003–2004 / "The Chocolate Rocket" playing overseas since 2006					
LUC ROBITAILLE (LW)—Montreal, QC	162	41	40	81	88
#20 / 2001–2003 / Hall of Famer "Lucky" got his Cup with Detroit in 16th NHL season					
ANDRE ST. LAURENT (C)—Rouyn-Noranda, QC	172	52	73	125	249
#16, 34 / 1977–1979, 1983–1984 / Versatile player had best offensive seasons with Wings					
TOMAS SANDSTROM (RW)—Jakobstad, Finland	34	9	9	18	36
#28 / 1997 / Nagging injuries slowed Swede born in Finland; now a fireman in Malmo					
RIC SEILING (RW)—Elmira, ON	74	3	8	11	49
#16 / 1986–1987 / Much younger brother of Rod; nine seasons in Buffalo before Detroit					

RED WINGS REGULAR SEASON STATISTICS	GP	G	A	PTS	PIM
BRENDAN SHANAHAN (LW)—Mimico, ON	716	309	324	633	1,037
#14 / 1996–2006 / Only player in history with more than 600 goals and 2,000 PIM					
RILEY SHEAHAN (C)—St. Catherines, ON	1	0	0	0	4
#15 / 2012 / Wings first round pick in 2010 played three seasons with Fighting Irish					
DOUG SHEDDEN (C)—Wallaceburg, ON	44	8	15	23	8
#14 / 1986–1987 / Bridged two seasons; coach in three minor leagues and in Europe					
BOBBY SHEEHAN (C)—Weymouth, MA	34	5	4	9	2
#17 / 1976–1977 / NHL numbers never came about for small whiz kid from Weymouth					
RAY SHEPPARD (RW)—Pembroke, ON	274	152	113	265	101
#26 / 1991–1995 / Had 52-goal season in Detroit, sent to San Jose for Igor Larionov					
DARRYL SITTLER (C)—Kitchener, ON	61	11	16	27	37
#27 / 1984–1985 / Hall of Famer wrapped up career with Wings; 1,121 career points					
FLOYD SMITH (RW)—Perth, ON	290	93	122	215	118
#8, 17 / 1962–1968 / Part of epic eight-player deal with Toronto on March 3, 1968					
DENNIS SOBCHUK (C)—Lang, SK	33	4	6	10	0
#14 / 1979–1980 / Tore up juniors and WHA; brother Gene played one NHL game					
FRED SPECK (C)—Thorold, ON	10	0	0	0	2
#15, 8 / 1968–1970 / AHL MVP, Rookie of the Year, and leading scorer in 1971					
TED SPEERS (RW)—Ann Arbor, MI	4	1	1	2	0
#11 / 1985–1986 / Former Wolverine helped win a Calder Cup with Adirondack in 1986					
PETE STEMKOWSKI (C)—Winnipeg, MB	170	51	114	165	207
#23, 19 / 1968–1970 / "Stemmer" was on Leafs last Cup win in '67; seven seasons with NYR					
STEVE THOMAS (LW)—Stockport, England	44	10	12	22	25
#32 / 2003–2004 / "Stumpy" was towel-snapped by Patrick Swayze in *Youngblood*					
ERROL THOMPSON (LW)—Summerside, PEI	200	76	58	134	102
#12 / 1978–1981 / "Spud" had a 43-goal season with the Maple Leafs					
NORM ULLMAN (C)—Provost, AB	875	324	434	758	552
#7 / 1955–1968 / One of the greatest players never to win a Cup; 11 All-Star Games					
GARRY UNGER (C)—Calgary, AB	216	84	88	172	165
#16, 7 / 1968–1971 / Held Iron Man record (914) until Doug Jarvis (964) topped it					
ERIC VAIL (LW)—Timmins, ON	52	10	14	24	35
#19 / 1981–1982 / Won Calder Trophy as Rookie of the Year for Atlanta in 1975; "Big Train"					
PAT VERBEEK (RW)—Sarnia, ON	135	37	41	78	168
#15 / 1999–2001 / "The Little Ball of Hate" won Cup with Dallas; 500 career goals					
TOM WEBSTER (RW)—Kirkland Lake, ON	84	31	38	69	44
#8, 16 / 1970–1971, 1979–1980 / Wings leading scorer in Howe's final Detroit season					
RAY WHITNEY (LW)—Fort Saskatchewan, AB	67	14	29	43	22
#41 / 2003–2004 / "The Wizard" won a Cup with Carolina in 2006					
JASON WILLIAMS (C)—London, ON	277	55	76	131	87
#29 / 2000–2004, 2009–2010 / Won Cup in 2002; serious head and leg injuries since					
WARREN YOUNG (C)—Toronto, ON	79	22	24	46	161
#35 / 1985–1986 / NHL All-Rookie in 1984–85 with 40 goals, then free agent to Detroit					
PAUL YSEBAERT (C)—Sarnia, ON	210	84	86	170	113
#21 / 1990–1993 / Traded to Winnipeg in 1993 for defenseman Aaron Ward					
STEVE YZERMAN (C)—Cranbrook, BC	1,514	692	1,063	1,755	924
#19 / 1983–2006 / "Stevie Wonder," "The Captain," led team to three Stanley Cups					
HENRIK ZETTERBERG (C/LW)—Njurunda, Sweden	668	252	372	624	271
#40 / 2002–2012 / Olympic and World Championship Gold in 2006, Stanley Cup in 2008					

13 Enforcers

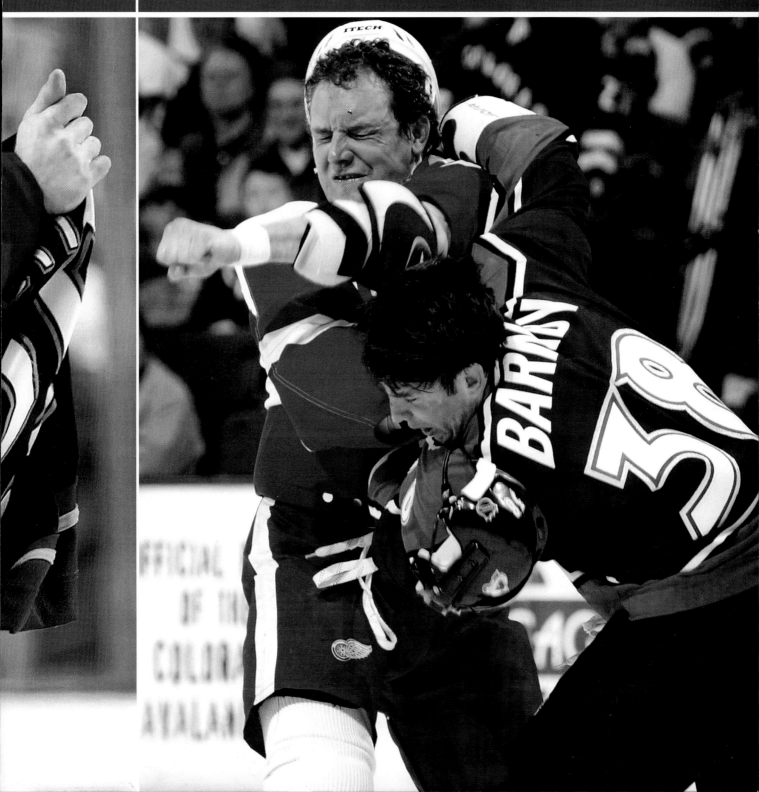

> *"Probert and Kocur were two tough guys, and two tough guys I never had to fight. I wouldn't have anyway, but I'm glad I didn't have to."*
>
> — DETROIT TEAMMATE Gerard Gallant

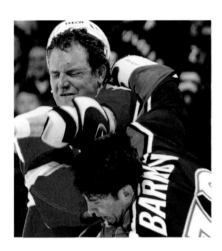

IN RECENT YEARS, THE RED WINGS have been very near the bottom of the statistical list as it relates to NHL teams with fighting majors. Apparently the organization got it out of its system in the late '80s and early '90s. At that time, Detroit dominated the enforcer category like it had never been dominated before.

"Two of the things we had going for us at the time: we had two of the toughest players all-time in the history of hockey in Bob Probert and Joe Kocur, in an era when tough hockey was in vogue, and we also had one of the best young players ever in Steve Yzerman," states former Detroit defenseman and assistant coach Colin Campbell. "That was augmented by Gerard Gallant, Petr Klima, Adam Oates. And Probert was a good player. The most important thing is to have a chance to win every night and for the players to think they could win every night. We were never going to get intimidated and we always had a chance to win."

Jim Nill, a right-winger who was no slouch himself, points out that even the secondary players were pretty close to heavyweights.

He says, "It was an exciting time in Detroit too, because the changing of the guard. They had some tough years and then all of a sudden you get the Proberts and Kocurs showing up, and you get Harold Snepsts and Mel Bridgman. What was neat about it, we had some young guys that were tough, and we had some old veterans that were real tough and hardened, and they knew how to really play the game."

"People loved the kind of hockey that came out of those teams, from 1985, '86, on," adds Campbell. "It was exciting hockey; scoring goals

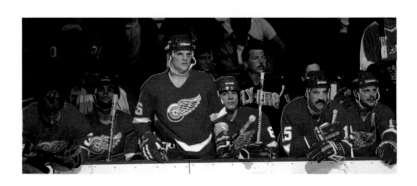

ABOVE: *The rage of Kocur, while taking on "The Missing" Link Gaetz, of the Minnesota North Stars in 1988.*

ABOVE RIGHT: *Kocur spent seven seasons in Detroit, left for New York for six, with a "cup of coffee" in Vancouver, and returned to Motown in time to partake in the 1997 Stanley Cup championship.*

and toughness. Keep in mind we were in the Norris, which became the 'Chuck Norris' Division, with a lot of black-and-blue battles. We had some epic battles with Toronto, St. Louis, and Chicago. Any given night you'd have Stevie scoring a great goal, Adam Oates setting up a great goal, Gerry Gallant scoring and fighting, and Probert and Kocur having an epic tilt."

"Probie" played most of nine seasons in Detroit from 1985 through 1993-94. In his third year he led the league in penalty minutes with a 398. Kocur had led the league two seasons earlier with 377. Appropriate terms for this Red Wings twosome may have been "Thunder and Lightning," "The Twin Terrors," or "Death and Destruction." Instead, they were the "Bruise Brothers."

"We could go in any building and not get intimidated," states team-mate Gerard Gallant. "It was a big part of the game at that time and we weren't gonna worry about anyone else's toughness. We played our game and those guys did a great job. They were very entertaining. Some nights it was a little scary because they hurt some people in some of those fights, and you don't like to see people get hurt, but they were two tough guys."

Against Boston, Kocur actually cracked Jay Miller's helmet with a punch. Kocur would end fights quickly with his massive right hand and a sneaky, powerful left. Meanwhile, Probert would ragdoll guys, dragging and shaking them around and pummeling them. They both had an overwhelming intimidation factor. They, and the Red Wings scorers, got plenty of room on the ice.

Keep in mind we were in the Norris, which became the "Chuck Norris" Division, with a lot of black-and-blue battles.

Mike Hartman, a former Sabre whose father, John, was the Red Wings' team photographer, remembers punching Probert during a game: "I one-punched him, got a lucky punch in. I think I punched his helmet into him, cut him pretty good. He got in the penalty box [where John

Hartman was taking photos] and told my dad, 'I'm gonna kill your son, I'm gonna effing kill him.' My dad said, 'Hey, you do what you have to do.'" Hartman laughs. "He came out and one-punched me in the head and got four minutes and a 10-minute misconduct."

Among hockey fans, the Bruise Brothers' more memorable battles simply became known by the participants' names, such as "Probert-Domi Two," "Cox-Probert Two," or "Kocur-Baumgartner."

"I remember Probert-[Troy] Crowder Two," says former Wings PR man Bill Jamieson. "That second one was in Detroit. Don Cherry came down [from Toronto] for that game, he was sitting in the stands. 'Grapes' didn't sit in the press box, he sat in the stands. It was bizarre; it was a fight crowd."

"Probert was a big man, with a big reach," Hall of Fame linesman Ray "Scampy" Scapinello recalls in the book *Between the Lines*. "He'd pull you in, drill you a few times, push you outside his range, get his wind, then pull you back in and drill you a few more times."

In March of 1992, former Maple Leafs and Blackhawks brawler Bob McGill was traded from San Jose to Detroit, and was confronted with an unusual situation.

"I'll never forget having to walk into that room," McGill says. "I had fought Kocur and Probert and Gallant so many times I had lost track.

They hated my guts. It was really weird, I had been with Toronto for six and Chicago for four and for 10 years I had fought all of those guys. It was really weird walking into that room."

Such is the life of an enforcer. But once inside, "Big Daddy" McGill and the rest of the team became brothers in arms. He fought three times during his Red Wings career, which lasted 12 regular-season and eight playoff games.

"We went down three–one to Minnesota and came back and won the first round and then we were swept by Chicago," adds McGill. "That was a downer, having basically just come from there."

> *I'll never forget having to walk into that room.*
> *I had fought Kocur and Probert and Gallant so many*
> *times I had lost track. They hated my guts.*

That summer he was scooped up by Tampa Bay in the expansion draft.

Unlike Probert, and Kocur, who won a Stanley Cup in New York and two more in Detroit during his career, most enforcers don't stick around one team for very long. In fact, many don't last that long in the league. It's a difficult, stressful, punishing job, one with a high attrition rate, especially for those with limited hockey skills.

A great majority of the fighters on the Red Wings career enforcer list spent just a handful of games with Detroit.

Jeff Brubaker, who played one game for the Wings, also auditioned for six other teams during his partial eight-season NHL career. Steve Martinson banged around with three teams over five years for a grand total of 49 games. Brian Johnson, part of a championship team at the AHL level and a bruiser in the minors, ended up with three total games in the big show.

These types of careers were the rule for enforcers, rather than the exception, especially in Detroit.

The biggest exception came from a guy who epitomizes the old saying, "looks can be deceiving." Dennis Polonich played his entire career with the Wings: 390 games from 1974 to 1982. He racked up 1,242 penalty minutes. Polonich was only five foot six, 166 pounds, and he was the 118th overall pick in 1973 out of the Flin Flon Bombers. After a year playing in Britain, Polonich showed up in Detroit.

"He was a great, great, great teammate," states Errol Thompson, a Red Wings forward from that era. "We were good buddies when I got there. Pound for pound there are not too many guys tougher. Team first. I was five eight and he was probably five six, and not afraid of anyone. Not a soul."

This Red Wing pit bull put together consecutive seasons of 302, 274, and 254 penalty minutes beginning in 1975.

During those same three seasons, Polonich received assistance from Dennis Hextall, and from a more traditional enforcer, six-foot-two, 195-pound left-wing Dan Maloney.

ABOVE: *Pound for pound, at five foot six, and 165 pounds, Dennis Polonich was as tough a hockey player as ever existed. For six full seasons and parts of two more in the 1970s, he took on anyone and everyone. On October 25, 1978, apparently purely out of frustration, Wilf Paiement of the Colorado Rockies slashed Polonich across the face resulting in a concussion and reconstructive face surgery. Paiement received the second-longest suspension in league history at the time, while Polonich sued and reached settlement four years later.*

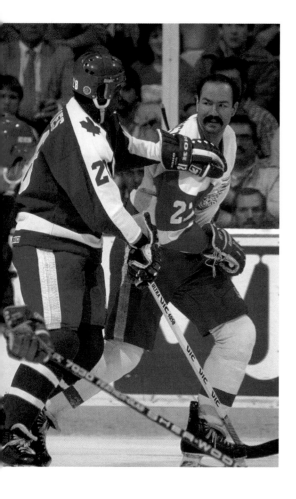

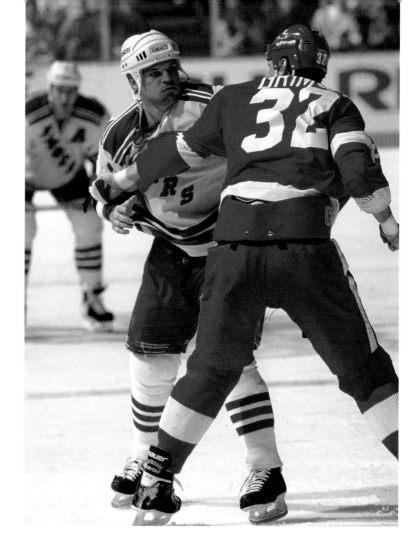

"I was always honored to play in the National Hockey League and being able to play in the Original Six is an honor for me," reflects Maloney. "To play in the old building, we were a team that struggled for a while, but they slowly turned it around and got it going."

In the decades that followed, the Red Wings saw some big-name fighters swing through town, none bigger than Stu Grimson, who stood six foot five and weighed in at about 230 pounds. In 68 games with Detroit he had 165 penalty minutes.

Jim Cummins, Gerry Hart, Aaron Downey, Brad May, Basil McRae, Troy Crowder, Randy McKay, Dennis Vial, and Warren Young were all men with reputations—some memorable—who dropped their mitts briefly for Detroit. Even the legendary Dave "Tiger" Williams, the all-time NHL penalty-minutes leader, swung through for 55 games.

Meanwhile, Darren McCarty, another big-name pugilist and also a renowned grinder, is a man that Red Wings fans will remember forever. Looking back from 2012, he was the last true long-term enforcer in Detroit, who also came up with big plays at big moments.

McCarty scored the Cup-winning goal in 1997 against Philadelphia, turning Flyers defenseman Janne Niinimaa inside out and beating goalie Ron Hextall for a 2–0 lead in the second period of Game 4. The Wings would hold on to win the game 2–1 and sweep the series.

The next spring McCarty finished with a career-high 11 playoff points in 22 games, helping the Wings win back-to-back Cups.

Four years later he was at it again, this time with a hat trick in Game 1 of the Western Conference finals against the Wings' arch nemesis, the Colorado Avalanche. Detroit would win that series in seven games and beat Carolina in a five-game final for the Cup.

After signing with Calgary following the lockout of 2004–05, McCarty returned to the Wings in time to help them win it all again in 2008.

During this time, McCarty suffered with substance abuse issues, an unfortunate trait he shared with the Wings most famous enforcer and his teammate for one season, Bob Probert.

Probert's many adventures and ordeals with drugs, alcohol, and the law were detailed in his autobiography, which was completed after he died from a heart attack in the summer of 2010.

Dave Strader remembers Probert's death coming as a shock to the hockey world.

"Because there was a period of time when you didn't hear much about him," he explains. "But I had this old saying that you can't fool your body. You can fool your mind into thinking things are okay, but you can't do what he did to his body over time without potentially paying the price. That's probably what happened. It was very sad; he was a happy

ABOVE LEFT: *As of 2012, Darren McCarty, or "D-Mac," was the Red Wings last true enforcer. In a playoff game from April 26, 2008, at the Joe Louis Arena, McCarty is about to put Avalanche fighter Cody McCormick in a very bad position.*

ABOVE RIGHT: *McCormick is in that very bad position.*

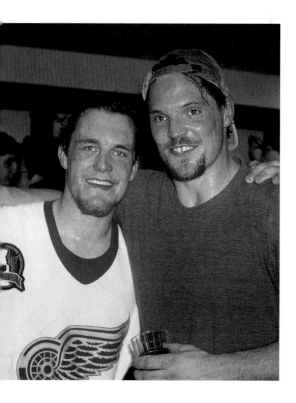

ABOVE LEFT: *McCarty and Kocur, on the right, celebrate the Red Wings 1997 Stanley Cup victory.*

ABOVE RIGHT: *Red Wing Danny Markov goes toe-to-toe with Anaheim Ducks enforcer Shawn Thornton during Game 1 of the 2007 Western Conference finals on May 11, 2007, at the Joe Louis Arena. Detroit won the game 2–1 but went on to lose the series to the eventual Cup champs.*

guy to be around, away from the ice a great guy to be around, and great with the fans."

Gallant agrees, saying, "Quality person, who had some problems as we know, but Bob Probert was a great guy, a team guy. I don't think you'll ever hear anyone say anything bad about Bob Probert. I know he had some troubles, but when he came to the rink he was a friendly guy, he'd give you the shirt off his back, and he'd fight for his teammates. He was a great person, a great friend of ours, and it was a shame he died so young."

"You couldn't stay mad at Bob," recalls Bill Jamieson. "He had this image as a violent enforcer, but he had the softest hands you ever saw around the net. He could have been Clark Gillies, could have been in the Hall of Fame. It's unfortunate he had to battle all those demons, which really affected him all the way from juniors into the NHL. He was a teddy bear, and you couldn't stay mad at him."

"I used to go with him and helped him out with his little speeches to kids as part of his rehab," remembers photographer John Hartman. "He beat up guys on the ice, and he had some drug problems, but he was a nice, great guy off the ice. He was polite, nice, never a bad guy."

"People just absolutely loved him, they loved to be around him," adds Strader. "I think that whole thing with Joey, the Bruise Brothers and all that . . . was a huge part of the resurrection of that franchise."

Probert epitomizes a common refrain heard around the hockey world, that enforcers are easily the toughest guys on the ice, but the biggest sweethearts off of it. He'll be remembered for that, and for being the face of a bygone Red Wings era.

Enforcers whose careers included or began after 1962–1963, a half century ago.

Defensemen included on this list were taken out of the Blueliners chapter list.

RED WINGS REGULAR SEASON STATISTICS	GP	G	A	PTS	PIM
RYAN BARNES (LW)—Dunnville, ON	2	0	0	0	0
#52 / 2003–2004 / Suspended 25 games in OHL for 1999 stick-swinging incident					
FRANK BATHE (D)—Oshawa, ON	26	0	5	5	40
#24 / 1974–1976 / Had 306 PIM with Spitfires in 1973–74 before signing in Detroit					
DARRYL BOOTLAND (RW)—Schomberg, ON	28	1	1	2	83
#27 / 2003–2004, 2006–2007 / Had 390 PIM with Grand Rapids in 2005–06					
JEFF BRUBAKER (LW)—Frederick, MD	1	0	0	0	0
#38 / 1988–1989 / Traded twice, free agent twice, picked up on waivers five times					
REJEAN CLOUTIER (D)—Windsor, QC	5	0	2	2	2
#16, 4 / 1979–1980, 1981–1982 / Ended his career playing in France					
TROY CROWDER (RW)—Sudbury, ON	7	0	0	0	35
#25 / 1991–1993 / Made a name for himself as NJ rookie by bloodying Probert in a fight					
JIM CUMMINS (RW)—Dearborn, MI	8	1	1	2	65
#47, 27 / 1991–1993 / 1,500 penalty minutes in 511 career NHL games					
AARON DOWNEY (RW)—Shelburne, ON	60	1	4	5	123
#20, 44 / 2007–2009 / Cup winner; became Wings part-time strength/conditioning coach					
RICK FOLEY (D)—Niagara Falls, ON	7	0	0	0	4
#19 / 1973–1974 / Played for the old Portland Buckaroos in the Western league					

ENFORCERS

RED WINGS REGULAR SEASON STATISTICS	GP	G	A	PTS	PIM
STU GRIMSON (LW)—Kamloops, BC	68	0	1	1	165
#32 / 1995–1996 / Wings career bridged three seasons; "The Grim Reaper" 6'5", 230 lbs					
BOB HALKIDIS (D)—Toronto, ON	32	1	5	6	99
#21 / 1993–1995 / Owns a hockey school in North Carolina					
DAVE HANSON (D)—Cumberland, WI	11	0	0	0	26
#17 / 1978–1979 / Yes, one of the Hanson Brothers from *Slap Shot*					
GERRY HART (D)—Flin Flon, MB	71	2	7	9	152
#21, 3, 18 / 1968–1972 / Seven seasons with Isles, pre-Cups, after arriving via expansion draft					
DENNIS HEXTALL (LW)—Poplar Point, MB	193	39	82	121	457
#22 / 1976–1979 / Traded to Detroit three months after his brother Bryan was traded away					
JOHN HILWORTH (D)—Jasper, AB	57	1	1	2	89
#19, 29, 4 / 1977–1980 / Edmonton grabbed him on waivers in '80 but no more NHL GP					
BRIAN JOHNSON (RW)—Montreal, QC	3	0	0	0	5
#24 / 1983–1984 / 31 points, 193 PIM, and a Calder Cup win for Adirondack in 1980–81					
KRIS KING (LW)—Bracebridge, ON	58	3	3	6	170
#37, 18 / 1987–1989 / Longtime executive in the NHL hockey operations department					
JOE KOCUR (RW)—Calgary, AB	533	66	66	132	1,963
#26 / 1984–1991, 1996–1999 / Three Cups (one with NYR) and 2,519 PIM in NHL					
JIM KORN (D/LW)—Hopkins, MN	185	11	35	46	458
#26 / 1979–1982 / Went to Toronto in 1982 trade for draft pick that became Joe Kocur					
CLAUDE LOISELLE (C)—Ottawa, ON	128	22	22	44	236
#8, 15, 21 / 1982–1986 / Fought, scored, won draws; veteran hockey exec and pro scout					
MARK MAJOR (LW)—Toronto, ON	2	0	0	0	5
#40 / 1996–1997 / Won a United League Colonial Cup with Flint Generals in 2000					
DAN MALONEY (LW)—Barrie, ON	177	56	81	137	418
#7 / 1975–1978 / To Detroit from LA with Terry Harper and pick in Marcel Dionne deal					
STEVE MARTINSON (D)—Minnetonka, MN	10	1	1	2	84
#36 / 1987–1988 / Longtime coach of the San Diego Gulls when in the WCHL					
BRAD MAY (LW)—Toronto, ON	40	0	1	1	66
#20, 24 / 2009–2010 / Wings his last NHL team of seven, won Cup with Anaheim					
DARREN MCCARTY (RW)—Burnaby, BC	659	120	155	275	1,302
#25 / 1993–2004, 2007–2009 / His "feeding" of Claude Lemieux in '97 a great moment					
KEVIN MCCLELLAND (RW)—Oshawa, ON	64	4	5	9	190
#18 / 1989–1991 / Four Cups with Edmonton, now a minor-league head coach					
BOB MCGILL (D)—Edmonton, AB	12	0	0	0	21
#4 / 1992 / "Big Daddy" went into coaching and hockey broadcasting after playing career					
RANDY MCKAY (RW)—Montreal, QC	83	4	13	17	234
#25, 29, 14 / 1988–1991 / Wings draft pick went on to win two Cups with New Jersey					
BASIL MCRAE (LW)—Beaverton, ON	40	2	2	4	198
#23, 18 / 1985–1987 / Seven clubs, almost 2,500 PIM, older brother of Chris					
CHRIS MCRAE (LW)—Beaverton, ON	7	1	0	1	45
#5 / 1989–1990 / Eye injury ended his Wings season prematurely; 21 NHL GP, 122 PIM					
BARRY MELROSE (D)—Kelvington, SK	35	0	1	1	144
#2 / 1983–1984, 1985–1986 / The face (and hair) of the NHL on ESPN-TV					
KRIS NEWBURY (LW)—Brampton, ON	4	1	0	1	4
#32 / 2009–2010 / Middleweight knocked cold rookie season by Ronald Petrovicky					
JIM NILL (RW)—Hanna, AB	122	11	20	31	156
#8 / 1988–1990 / Longtime assistant GM of Wings was never afraid to drop the mitts					

LEFT: *Long before he went on to become a scout and hockey executive, Claude Loiselle was a scrappy centerman and fine all-around player for the Red Wings between 1981 and 1986.*

ENFORCERS

RED WINGS REGULAR SEASON STATISTICS	GP	G	A	PTS	PIM
BRAD NORTON (D)—Cambridge, MA	6	0	1	1	20
#17 / 2006–2007 / His older brother Jeff went to Michigan and played 725 NHL games					
JOE PATERSON (LW)—Toronto, ON	115	6	11	17	215
#29, 8, 7 / 1980–1984 / Lengthy minor-league coaching career, mostly AHL, since 1992					
JIM PAVESE (D)—New York, NY	46	3	9	12	151
#25 / 1987–1989 / Played 47 games in 1983–84 for the Central League's Montana Magic					
DENNIS POLONICH (RW)—Foam Lake, SK	390	59	82	141	1,242
#22, 8 / 1974–1981, 1982–1983 / 5'6", 165 pounds, hockey's littlest fearless enforcer					
MARC POTVIN (RW)—Ottawa, ON	14	1	0	1	107
#46, 20 / 1990–1992 / Minor-league coach in ECHL and AHL; took his own life in 2006					
BOB PROBERT (LW)—Windsor, ON	474	114	145	259	2,090
#24 / 1985–1994 / One of the greatest enforcers in history; "Bruise Brother" died in 2010					
STEVE RICHMOND (D)—Chicago, IL	29	1	2	3	82
#7 / 1985–1986 / Michigan Wolverine turned fighter as a pro					
TORRIE ROBERTSON (LW)—Victoria, BC	54	3	7	10	175
#14 / 1989–1990 / Brought over to fill in for Probert during his legal troubles					
DANIEL SHANK (RW)—Montreal, QC	64	11	14	25	157
#34 / 1989–1991 / Had 495 PIM for San Diego in the IHL in 77 games in 1992–93					
BRAD SMITH (RW)—Windsor, ON	63	10	3	13	214
#27, 17, 21, 11, 72 / 1981–1985 / "Motor City Smitty" an Avalanche scout for years					
HAROLD SNEPSTS (D)—Edmonton, AB	120	2	23	25	271
#27 / 1985–1988 / It's believed he invented the popular minor-league card game "Snarples"					
DENNIS VIAL (D)—Sault Ste. Marie, ON	45	1	1	2	108
#36, 29 / 1991–1993 / "Dancin' Bear" helped start crazy 2001 brawl in British pro league					
BRYAN WATSON (D)—Bancroft, ON	302	3	44	47	897
#18 / 1965–1967, 1974–1976 / Great pizza at his bar "Bugsy's" in Alexandria, Virginia					
DAVE "TIGER" WILLIAMS (LW)—Weyburn, SK	55	3	8	11	158
#55 / 1984–1985 / NHL career penalty minutes leader; led the league three separate seasons					
BJ YOUNG (RW)—Anchorage, AK	1	0	0	0	0
#36 / 1999–2000 / Career minor-league fighter killed in a car accident in 2005					
HOWIE YOUNG (D)—Toronto, ON	229	9	46	55	660
#2, 22, 4 / 1960–1963, 1966–1968 / Led NHL in PIM 1962–63; "Wild Thing" died in '99					

14 | Muckers and Grinders

> *"The beauty of it is, you come here as a hockey player and you make friends for life within this organization."*
>
> — 17-YEAR RED WINGS GRINDER Kris Draper

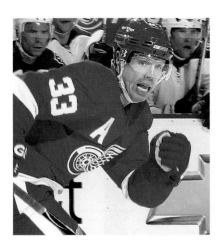

ABOVE: *Two thirds of Detroit's famous "Grind Line," the two permanent members Kirk Maltby and Kris Draper. They both were involved in all four Stanley Cups from 1997 to 2008, and they both still work within the organization following retirement.*

GRINDERS WIN CHAMPIONSHIPS. While the Red Wings legends, whose sweaters hang from the rafters, have played the biggest role in expanding the organization's legacy, it's the unsung muckers and plumbers who contribute the key elements to adding title banners. Whether it's a scorer turned checker, or an ace penalty killer, or shift disturber extraordinaire, the Red Wings have been blessed with some classic, blue-collar grinders.

Kirk Maltby arrived in a trade from Edmonton in 1996, just months before Joey Kocur joined the club for a second time as a free agent. Those two, along with Kris Draper, formed a line together for a while, only to see Kocur gradually give way to Darren McCarty, who was drafted by Detroit and arrived with the big club in 1993. The McCarty, Draper, Maltby threesome became the trademark Grind Line.

"When the Grind Line came out, the next thing you know we've got T-shirts and stuff like that," says Maltby, a Red Wing for 13-plus seasons. "So it was definitely a very prideful thing, and something I'm extremely glad and happy to be a part of. It's nothing like the Production Line . . . we're not trying to kid ourselves, but we feel we had a role and a part in some of the success that we had as a team. It was a nice little perk to have been a part of."

"After family, the thing I'm most proud of is being a part of this organization," states Draper. "I don't have a tattoo, but if I had one it would be that right there," he adds, pointing at the Winged Wheel painted on the wall. "Proud to have played as many games as I have, regular season, postseason with the Detroit Red Wings, and this is my home."

The Grind Line played a part in all four of the club's most recent Stanley Cups. Not bad when you consider Draper was obtained by Wings GM Bryan Murray in 1993 for a dollar.

Draper explains, "I had been traded for future considerations, but nothing had ever been agreed upon. The day that I got called up here, from Adirondack to Detroit, the league called Detroit and said, 'You realize there hasn't been an official trade for Kris Draper.' So my recollection is Bryan Murray called [Winnipeg GM] Mike Smith and said, 'Draper is playing tonight, we need to finish that deal,' and Mike Smith said, 'Give us a dollar and we'll call it a trade.'"

Draper retired in the summer of 2011, a year after Maltby, who retired a year after enforcer McCarty. The previous two are still working within

ABOVE: *The element of speed added to the grinders' effectiveness and Draper had speed to burn. Here he blazes around Maple Leafs defenseman Tomas Kaberle and teammate Tomas Kopecky on October 1, 2006, in Toronto.*

LEFT: *Maltby collides with Pittsburgh Penguins defenseman Kris Letang during Game 1 of the Stanley Cup final in Detroit on May 30, 2009.*

ABOVE: *Nothing friendlier than a little face-wash, as exhibited by Red Wing Mikael Samuelsson against Penguin Ruslan Fedotenko during Game 4 of the Cup final in Pittsburgh on June 4, 2009.*

the organization, which comes as no surprise to Wings assistant general manager Jim Nill, who followed a similar, although less prolific path playing with the Red Wings.

"I was very blessed," says Nill, who, like McCarty, was never afraid to drop the mitts. "I got to come in and play for three years at the end of my career, and Jimmy Devellano took a liking to me and offered me a position. I went down to the minor leagues and started coaching and got a feel for things. From there it's blossomed into this, and it's been 18 years in the front office. We've got a great group of people from the ownership, to Jimmy D, to Kenny Holland, to our scouting staff. We've been together about 15 years, so we know who everybody is, we know how everybody thinks, and we know what type of players we like, so it's been good."

"If you're part of this organization or you come in and see what's going on, you definitely understand why people want to be here and why they try to stay here as long as they can," says Maltby, who began

ABOVE: *Muckers and grinders not only check hard, harass the opposition, and backcheck against the other team's best players, they do whatever they have to do to score. Dan Cleary creates a screen by going airborne, à la Ted Lindsay, against Chicago D-man Matt Walker and goalie Cristobal Huet, during a playoff game on May 27, 2009.*

LEFT: *Grinders on the bench for the national anthem before Game 1 of the 2008 Stanley Cup final: left to right, Kirk Maltby, Mikael Samuelsson, Darren McCarty, and Kris Draper.*

ABOVE: *Paul Woods, who prided himself on shutting down the opposition's best scorers, is shown here shadowing Eric Vail of the Atlanta Flames. Vail won the Calder Trophy as Rookie of the Year in 1975 with a 39-goal, 60-point season.*

work as a scout after leaving the ice. "It really starts right with Mr. and Mrs. Ilitch right on down. It's a great organization to be a part of whether you're on the management side of it or on the sporting side of it playing. Either way, if you're loyal to them, it works both ways, and the key is just working hard."

Longtime Red Wings radio analyst Paul Woods filled that hardworking role in Detroit for seven seasons as a winger, beginning with the upstart 1977–78 club.

"Every day in the NHL is a good day," states Woods. "I look back on nothing but great memories to be able to get on that ice and do whatever. Back in those days the checking lines always played against the top lines, and a chance to play against the best players in the world, that was very exciting and rewarding too."

It's not surprising the fans in Detroit grasp the grinders and hold them high. In a union town, a blue-collar bastion, an industrial-belt stronghold, the guys that dig deep are wildly appreciated. It's why penalty-killing units often get post-shift standing ovations. Whether it was Alex Faulkner or Larry Jeffrey in the '60s, Phil Roberto or J.P. Leblanc in the '70s, Tim Higgins or Ted Nolan in the '80s, or the Grind Line in the '90s and beyond, Detroit fans have always loved versatile forwards that could muck, fight, and contribute some scoring.

Gerard Gallant's name pops to the forefront as a player who would consistently contribute every element. He's the leader and poster boy for the grinder category. He had too many goals to be listed as an enforcer, and too many fights to be listed as a scorer. He was a man who literally did it all.

In a union town, a blue-collar bastion, an industrial-belt stronghold, the guys that dig deep are wildly appreciated.

Gallant played nine memorable seasons with the Red Wings, and set the stage for the grinders that followed. Draper, although not a fighter, arrived the season after Gallant departed. They shared a work ethic, a passion, and a love for the city.

"This is where my kids were born, this is where we're gonna stay, this is where we're gonna live. That's how much it means to me," declares Draper. "It's just an amazing place to play—the people, the friends I've made away from the game, the friends that my family and kids have made, everything about it, it's all because I've been able to stay here as long as I have with this great organization."

ABOVE LEFT: *Gerard Gallant could have been listed as a scorer, a fighter, or a grinder—he was that effective as an all-around player. His numbers back it up. Here, he fronts Montreal Canadiens goalie Brian Hayward.*

ABOVE RIGHT: *Darren McCarty says no-no to future Red Wing Jordin Tootoo of the Predators on April 17, 2004, in Nashville.*

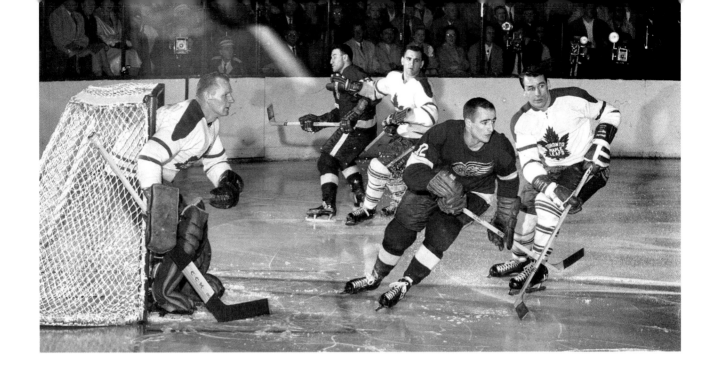

Red Wing Val Fonteyne swoops in front of Maple Leafs goalie Johnny Bower while being pursued by Toronto's Larry Regan.

Forwards whose Red Wings career included or began after 1962–1963, a half century ago.

This section includes not only prolific hard workers, but also everyone else: a few players who were supposed to score and didn't, penalty killers, checkers and middleweights, and those who had less impact than necessary in any specific category.

RED WINGS REGULAR SEASON STATISTICS	GP	G	A	PTS	PIM
JUSTIN ABDELKADER (LW)—Muskegon, MI	209	18	29	47	160
#8 / 2007–2012 / Scored NCAA championship–winning goal for Michigan State in 2007					
GERRY ABEL (LW)—Detroit, MI	1	0	0	0	0
#11 / 1967 / Christmas baby and son of Hall of Famer and GM/coach Sid					
MICAH AIVAZOFF (C)—Powell River, BC	59	4	4	8	58
#27 / 1993–1994 / Of Armenian descent, finished his pro career in Germany					
EARL ANDERSON (RW)—Roseau, MN	45	7	3	10	12
#16 / 1974–1975 / Popular while in Boston, injuries shortened career					
RON ANDERSON (RW)—Red Deer, AB	25	2	0	2	21
#22, 15 / 1967–1968 / Scored the first goal in WHA history					
JOAKIM ANDERSSON (C)—Munkedal, Sweden	5	0	0	0	0
#63 / 2011–2012 / All-time leader for Sweden in international games played as a junior					
PHILIPPE AUDET (LW)—Ottawa, ON	4	0	0	0	0
#22 / 1989–1990 / Might have been listed as an "enforcer" if he hadn't lost all his fights					
SEAN AVERY (LW)—North York, ON	75	7	8	15	188
#42 / 2001–2003 / Named "Little Pup" by vets when he showed up acting like a big dog					
GARNET "ACE" BAILEY (LW)—Lloydminster, SK	58	11	25	36	49
#12 / 1973–1974 / Died when his plane hit World Trade Center, 9/11/2001					
DAVE BARR (RW)—Toronto, ON	293	82	118	200	276
#22 / 1986–1991 / Assistant coach in IHL and NHL since playing days					

GRINDERS

RED WINGS REGULAR SEASON STATISTICS	GP	G	A	PTS	PIM
TODD BERTUZZI (LW/C)—Sudbury, ON	242	50	81	131	221
#44 / 2006–2007, 2009–2012 / Versatile; remembered most as Canuck for Steve Moore attack					
MIKE BLOOM (LW)—Ottawa, ON	134	23	28	51	131
#25 / 1975–1977 / Played on a line with Marcel Dionne in St. Catharines in the OHA					
DAN BOLDUC (LW)—Waterville, ME	100	22	18	40	33
#19 / 1978–1980 / Harvard grad played for U.S. Olympic team in 1976					
HENRY BOUCHA (C)—Warroad, MN	159	34	26	60	116
#12, 16 / 1972–1974 / Full-blooded Chippewa Indian, known for his red headband					
RICK BOWNESS (RW)—Moncton, NB	61	8	11	19	76
#11 / 1977–1978 / Coached in NHL off and on since 1984					
JOHN BRENNEMAN (LW)—Fort Erie, ON	9	0	2	2	0
#21 / 1967–1968 / Finished playing career in Austria					
DOUG BROWN (RW)—Southborough, MA	427	74	97	171	108
#17 / 1994–2001 / Claimed by Nashville in '98 expansion draft, then traded back					
YURI BUTSAYEV (C/LW)—Togliatti, Russia	75	6	4	10	16
#22 / 1999–2001 / After stop with Atlanta, has played in Russian pro leagues since 2002					
KYLE CALDER (LW)—Mannville, AB	19	5	9	14	8
#17 / 2007 / Fine junior player in Regina, showed flashes of being an NHL scorer					
CRAIG CAMERON (RW)—Edmonton, AB	1	0	0	0	0
#14 / 1966–1967 / Online, there is a Craig Cameron ("ugliest player of all time") fan club					
BILLY CARROLL (C)—Toronto, ON	52	3	6	9	17
#12 / 1985–1987 / Blessed: seven NHL seasons; three Cups with Islanders, one with Edmonton					
GREG CARROLL (C)—Gimley, MB	36	2	9	11	8
#25 / 1979 / Played for the New England Whalers and Cincinnati Stingers in the WHA					
CHRIS CICHOCKI (RW)—Detroit, MI	61	10	11	21	23
#15 / 1985–1986 / Prolific goal scorer at Michigan Tech					
STEVE COATES (RW)—Toronto, ON	5	1	0	1	24
#17 / 1976–1977 / Blew groin on breakaway, dumped puck in the corner, Olympia booed					
BILL COLLINS (RW)—Ottawa, ON	239	54	77	131	129
#22 / 1971–1974 / Came from Montreal with Redmond and Charron for Mahovlich					
BRIAN CONACHER (LW)—Toronto, ON	22	3	1	4	4
#24 / 1971–1972 / Uncles Roy and Charlie, former Wings, and dad Lionel, all HOF					
CHRIS CONNER (RW)—Westland, MI	8	1	2	3	0
#41 / 2011–2012 / Grew up & played hockey in Livonia with Canucks forward Ryan Kesler					
BOB COOK (RW)—Sudbury, ON	13	3	1	4	4
#12 / 1971–1972 / Canucks sold "Cookie" to the Wings in November 1971					
GARY CROTEAU (LW)—Sudbury, ON	10	0	2	2	2
#11 / 1969–1970 / Expansion team specialist; played for Kings, Seals, Scouts, Rockies					
BILLY DEA (LW)—Edmonton, AB	210	35	25	60	28
#21 / 1956–1958, 1969–1971 / "Hard Rock" also listed in the "Bench Bosses" chapter					
NELSON DEBENEDET (LW)—Cordeno, Italy	15	4	1	5	2
#23 / 1973–1974 / Played three seasons at Michigan State; later 31 games with Pittsburgh					
BOYD DEVEREAUX (C)—Seaforth, ON	256	23	40	63	74
#21 / 2000–2004 / Former sixth-overall pick of Oilers, won a Cup with Wings in '02					
BOB DILLABOUGH (LW)—Belleville, ON	9	0	0	0	4
#22, 12, 11, 24 / 1961–1965 / One playoff game in '63 and '64 after no regular-season games					
DALLAS DRAKE (LW/RW)—Trail, BC	184	31	51	82	171
#28, 17 / 1992–1994, 2007–2008 / NCAA title at Northern Michigan in '91; Cup in 2008					

ABOVE: *Martin Lapointe is congratulated by Mathieu Dandenault after scoring against the Los Angeles Kings in a playoff game at the Joe, April 15, 2000. Lapointe was a borderline checker/scorer, who cashed in big time with Boston in 2001 free agency.*

OPPOSITE TOP: *Dan Cleary sandwiched between Penguins goalie Marc-Andre Fleury and defenseman Mark Eaton during Game 5 of the Stanley Cup final in Detroit on June 6, 2009.*

GRINDERS

RED WINGS REGULAR SEASON STATISTICS	GP	G	A	PTS	PIM
KRIS DRAPER (C)—Toronto, ON	1,137	158	203	361	781
#33 / 1993–2011 / Acquired from Jets for $1; Game 2, 1998 final, overtime GWG					
MURRAY EAVES (LW)—Calgary, AB	8	0	1	1	2
#38, 43 / 1987–1988, 1989–1990 / Younger brother of longtime collegiate coach Mike					
PATRICK EAVES (RW)—Calgary, AB	138	25	18	43	42
#17 / 2009–2012 / Played at Boston College while his dad Mike coached at Wisconsin					
TIM ECCLESTONE (LW/RW)—Toronto, ON	191	40	80	120	90
#17 / 1971–1973 / Came from Blues with Berenson for Garry Unger and Wayne Connelly					
BO ELIK (LW)—Geralton, ON	3	0	0	0	0
#17 / 1962–1963 / Barely made the book on two counts; AHL Rookie of the Year in 1957					
MATT ELLIS (LW)—Welland, ON	51	2	4	6	12
#8 / 2006–2008 / In 2005–06 was Grand Rapids Griffins' youngest captain in history					
CORY EMMERTON (C)—St. Thomas, ON	73	7	4	11	14
#48 / 2010–2012 / First goal came in first NHL game, January 22, 2011, in loss to Chicago					
BOB ERREY (LW)—Montreal, QC	137	18	34	52	124
#12, 21 / 1995–1997 / 53 goals his final year of junior in Peterborough; two Cups in Pitt					
ALEX FAULKNER (C)—Bishop Falls, NL	100	15	17	32	15
#12 / 1962–1964 / Played senior league for the Woodsmen, Kinsemen, and Cee Bees					

GRINDERS

RED WINGS REGULAR SEASON STATISTICS	GP	G	A	PTS	PIM
BRENT FEDYK (LW)—Yorkton, SK	162	24	32	56	88
#28, 39, 7, 15, 14 / 1987–1992 / Calder Cup with Adirondack in '89; three-plus seasons in Philly					
VALTTERI FILPPULA (C, LW)—Vantaa, Finland	442	91	143	234	152
#41, 51 / 2005–2012 / Emerging scorer the first Finnish player to ever play for Detroit					
VAL FONTEYNE (LW)—Wetaskiwin, AB	375	29	53	82	16
#19, 21, 11, 8 / 1959–1963, 1965–1967 / Lost three Cup finals; five seasons with no penalties					
JODY GAGE (RW)—Toronto, ON	50	11	12	23	24
#16, 17, 21 / 1980–1982, 1983–1984 / AHL MVP with 60 goals for Rochester in '88					
GERARD GALLANT (LW)—Summerside, PEI	563	207	260	467	1,600
#17 / 1984–1993 / Fighter, grinder, and scorer; later head coach of Columbus					
JOHAN GARPENLOV (LW)—Stockholm, Sweden	87	19	23	42	22
#15 / 1990–1992 / With Sharks that upset Wings in '94; with Florida for Cup final '96					
BRENT GILCHRIST (LW)—Moose Jaw, SK	169	20	25	45	113
#40 / 1997–2002 / Won Cup in 1998; missed most of next season after hernia surgery					
DANNY GRUEN (LW)—Thunder Bay, ON	20	1	3	4	7
#23, 12 / 1972–1974 / Grinder could score; led Central League in points/PIMs in 1972–73					
MARC HABSCHEID (C/RW)—Swift Current, SK	112	24	19	43	55
#25 / 1989–1991 / Scored 64 goals in last season of junior for Saskatoon Blades					

ABOVE: *If he wasn't such a pest, he'd be listed as a scorer. Tomas Holmstrom in his familiar stomping ground, in, near, or around the opponent's crease. Marc-Andre Fleury coughs up the rebound as "Homer" battles with Penguins defenseman Darryl Sydor at the Joe on November 11, 2008.*

GRINDERS

RED WINGS REGULAR SEASON STATISTICS	GP	G	A	PTS	PIM
MURRAY HALL (RW)—Kirkland Lake, ON	13	4	3	7	4
#25, 20, 14 / 1965–1967 / Played three seasons with Gordie Howe in Houston in WHA					
TED HAMPSON (C)—Togo, SK	110	22	54	76	14
#20, 17, 16 / 1963–1965, 1966–1968 / Son Gord played at Michigan and four games in NHL					
BILLY HARRIS (C)—Toronto, ON	24	1	4	5	6
#14 / 1965–1966 / "Hinky" won three Cups with Toronto from 1962–64					
MARK HARTIGAN (C)—St. John, BC	23	3	1	4	16
#44 / 2007–2008 / Cup rings with Anaheim and Detroit, but name not etched either time					
BUSTER HARVEY (RW)—Fredericton, NB	89	19	20	39	43
#27 / 1976–1977 / Frederick John Charles was Minnesota's first-round pick in 1970					
ED HATOUM (RW)—Beirut, Lebanon	21	2	3	5	4
#18, 20 / 1968–1970 / First player from Lebanon to make it to the NHL					
DARREN HELM (C)—Winnipeg, MB	248	32	51	83	52
#43 / 2007–2012 / Speedster suffered lacerated forearm in first game of 2012 playoffs					
BRYAN HEXTALL JR. (C)—Winnipeg, MB	21	0	4	4	29
#12 / 1975–1976 / Dad a Hall of Famer, brother a Red Wing, son Ron an All-Star goalie					
GLENN HICKS (LW)—Red Deer, AB	108	6	12	18	127
#23, 22 / 1979–1981 / Borderline enforcer; brother Doug was NHL D-man for nine seasons					
TIM HIGGINS (RW)—Ottawa, ON	181	29	36	65	280
#20 / 1986–1989 / 10th-overall pick in the 1978 draft for Chicago					
JIM HILLER (RW)—Port Alberni, BC	21	2	6	8	19
#14 / 1993 / With Dallas Drake for NCAA title at N. Michigan and while a Red Wing					
BILL HOGABOAM (C)—Swift Current, SK	221	61	84	145	74
#23, 15, 22 / 1972–1976, 1979–1980 / "Hogi" took grief at Olympia during lean years					
TOMAS HOLMSTROM (LW)—Pitea, Sweden	1,026	243	287	530	769
#15, 96 / 1996–2012 / A fearless warrior and goal scorer in front of the net					

GRINDERS

RED WINGS REGULAR SEASON STATISTICS	GP	G	A	PTS	PIM
JIRI HUDLER (C)—Olomouc, Czech	409	87	127	214	160
#26 / 2003–2009, 2010–2012 / Left in 2009 for a season to play for Moscow Dynamo (KHL)					
MATT HUSSEY (C)—New Haven, CT	5	0	0	0	2
#43 / 2006–2007 / Former Wisconsin Badger has spent the last few years in Germany					
MIROSLAV IHNACAK (LW)—Poprad, Czech	1	0	0	0	0
#35 / 1988–1989 / Played 55 games in Toronto with brother Peter, who played eight seasons					
EARL INGARFIELD JR. (C)—New York, NY	22	2	1	3	16
#21 / 1981 / His dad a popular Ranger; Jr. moved with Flames from Atlanta to Calgary					
GARY JARRETT (LW)—Toronto, ON	72	18	21	39	20
#15, 8 / 1966–1968 / Part of an eight-player deal from Toronto and a six-player deal to Oakland					
LARRY JEFFREY (LW)—Goderich, ON	160	24	34	58	217
#21, 14 / 1961–1964, 1969 / Traded back in '69 but didn't play; car accident ended career					
AL JOHNSON (RW)—Winnipeg, MB	103	21	27	48	28
#15 / 1960–1963 / Won Allan Cup, senior league's top prize, with '64 Winnipeg Maroons					
DANNY JOHNSON (C)—Winnipegosis, MB	43	2	5	7	8
#8 / 1971–1972 / Former Central League MVP died in 1993					
GREG JOHNSON (C)—Thunder Bay, ON	177	33	48	81	78
#23 / 1993–1997 / Traded to Pittsburgh for Tomas Sandstrom before the Cup win					
EDDIE JOHNSTONE (RW)—Brandon, MB	55	13	11	24	56
#17, 34, 7 / 1983–1984, 1985–1987 / Came with Eddie Mio and Ron Duguay from NYR					
EDDIE JOYAL (C)—Edmonton, AB	107	20	29	49	53
#21 / 1962–1965 / Found his scoring touch as original member of LA Kings					
AL KARLANDER (C)—Lac La Hache, BC	212	36	56	92	70
#15 / 1969–1973 / Played two seasons for Indianapolis Racers and coach Jacques Demers					
DAVE KELLY (RW)—Chatham, ON	16	2	0	2	4
#25 / 1976–1977 / Played with Brian Burke and Ron Wilson at Providence College					
SHELDON KENNEDY (RW)—Elkhorn, MB	183	31	33	64	122
#12, 28, 15 / 1989–1994 / Career disrupted by car accident in '90 and cycling crash in '97					
ALAN KERR (RW)—Hazelton, BC	58	3	8	11	133
#18 / 1991–1992 / Spent seven seasons with Islanders just after their Cups					
MARK KIRTON (C)—Regina, SK	134	33	42	75	92
#23, 16 / 1980–1982 / Traded in for Jim Rutherford (Tor), out for Ivan Boldirev (Vanc)					
MIKE KNUBLE (RW)—Toronto, ON	62	8	6	14	16
#22 / 1996–1998 / Power forward got name on Cup in '98; still playing with Washington					
LADISLAV KOHN (RW)—Uherske Hradiste, Czech	4	0	0	0	4
#15 / 2001 / Left NHL to play in Finland, Russia, and Czech Republic					
TOMAS KOPECKY (RW)—Ilava, Czech	183	12	20	32	113
#32, 28, 82 / 2005–2009 / Cups with Detroit and Chicago; GWG in Game 1 of 2010 final					
MIKE KORNEY (RW)—Dauphin, MB	59	9	9	18	41
#2, 19 / 1973–1976 / Played with eight different minor-league teams during stint in Detroit					
DALE KRENTZ (LW)—Steinbach, MB	30	5	3	8	9
#28, 39 / 1986–1989 / Former MSU Spartan finished career with six seasons in Germany					
JIM KRULICKI (LW)—Kitchener, ON	14	0	1	1	0
#19 / 1971 / Won Central League title and then AHL Calder Cup the same season ('70)					
MIKE KRUSHELNYSKI (C/LW)—Montreal, QC	20	2	3	5	6
#18 / 1994–1995 / "Krusher" won face-offs and three Cups with the Oilers dynasty					
DAVE KRYSKOW (LW)—Edmonton, AB	18	1	4	5	4
#7 / 1975 / Played most of 1974–75 season for expansion Capitals team that went 8–67–5					

GRINDERS

RED WINGS REGULAR SEASON STATISTICS	GP	G	A	PTS	PIM
MARK KUMPEL (RW)—Wakefield, MA	18	0	3	3	4
#18 / 1987–1988 / Bridged two seasons in Detroit, traded to Winnipeg for winger Jim Nill					
CLAUDE LAFORGE (LW)—Sorel, QC	123	15	17	32	46
#8, 21 / 1958–1959, 1960–1962, 1963–1965 / Member of expansion Philadelphia Flyers					
MARK LAMB (C)—Ponteix, SK	22	2	1	3	8
#8 / 1986–1987 / 17 points in 22 playoff games with Oilers Cup team in 1990					
LANE LAMBERT (RW)—Melfort, SK	176	36	29	65	349
#14 / 1983–1986 / Won Calder Cup with Adirondack in '86; a head coach in Milwaukee					
JOSH LANGFELD (RW)—Fridley, MN	33	0	2	2	12
#15 / 2006–2007 / Scored GWG for Michigan over BC in NCAA title game in '98					
DARRYL LAPLANTE (C)—Calgary, AB	35	0	6	6	10
#21 / 1997–2000 / Two games in 1997–98 regular season, no playoffs, name not on Cup					
MARTIN LAPOINTE (RW)—Ville Ste. Pierre, QC	552	108	122	230	888
#22, 20 / 1991–2001 / Two Cups in Detroit, Boston signed him to $20 million deal in 2001					
BRIAN LAVENDER (LW)—Edmonton, AB	30	2	2	4	25
#11, 18 / 1973–1974 / Bridged two seasons in Detroit; original member of Isles expansion					
DANNY LAWSON (RW)—Toronto, ON	45	5	7	12	21
#22, 18 / 1968–1969 / Scorer in juniors, reignited in WHA, led league in goals in 1972–73					
J.P. LEBLANC (C)—South Durham, QC	147	13	28	41	87
#22, 18, 21 / 1975–1978 / Former Michigan Stag went on to coach K-Wings in IHL					
RENE LECLERC (RW)—Ville de Vanier, QC	87	10	11	21	105
#8, 15 / 1968–1969, 1970–1971 / Wayne Gretzky's teammate with Indianapolis Racers					
VILLE LEINO (LW/RW)—Savonlinna, Finland	55	9	7	16	12
#21 / 2008–2009 / Blossomed in playoffs for Philly in 2010					
REAL LEMIEUX (LW)—Victoriaville, QC	1	0	0	0	0
#14 / 1966–1967 / 211 PIM same year in Memphis; never more than 68 in seven NHL seasons					
LOWELL MACDONALD (LW)—New Glasgow, NS	46	5	6	11	10
#10, 8, 11 / 1962–1965 / Led in goals and points for Hamilton's '62 Memorial Cup win					
BRIAN MACLELLAN (LW)—Guelph, ON	23	1	5	6	38
#27 / 1991–1992 / Bowling Green Falcon had two 30-plus goal seasons in NHL					
JOHN MACMILLAN (LW)—Lethbridge, AB	23	0	4	4	6
#12, 19, 11 / 1963–1965 / Two Cups in Toronto; rare, early collegian to reach NHL					
KIRK MALTBY (RW)—Guelph, ON	908	107	115	222	683
#18 / 1996–2010 / "Malts" helped make Grind Line famous with Draper and McCarty					
KEN MANN (RW)—Hamilton, ON	1	0	0	0	0
#17 / 1975–1976 / A scorer in juniors and minors; took one NHL shot and was a minus-1					
GARY MARSH (LW)—Toronto, ON	6	1	3	4	4
#14 / 1967–1968 / Allan Cup as player, Centennial Cup as coach, both in Orillia, Ontario					
DON MARTINEAU (RW)—Kimberley, BC	10	0	1	1	0
#29, 20 / 1975–1977 / Former Atlanta Flames draft pick; died in 2006					
GARY MCADAM (LW)—Smiths Falls, ON	40	5	14	19	27
#19 / 1981 / Scored 40 goals for Rochester Americans team that won Calder Cup in 1983					
RICK MCCANN (C)—Hamilton, ON	43	1	4	5	6
#8, 22, 18, 24 / 1967–1972, 1974–1975 / Michigan Tech and Team Canada pre-NHL					
BRIAN MCCUTCHEON (LW)—Toronto, ON	37	3	1	4	7
#27, 29, 8 / 1974–1977 / Coached in college, in Austria, in minors, and NHL since 1978					
AB MCDONALD (LW)—Winnipeg, MB	74	10	19	29	8
#22, 12 / 1965–1966, 1971–1972 / Won Cups his first four years in the league					

RED WINGS REGULAR SEASON STATISTICS	GP	G	A	PTS	PIM
BILLY MCNEILL (RW)—Edmonton, AB	257	21	46	67	142
#14 / 1956–1960, 1962–1964 / Traded to NYR in '60, refused to report, suspended, retired					
HOWIE MENARD (C)—Timmins, ON	3	0	0	0	0
#12 / 1963–1964 / Had 13 assists in 14 Memorial Cup games in 1962 title with Hamilton					
DREW MILLER (LW)—Dover, NJ	213	34	28	62	43
#20 / 2009–2012 / Won a Cup as rookie in '07; a Spartan, like cousins Kevin, Kip, and Kelly					
KEVIN MILLER (C)—Lansing, MI	95	25	30	55	57
#23, 28 / 1991–1992, 2003–2004 / National title in 1986 with Michigan State					
TOM MILLER (C)—Kitchener, ON	29	1	7	8	9
#12 / 1970–1971 / Part of back-to-back national championships at University of Denver					
GARRY MONAHAN (LW)—Barrie, ON	51	3	4	7	24
#11 / 1969–1970 / Played junior hockey with Mickey Redmond; finished career in Japan					
HANK MONTEITH (LW)—Stratford, ON	77	5	12	17	6
#15, 11, 19 / 1968–1971 / Scored a lot over five (!) seasons at the University of Toronto					
MARK MOWERS (RW)—Whitesboro, NY	98	7	19	26	20
#20, 44 / 2003–2004, 2005–2006 / Played in Switzerland after finishing in NHL					
BRIAN MURPHY (C)—Toronto, ON	1	0	0	0	0
#17 / 1974–1975 / Rights traded from Toronto to LA, and then LA to Toronto two years later					
RON MURPHY (LW)—Hamilton, ON	90	30	26	56	42
#12 / 1964–1966 / Name on Stanley Cup with Chicago (1961) and Boston (1970)					
JAN MURSAK (LW)—Maribor, Slovenia	44	2	2	4	4
#39 / 2010–2012 / One of two Slovenians ever to play in the NHL (Anze Kopitar—Kings)					
TED NOLAN (C)—Sault Ste. Marie, ON	60	5	15	20	71
#29, 8 / 1981–1982, 1983–1984 / Borderline enforcer added offense; NHL head coach					
HANK NOWAK (LW)—Oshawa, ON	56	8	14	22	69
#11 / 1974–1975 / Played for six minor-league teams between 1977 and 1980					
MARK PEDERSON (LW)—Prelate, SK	2	0	0	0	2
#18 / 1993–1994 / Went to play in Austria, Sweden, Switzerland, and Germany					
JIM PETERS JR. (C)—Montreal, QC	54	6	7	13	10
#25, 11, 21 / 1965–1968 / Claim to fame was trade to LA for Terry Sawchuk in 1968					
BRENT PETERSON (C)—Calgary, AB	91	8	20	28	32
#27, 12 / 1978–1981 / Part of awful trade to Buffalo with Mike Foligno and Dale McCourt					
ALEX PIRUS (RW)—Toronto, ON	4	0	2	2	0
#14 / 1979–1980 / Scorer at Notre Dame long before Irish were known for hockey					
ROB PLUMB (LW)—Kingston, ON	14	3	2	5	2
#18, 17 / 1977–1979 / Too little for the big show, lit up Swiss-league scoring later					
ANDRE PRONOVOST (LW)—Shawinigan Falls, QC	120	20	22	42	72
#15, 21 / 1962–1965 / Won four Cups with Montreal his first four years in the league					
NELSON PYATT (C)—Port Arthur, ON	14	0	0	0	2
#26, 23, 22 / 1973–1975 / Father of NHLers Tom and Taylor Pyatt					
DAVE RICHARDSON (LW)—St. Boniface, MB	1	0	0	0	0
#21 / 1967–1968 / Minor-league scrapper was 1962 IHL Rookie of the Year in Fort Wayne					
MATTIAS RITOLA (LW)—Borlange, Sweden	7	0	1	1	0
#42 / 2007–2008, 2009–2010 / Waiver pickup by Tampa, saw little playoff action in 2011					
PHIL ROBERTO (RW)—Niagara Falls, ON	83	14	34	48	98
#27 / 1974–1976 / Went on to play for NHL's Scouts, Rockies, and Barons					
DOUG ROBERTS (RW)—Detroit, MI	134	27	39	66	53
#25, 14, 26 / 1966–1968, 1973–1975 / Former Spartan, brother of Gord and dad of David					

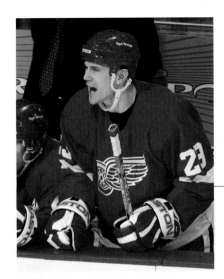

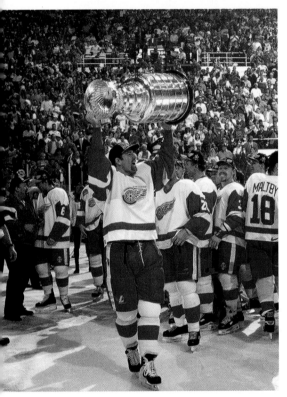

GRINDERS

RED WINGS REGULAR SEASON STATISTICS	GP	G	A	PTS	PIM
DAVE ROCHEFORT (C)—Red Deer, AB #23 / 1966–1967 / Won a Memorial Cup with Edmonton Oil Kings in 1966	1	0	0	0	0
LEON ROCHEFORT (RW)—Cap-de-la-Madeleine, QC #11 / 1971–1972 / Bridged two seasons, an All-Star with Flyers in '68, Montreal Cup in '71	84	19	16	35	12
MARC RODGERS (RW)—Shawville, QC #37 / 1999–2000 / Won IHL Turner Cups with Utah and Chicago two years apart	21	1	1	2	10
STACY ROEST (C)—Lethbridge, AB #23, 39 / 1998–2000 / Minnesota Wild's expansion draft pick from Detroit in June, 2000	108	11	17	28	26
TOM ROWE (RW)—Lynn, MA #8, 12 / 1982–1983 / First American with 30-goal NHL season; asst. coach Cup win in '06	51	6	10	16	44
MIKAEL SAMUELSSON (RW)—Mariefred, Sweden #37 / 2005–2009 / Member of Triple Gold Club; Cup, World Championship, Olympics	278	67	92	159	146
KEVIN SCHAMEHORN (RW)—Calgary, AB #18, 25 / 1976–1977, 1979–1980 / Minor-league scorer with zero points in 10 NHL games	5	0	0	0	13
TIM SHEEHY (RW)—Fort Frances, ON #29 / 1977–1978 / Minus-13 in Detroit; good scorer during six seasons in WHA	15	0	0	0	0
JIM SHIRES (LW)—Edmonton, AB #23 / 1970–1971 / Senior on University of Denver's National Championship team in 1968	20	2	1	3	22
GARY SHUCHUK (RW)—Edmonton, AB #48 / 1990–1991 / Led NCAA in scoring and Wisconsin to title at "The Joe" in 1990	6	1	2	3	6
DAVE SILK (RW)—Scituate, MA #8 / 1984–1985 / Member of "Miracle on Ice" 1980 U.S. Olympic team	12	2	0	2	10
MIKE SILLINGER (C)—Regina, SK #23, 12 / 1991–1995 / Played for a record 12 NHL teams and was traded nine times	129	14	45	59	28
BJORN SKAARE (C)—Oslo, Norway #25 / 1978–1979 / Led Norwegian league in scoring in '81; killed in car accident in 1989	1	0	0	0	0
DEREK SMITH (C)—Quebec City, QC #24 / 1981–1983 / With Gare, Schoenfeld from Buffalo for Foligno, Peterson, McCourt	91	13	18	31	22
TED SNELL (RW)—Ottawa, ON #8 / 1974–1975 / Returned to his longtime Hershey club, only to lose Calder final in '76	20	0	4	4	6
SANDY SNOW (RW)—Glace Bay, NS #15 / 1968–1969 / Traded with Terry Sawchuk to New York for Larry Jeffrey in 1969	3	0	0	0	2
KEN SOLHEIM (LW)—Hythe, AB #26 / 1983 / Scored goal in his first NHL game; Gretzky's 1,000th assist came on later goal	10	0	0	0	2
VIC STASIUK (LW)—Lethbridge, AB #11 / 1950–1955, 1961–1963 / Three Cups in first stint with Wings; scorer in Boston	330	52	84	136	200
RAY STASZAK (RW)—Philadelphia, PA #8 / 1985 / Suffered a career-ending groin injury against the North Stars	4	0	1	1	7
BLAIR STEWART (C)—Winnipeg, MB #22, 18, 25 / 1973–1975 / Shipped to DC to drop the mitts for a bad Capitals team	36	0	9	9	54
ART STRATTON (C)—Winnipeg, MB #8 / 1963–1964 / Original Pittsburgh Penguin and MVP in three different minor leagues	5	0	3	3	2
BILL SUTHERLAND (C)—Regina, SK #8, 18 / 1971–1972 / 12 years in minors, then regular-season NHL debut as original Flyer	5	0	1	1	2
CHRIS TANCILL (C)—Livonia, MI #48, 18 / 1991–1993 / NCAA Championship MVP for Wisconsin in 1990; four NHL teams	5	1	0	1	2
TED TAYLOR (LW)—Oak Lake, MB #18 / 1966–1967 / Played with Gordie and sons in Houston in WHA from 1973–77	2	0	0	0	0

GRINDERS

RED WINGS REGULAR SEASON STATISTICS	GP	G	A	PTS	PIM
TIM TAYLOR (C)—Stratford, ON	139	15	22	37	107
#38, 37 / 1993–1997 / "The Tool Man" won Cup with Detroit and then with Tampa in '04					
DOUG VOLMAR (RW)—Cleveland, OH	41	9	6	15	10
#23, 19, 27 / 1969–1972 / All-America at MSU, only appeared in playoffs first NHL year					
WES WALZ (C)—Calgary, AB	2	0	0	0	0
#26 / 1995–1996 / Original member of the Minnesota Wild after four seasons in Switzerland					
BRIAN WATTS (LW)—Hagersville, ON	4	0	0	0	0
#15 / 1975–1976 / Former Michigan Tech Huskie finished his career in Sweden					
STAN WEIR (C)—Ponoka, AB	57	5	24	29	2
#14 / 1982–1983 / Grew up going to Glen Sather hockey camps; played for him in NHL					
FRED WILLIAMS (C)—Saskatoon, SK	44	2	5	7	10
#15 / 1976–1977 / Lost Calder Cup to Adirondack with Maine; brother Gord a Flyer					
MIKE WONG (C)—Minneapolis, MN	22	1	1	2	12
#19, 22 / 1975–1976 / Part Chinese and Native American, played for U.S. in 1974 WJC					
PAUL WOODS (LW)—Hespeler, ON	501	72	124	196	276
#15 / 1977–1984 / "Woodsy" known to fans as the Wings longtime radio commentator					
LARRY WRIGHT (C)—Regina, SK	66	3	6	9	13
#25 / 1977–1978 / Eighth overall pick of Philly in '71 played in Germany before Detroit					

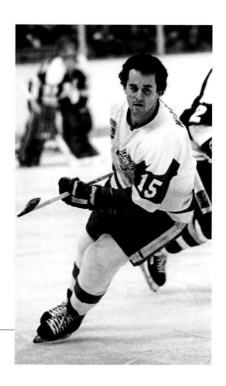

15 | Shooters

> *"It's a privilege that I don't take for granted, how special it is to go to work there every day, how cool and unique, and what a tremendous opportunity I have in front of me."*
>
> — Dave Reginek, RED WINGS PHOTOGRAPHER SINCE 2003

OPENING SPREAD: The before and after in less than a second: the shot on the left of the Blackhawks Michael Frolik and the Red Wings Valtteri Filppula was taken by Red Wings photographer Dave Reginek through a photographer's hole in the glass at the Joe Louis Arena. In an instant, as the two players meet for the puck, Frolik's stick comes through that hole and strikes Reginek in the face, just as his friend Terri Coppens took this photo. "Thwak! It sounded and felt like a firecracker went off in my head," Reginek remembers. All a part of the job. A great job.

BOTTOM: Hockey photographers, among other talents, left to right, Bob "Red" Wimmer, JD McCarthy, and Jim Mackey.

THESE SHOOTERS DON'T GO TOP SHELF, where mama keeps the Ripple; these shooters go high and low, from the rafters to along the ice, to take snapshots no one else gets to take. They don't slap, they click. These are the guys responsible for many of the great photographs in this book and throughout the last 50 years of Red Wings hockey.

Bob "Red" Wimmer, a Wings photographer from 1959 to 1988, was the only extra person on hand for what's likely considered the most important moment in the franchise's last 50 years.

"Mike Ilitch made me wait in the lobby outside Bruce Norris's office for a while," Wimmer recalls. "And then he told me 'I'm buying the Red Wings, I'm here to sign the papers.'"

That was in 1982, for $8 million, and the change of ownership turned the franchise around. Wimmer captured the moment—a pretty amazing scene for a guy who only took photos part time while working for 32 years as a school teacher.

All of the Wings photographers have been moonlighters. Wimmer's cohort Jim Mackey also took shots on the side at Wings games while working full time in the art department at WJBK-TV.

"I was an artist; sketches, cartoons," Mackey says. "So I guess the photography was a natural extension."

Standout moments for Mackey are simple ones. "I just remember being wowed by the fights. I remember one guy from Edmonton getting pummeled. It was incredible to watch from the penalty box."

The next part-time team photographer, John Hartman, began his gig through a stroke of luck. It started as a simple gesture in 1980 for the parents of Calgary rookie Steve Konroyd. Roaming around as a fan with a camera, Hartman took pictures during a Flames game in Detroit at the Joe Louis Arena.

Hartman says, "My son Mike had gone to hockey camp in Oakville, where Konroyd had taken him under his wing, given advice, guidance, so I took pictures of Steve to return the favor, and used to send them to his parents. That night, I managed to get downstairs, and I shot the third period. I ended up taking the photos to the Wings the next season and they hired me to be their color photographer."

It didn't take long to become part of the Red Wings family.

"My younger son Ricky played in a local league," remembers Hartman, "and there was a spring league in Redford, and they'd only get the ice for an hour every once in a while for practice. [Wings player] Dwight Foster put a note up on the Red Wings wall to get anyone interested in coming out. They all knew Ricky, and they loved Ricky, as he'd go in the room all the time. We go to practice, and eight Red Wing players showed up for this one practice as a favor to me. I mean, there were two guys —Eddie Mio was one of them—two NHLers coaching our goalie!"

Hartman's older son Mike actually developed enough to get to hockey's highest level, also with some assistance from the Wings. The scrappy left-winger, who developed in Detroit-area youth programs, went on to play almost 400 games in the NHL.

"Those players were absolutely fabulous with Mike, helping him along," adds Hartman.

Hartman became a mentor himself, eventually passing on his puck-photography gig to his former assistant Mark Hicks. Before departing, he left a league-wide legacy with his installation of strobes in the ceiling of the Joe. The remote-controlled flashes allow photographers to get instantaneous light while taking shots from anywhere in the building.

"Jimmy Varon [of *The Detroit News*] and I went up there during the summer during a practice and put up strobes and tried them," he recalls. "Greg Stefan was the Red Wings goalie at the time; we went up to see if they bothered him, then we got permission to use them at a game, and then a couple more games. That was it. A couple years later *Sports Illustrated* came out with a memo: if your photo isn't strobed, don't bother submitting it. We started the strobes in the NHL."

"The technology that has evolved is incredible," points out Hicks. "The digital photography has changed everything. The guys before me, everyone came with their own camera. Now, instead of six camera guys, it's one guy with six cameras. We could remote-control cameras around the building. I really started to move them around."

While Hicks was an early pioneer in net-cam technology, among other things, he also started less technical initiatives.

He says, "We cut a hole in the door at Joe Louis. When the Zamboni comes off the ice it drops down right, so we cut a hole right at the very bottom, so I can lie on the cement and actually shoot up at the players right behind the net. I'd lie on my belly and shoot out of that hole. Some of that angle stuff we pioneered in Detroit.

TOP: *Bruce Norris signing over the ownership of the Detroit Red Wings to Mike Ilitch.*

BOTTOM: *The late James Varon, left, of the* Detroit News, *with Wings photographer John Hartman at the Joe Louis Arena, where the two men first installed strobe lighting.*

ABOVE: *A remote-controlled self-portrait, by photographer Dave Reginek.*

OPPOSITE TOP: *Former Wings photographer, the very innovative Mark Hicks.*

OPPOSITE BOTTOM: *You never know who might be critiquing your work: Dave Reginek with Red Wing Todd Bertuzzi looking over his shoulder.*

"I went through a lot," Hicks continues. "When I started, the team sucked. It was the year they drafted Yzerman, and through the team's transformation, a lot of things changed. The hockey changed, the dasher boards changed a lot in the background, the technology changed when strobes came in, and tech guys started running cameras everywhere."

Coincidentally, as the photography improved, so did the hockey team. Hard work and patience allowed Hicks to stick around for 18 seasons, long enough to see the Red Wings end their Stanley Cup drought. This led to more spontaneous innovation.

"We flew to Washington, DC, to take the Cup to the White House," Hicks recalls. "The bus ride from the airport to the White House is phenomenal because you get the police escort. You go right through every red light, right through town, just blasting on the bus, about 40 miles per hour, right through it. All the guys stand up, there are motorcycles swarmed all around you, like you're coming with a nuclear bomb or something. So we had bolted a camera to the front of the bus, which I wired with airplane wire. So when the time came, I just put two wires together and got a shot of the guys all at the front of the bus checking out the motorcycles."

And being part of the hockey family meant being part of the entire celebration, from having your own family's picture taken with superstar players and the Cup, to seven-hour parade gigs, to Cup party after Cup party.

"We got Stevie [Yzerman] with the Cup on a Jet Ski, he and [former Tigers great] Kirk Gibson," remembers Hicks. "We went out boating one day, all of us went out and put the Cup on the boat, and Kirk and Stevie put the Cup on a Jet Ski. The Cup guy was going nuts, so they put a life jacket on the Cup, snapped a ski jacket on it and tied it with anchor ropes to secure it. Then the Jet Ski broke down and we had to tow it two miles. So we had Stevie, the Cup, and a flotilla of boats, which began following them as they were towed up the Detroit River."

A decade later, photographer Dave Reginek enjoyed similar experiences. When the Wings won it all in 2008, Reginek found himself on a beach in California with Chris Chelios and Hollywood A-listers, at private parties around America, and back in Detroit with thousands of Wing Nuts.

"Cheli's Bar, when we had the Cup there, it was just packed with people," says Reginek. "You could literally just walk on the heads from one end of the building to the other. Players were dumping beers on them and spraying champagne. It was hotter than hell, and it was just crazy."

The regular season brings its fair share of surprises as well, and not every photo goes public.

Reginek says, "There was a photo shoot I did with Brett Hull, I think it was around Valentine's Day. The players were done practicing and he was out skating around with his little ones, I think he has two girls and a boy, and they were just kind of beating pucks around. He had chopped down some sticks for them to use. I don't remember specifically why I was around that day, but I seen Brett and his kids skating around out there and I asked him if he wanted to do a family picture. It was a spontaneous thing, they just knelt down by the net there, they put their elbows on his shoulder, and he hugged the girls, and then they piled on him. That was pretty cool."

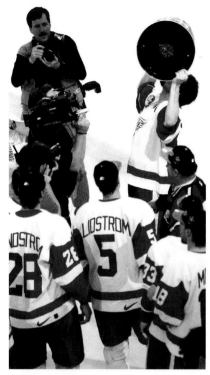

The regular season brings its fair share of surprises as well, and not every photo goes public.

Reginek has also had on-ice family shoots with the Lidstroms, the Holmstroms, and the Liljas, among others. For a lifelong Red Wings fan, it's just the latest generation of greatness.

"My first hockey game [at Olympia], Roger Crozier was in net, and Gordie was still playing, and Alex Delvecchio and Nick Libett, and Bruce MacGregor, and those kind of guys, and now I get to meet and talk to them; Dennis Hextall another," marvels Reginek. "Seeing these guys and talking to them, I'm still in awe of them as much as I am of the guys playing now, because I was a kid. Mickey Redmond, he was my childhood idol growing up. I used to tape my stick like him, and I used to try to pull off that little toe-drag snapshot he perfected. Now I can say he's my friend and I talk to him on a regular basis. I don't take those little situations for granted either. It's special. The fact that they know my name is a tremendous honor."

It's life in a hockey family as the Red Wings shooter.

Scrapbook

"The Winged Wheel is part of family, friends, and memories of home."

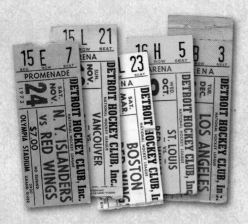

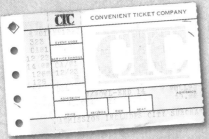

ABOVE: *At the Olympia and the first year at the Joe Louis Arena, fans received traditional colorful ticket stubs that included the opponent, the date, the seats clearly marked, and a 50-cent-off dinner coupon to Ponderosa or the Red Barn restaurant on the back.*

BOTTOM: *After 1980, the team sub-contracted out to CTC, the Convenient Ticket Company, which printed computerized tickets that looked like this.*

I HAVE COUNTLESS RED WINGS memories. They're in small bits and pieces; or, to use the photography vernacular, they're thumbnails.

We used to go to the Olympia as a family; Dad used to get tickets "through work" at Chevrolet. He was an engineer who designed Corvettes and later pickup trucks over at the Tech Center in Warren, Michigan.

He, my two older brothers and I, and occasionally Mom as well, would probably go to one or two games a year. We're talking late '60s, early '70s here.

Aside from the time we got to meet Gordie Howe on the concourse after a game, one other substantial moment stands out from those days when I was still a wee lad, 5 or 6 years old.

Chicago was visiting Detroit about 1970. For whatever reason, we ended up getting seats split apart, so my oldest brother Jim and I sat down in the right-wing corner, two rows from the glass, and my dad and middle brother Tom sat up about 10 rows over our right shoulders, with a great view down the rink inside the glass. Essentially they were scouts' seats.

Bobby Hull came down the left wing and ripped a slap shot that was deflected and rose over the net and wide, and just clipped the glass about two inches from the top, falling back into play. This was decades before the safety netting was introduced. You came to watch hockey.

I remember imagining, over and over, the trajectory of the puck if it had not hit the glass, if it was about four inches higher. It would have hit my dad right in the face, or so I thought. He was my dad, and as a 6-year-old I was worried about his well-being and therefore ours. I remember trying to explain this concept to my brother.

"Probably would have killed him, or at least knocked all his teeth out," he replied.

Thanks. I was nervous the rest of the night.

Years later, on November 16, 1977, to be exact, I recall sitting just above the walkway with my brother in our neighbor's reserved seats watching the Red Wings crush the St. Louis Blues 10–1. The score made it a game I'd never forget, every time the Wings touched the puck it went in. Also, I collected hockey cards at that time and the Blues had a goalie with a really cool photo on his card. When he entered the game to mop up, I recall exclaiming, "Cool! Ed Staniowski! He must stink, but he's got a great hockey card."

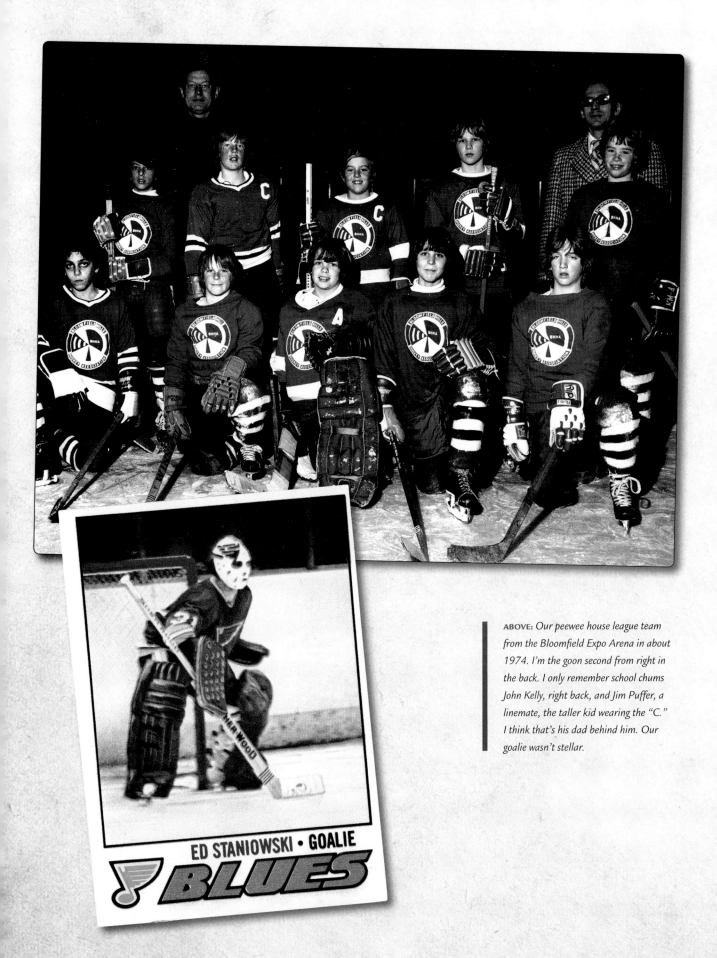

ED STANIOWSKI • GOALIE
BLUES

ABOVE: *Our peewee house league team from the Bloomfield Expo Arena in about 1974. I'm the goon second from right in the back. I only remember school chums John Kelly, right back, and Jim Puffer, a linemate, the taller kid wearing the "C." I think that's his dad behind him. Our goalie wasn't stellar.*

Three years later, I would attend a game with my father for the last time, this time at the new Joe Louis Arena. Someone had given me a certificate for the first game ever at the Joe from December 27, 1979, but I wasn't there. It was a passed-on memento. We were there for something better two weeks later, on January 12, 1980: the return of Gordie Howe with the Hartford Whalers. I had a lump in my throat the size of a grapefruit and misty eyeballs all night as the crowd kept chanting "Gordie, Gordie, Gordie." Dad was a tough man; I recall uncomfortably attempting to hide the emotion, but I'm sure it was an unbelievable memory for him as well. This was an authentic regular season NHL game, three weeks before Gordie came back and got his big ovation at the All-Star Game.

My first Red Wings road game on December 2, 1992.
It just happened to be Domi–Probert Two.

My final snippet involves a road game, being a "Wing Nut" away from home. It was 1992. I actually lived in Hawaii at the time, but had begun regular visits to New York for fun and potential future employment. I had never been inside Madison Square Garden.

Four of us, a reunion of high school buddies, found ourselves sitting about 10 rows back near center ice for what would be my first Red Wings road game on December 2, 1992. It just happened to be Domi–Probert Two. Oh my God! They dropped the mitts first shift, the place went crazy, the fight lasted forever, and Probie pretty much beat the crap out of Domi. "I like this place," I said.

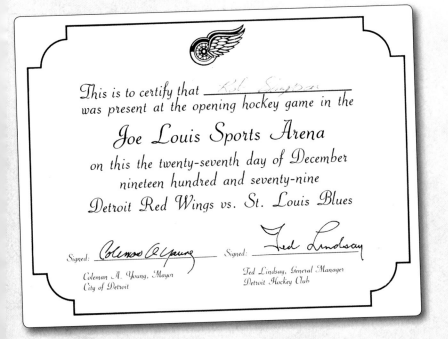

This is to certify that _Rob Simpson_
was present at the opening hockey game in the

Joe Louis Sports Arena

on this the twenty-seventh day of December
nineteen hundred and seventy-nine
Detroit Red Wings vs. St. Louis Blues

Signed: _Coleman A. Young_   Signed: _Ted Lindsay_

Coleman A. Young, Mayor   Ted Lindsay, General Manager
City of Detroit   Detroit Hockey Club

Since then it's been dozens of mostly playoff games for me, usually at the Joe, more often than not in a media capacity. I was there for the first two games when the Wings swept Washington in 1998, and a decade later I was on the ice when Pittsburgh was presented the Cup in 2009. On those nights, much like for the dozen or so home visits in between, postgame usually involved a trip to the Post Bar, and/or the Old Shillelagh.

Ultimately, it comes back to family and friends. Over the years, October to spring, calls back to Detroit always involved a "Did you see the Wings game?" Or if abroad or a little out of touch, the conversation would instead begin, "How are the Wings doing?"

My wife actually grew up in the City of Detroit, as did her parents and her many siblings. Most of them still follow the Red Wings religiously. Our son, who has never lived in Michigan, has gradually become a Red Wings fan as well, although he still ranks the Bruins tops on his list, mainly because of his acquaintance Zdeno Chara.

Hockey with family for me hit a high note with an event I organized while working for the Bruins and NESN-TV in Boston. On February 2, 2008, the Wings played the Bruins on a Saturday night. Besides relocated Detroit pals who lived in the area, old friends from high school and college, family, and other interested hockey folks all flew in from around the country and converged on Beacon Hill for a weekend of socializing, buzzing around, and a Red Wings game. I worked the telecast while the Bruins generously provided our group a suite. The weekend of frivolity was memorable, and the Red Wings won 3–1.

Here's to more of everything!

— Rob Simpson

About the Author

ROB SIMPSON began his broadcasting career in Detroit, covering the Pistons and Red Wings, at the ripe old age of 17. Since then, he's never been far from an NHL rink while handling TV, radio, and writing assignments. Along the way he's penned two other books for Wiley: *Between the Lines: Not-So-Tall Tales from Ray "Scampy" Scapinello's Four Decades in the NHL* and *Black and Gold: Four Decades of the Boston Bruins in Photographs*. Here are a few of his other favorite Red Wings photos—a gallery of parting shots.

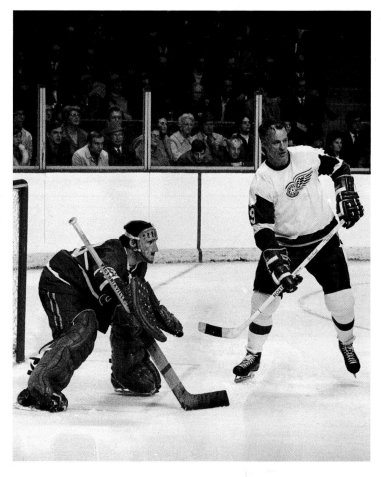

Photography Credits

AFP/Getty Images/Cris Bouroncle: 115(T)

Steve Babineau/Hockey Hall of Fame: 148(M)

Paul Bereswill/Hockey Hall of Fame: 144(L), 146(T, B), 149(MT), 160, 166(T), 177(B), 185(B), 198(L)

Terri Coppens: 223, 224(T)

Courtesy of Mike Emrick: 9

Courtesy of Greg Innis: 24(B)

Courtesy of Rob Simpson: 228–231

DRW Archives: 8, 17, 18, 19(TL, BR), 20, 21, 22, 27(T, M), 46, 68, 69, 70, 71(BL, BR), 122, 123, 125(BR), 133(B), 161(TL), 173, 178(T), 210, 213(M), 217(T), 219(T), 221(B), 227(T)

DRW Archives/Albert Barg: 19(TR)

DRW Archives/John Hartman: 178(B)

DRW Archives/Mark Hicks: 183, 194(L)

Getty Images/Justin K. Aller: 181(L)

Getty Images/P Angers: 202(B)

Getty Images/Brian Bahr: 148(T), 191, 192(T)

Getty Images/Al Bello: 145(R), 194(R)

Getty Images/Bruce Bennett: 11, 28, 29, 30, 32, 33(TL, TR), 34, 35(L, TR), 36, 37(L, BR), 38, 39, 40(T), 42, 43, 44, 47, 54, 57(T), 58, 61(L), 62, 63, 65, 67(B), 74, 76, 78, 79, 81, 82, 84, 90, 95, 99, 100(L), 118, 120, 127, 131, 157, 182, 188(T), 192(B), 198(R), 203(T), 203(B), 207(B), 208, 209(B), 213(B), 215(B), 220(B), 233(TL, TR), 234(BL)

Getty Images/Glenn Cratty: 189(T)

Getty Images/Scott Cunningham: 211(R)

Getty Images/DK Photo: 128(R), 129

Getty Images/Georges DeKeerle: 85(T)

Getty Images/Melchior DiGiacomo: 73(T)

Getty Images/Jed Jacobsohn: 86

Getty Images/Elsa: 85(BL), 98(R), 100(R)

Getty Images/Harry How: 195(L)

Getty Images/Robert Laberge: 97, 195(R),

Getty Images/Ronald Martinez: 190

Getty Images/Jim McIsaac: 75, 104, 105, 110, 215(T)

Getty Images/B Miller: 184, 203(M)

Getty Images/Christian Petersen: 134, 136

Getty Images/Tom Pidgeon: 80, 87(L), 101(T), 179, 214

Getty Images/Mike Ridewood: 132

Getty Images/Robert Riger: 48, 60

Getty Images/J Russel: 83

Getty Images/Jamie Sabau: 113

Getty Images/Dave Sandford: 73(B), 88, 103(TL), 117(T), 137, 145(L), 164, 207(T), 221(T)

Getty Images/Scott A. Schneider: 53

Getty Images/Harry Scull Jr.: 193

Getty Images/Gregory Shamus: 87(R), 138, 150, 152, 199(L), 200(R), 201

Getty Images/Ezra Shaw: 91, 92

Getty Images/Rick Stewart: 96, 102

Getty Images/Jeff Vinnick: 89

Getty Images/NHLI/Jonathan Daniel: 94(T)

Getty Images/NHLI/Elsa: 109(L), 130

Getty Images/NHLI/Mitchell Layton: 220(T)

Getty Images/NHLI/Dave Sandford: 137

Getty Images/NHLI/Jeff Vinnick: 133(T)

Graphic Artists/Hockey Hall of Fame: 31, 71(T), 72(B), 121(B), 125(TR, BL, BM), 126(TL, BL, BR), 140(T, BR), 141(L), 147(B), 148(B), 167(B), 169(B), 174, 175(BR), 186(T), 188(M), 189(B), 218(B)

John Hartman: 225(B)

Hockey Hall of Fame: 4, 15, 16, 55, 56, 125(TL, ML), 126(TR), 140(BL), 141(R), 143(M), 149(MB), 161(B), 162(M), 165(T, B), 168(M), 176(R), 177(T), 187(B), 213(T)

Doug MacLellan/Hockey Hall of Fame: 94(B), 139, 147(M), 167(T), 168(T), 188(B)

Matthew Manor/Hockey Hall of Fame: 156(T), 158(T, M)

Jack Mecca/Hockey Hall of Fame Images: 161(TR)

Peter S. Mecca/Hockey Hall of Fame: 176(TL)

NHLI via Getty Images/Brian Babineau: 101(B)

NHLI via Getty Images/Steve Babineau: 85(BR), 128(L), 165(M), 186(M, B), 197, 200(L), 202(T), 216(B), 218(T), 219(B)

NHLI via Getty Images/Denis Brodeur: 33(B), 37(TR), 50(L), 64, 66, 162(B), 180(L), 211(L), 234(BR)

NHLI via Getty Images/Andy Devlin: 233(B)

NHLI via Getty Images/Dave Reginek: 2, 7, 23, 24(T), 25, 26, 27(B), 45, 50(R), 51, 52, 107, 108, 110(T, B), 111, 112, 114, 116, 117(B), 143(T), 170, 172, 180(R), 185(T), 204, 206, 209(T), 216(T), 218(M), 232, 234(T)

NHLI via Getty Images/Debora Robinson: 217(B)

NHLI via Getty Images/John Russell: 181(L)

NHLI via Getty Images/Dave Sandford: 6, 14

NHLI via Getty Images/Gregory Shamus: 115(B)

NHLI via Getty Images/Eliot J. Schechter: 144(R)

NHLI via Getty Images/Bill Smith: 149(T)

NHLI via Getty Images/Tom Turrill: 199(R)

O-Pee-Chee/Hockey Hall of Fame: 142, 168(B), 169(T)

Lewis Portnoy/Hockey Hall of Fame: 167(M), 175(TR)

Frank Prazak/Hockey Hall of Fame: 10, 13, 67(T), 154, 159, 162(T), 175(L), 187(T), 212(B)

Dave Reginek: 222, 226

Dave Reginek/Paul Sancya: 227(B)

Chris Relke/Hockey Hall of Fame: 149(B), 156(B)

Dave Sandford/Hockey Hall of Fame: 11, 12, 77, 93, 98(L), 103(TR, B), 109(R), 143(B), 155, 158(B), 163, 166(B)

Sporting News via Getty Images: 41

Time & Life Pictures/Getty Images/ Ralph Morse: 61(R)

Time & Life Pictures/Getty Images/ Art Rickerby: 196

Turofsky/Hockey Hall of Fame: 72(T)

Nat Turofsky/Hockey Hall of Fame: 49, 57(B), 59, 121(T), 147(T), 153, 212(T)

Robert Wimmer 224(B), 225(T)

WireImage/Ron Galella, Ltd.: 40(B)

WireImage/SGranitz: 35(BR)

Index